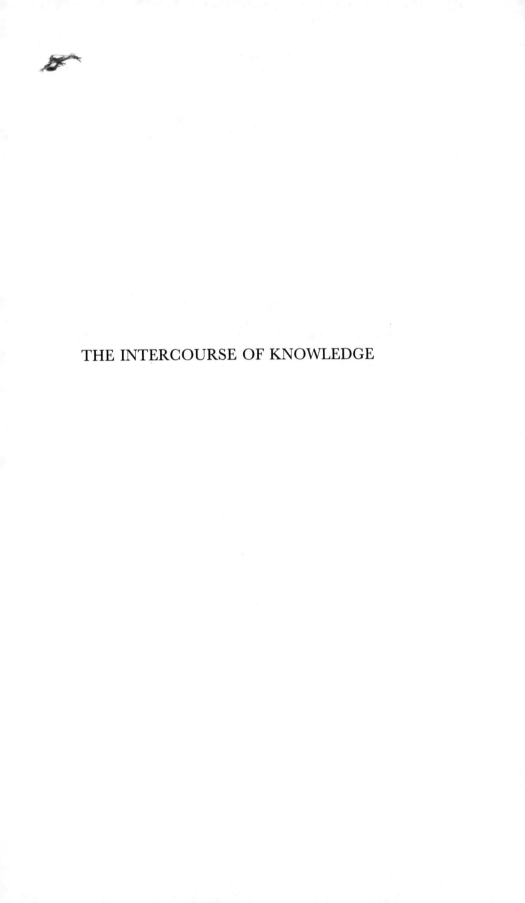

THE INTERCOURSE OF KNOWLEDGE

BIBLICAL INTERPRETATION SERIES

Editors
R. ALAN CULPEPPER
ROLF RENDTORFF

Assistant Editor
DAVID E. ORTON

Editorial Advisory Board
JANICE CAPEL ANDERSON · MIEKE BAL
PHYLLIS A. BIRD · ERHARD BLUM · ROBERT P. CARROLL
WERNER H. KELBER · EKKEHARD STEGEMANN
ANTHONY C. THISELTON · VINCENT L. WIMBUSH · JEAN ZUMSTEIN

VOLUME 26

THE INTERCOURSE
OF KNOWLEDGE

On Gendering Desire and 'Sexuality'
in the Hebrew Bible

BY

ATHALYA BRENNER

BRILL
LEIDEN · NEW YORK · KÖLN
1997

This book is printed on acid-free paper.

Library of Congress Cataloging-in-Publication Data

Brenner, Athhalya.
  The intercourse of knowledge : on gendering desire and 'sexuality'
in the Hebrew Bible / by Athalya Brenner.
    p.   cm. — (Biblical interpretation series, ISSN 0928-0731 ;
v. 26
    Includes bibliographical references and index.
    ISBN 9004101551 (cloth : alk. paper)
    1. Sex in the Bible.   2. Women in the Bible.   3. Sexual deviation-
-Biblical teaching.   4. Bible.   O.T.—Feminist criticism.   5. Bible.
O.T.—Terminology.   I. Title.   II. Series.
BS1199.S45.B74   1996
221.8'3067—cd20
                                                                96-46460
                                                                  CIP

Die Deutsche Bibliothek – CIP-Einheitsaufnahme

Brenner, Atalya:
The intercourse of knowledge : on gendering desire and
"sexuality" in the Hebrew Bible / by Athalya Brenner. - Leiden
; New York ; Köln : Brill, 1997
  (Biblical interpretation series : Vol. 26)
  ISBN 90-04-10155-1
NE: GT

ISSN   0928-0731
ISBN   90 04 10155 1

CONTENTS

A PERSONAL NOTE

This book was planned together with the late Fokkelien van Dijk-Hemmes as a sequel to the book we wrote separately and together, *On Gendering Texts: Female and Male Voices in the Hebrew Bible* (1993). When *On Gendering Texts* was completed we felt happy with our cooperation and decided to take it further. We believed that the gendering of desire in the Hebrew Bible was as important and difficult as the gendering of the literary voices in it. We submitted an outline to E.J. Brill and started to discuss the various issues we wanted to write about. As previously, our plan was to divide the work so that each chapter would be the sole responsibility of its individual writer, while both of us would criticize each other's work during the process.

Fokkelien died in February, 1994. After initial hesitation, I decided to tackle this project on my own. In the process, the original project was modified, then completely changed. But, as I was writing, I sometimes still had the feeling that Fokkelien was peering over my shoulder. I miss her, as a colleague and as a friend.

One of Fokkelien's last requests was, Remember my voice. I remember. Fokkelien's voice is certainly with us: the voice of a woman, a mother, a friend, a scholar.

Several friends and colleagues were generous in extending valuable assistance while I was writing. Special thanks are due to Ra'anan Abusch (who compiled the Bibliography and did much library legwork on my behalf); Jan Willem van Henten and David Orton, who read parts of the unfinished work and made valuable comments; Carole Fontaine, for her general good sense and for regaling me with literature on magic and witchcraft; Dick Bruggeman, for reading the proofs with interest and patience; and the staff and faculty members of Theology faculties at the Catholic University of Nijmegen and the University of Amsterdam.

Haifa-Amsterdam, June 1996.

CHAPTER ONE

INTRODUCTION

Strictly speaking, texts are gender-free in the grammatical as well as the social sense. But, as shown in *On Gendering Texts*[1] in keeping with many other recent publications, neither readers nor authors are gender-free or gender-neutral. Most humans are socialized into their gender roles according to the norms prevalent in or aimed at by their communities. Literature reflects this gendering process and also serves as one of its agents. In that sense, the result produced by authorly and readerly activities, a text, is gendered by its producers and its consumers. To the extent that a text is a cultural product and a commodity, it cannot be gender-neutral because both its conception and reception are not neutral. The chain of gendering is then reciprocal. Authors and readers gender texts as well as being gendered by them.

Recognition of this premise is of course relevant to the reading of the Hebrew Bible. In *On Gendering Texts*, Fokkelien van Dijk-Hemmes and I tried to show that although some, or many, Bible scholars may still insist that the implied authors and transmitters of most biblical texts were M (male/masculine), and this indeed appears to be the case, the possibility of F (female/feminine) voices within it cannot be excluded from the outset. Such F texts might have to be searched for, and with caution. However, their existence should at least be suspected.[2] We also tried to re-define how texts are qualified as either F or else M texts.

The project of this book is different from the previous one, albeit related to it. The project here is to study how, by what means and to what extent human love, desire and sex, possibly even 'sexuality' (the sexual characteristics or impulse, as experienced by an individual or group of either gender), are gendered in the Hebrew Bible (HB). In other words, how are sex (biological, anatomical, physical) differences

---

[1] A. Brenner and F. van Dijk-Hemmes, *On Gendering Texts: Female and Male Voices in the Hebrew Bible* (Leiden: Brill, 1993).

[2] For the terminology and summary of methodology and results, cf. *On Gendering Texts*, 'Introduction', pp. 1–11.

and similarities conceived of, and converted into, gender (social, functional) differences and similarities between women and men in HB
language and various literary genres. The question that I repeatedly
ask myself is, How is gender constructed by sex in the HB and, in
as much as this can be gleaned, in the societies that we conveniently
name 'ancient Israel' or 'biblical Israel'?[3]

These questions are asked specifically about the Hebrew Bible. Yet,
they are anchored in the ongoing and unresolved feminist debates
about 'gender' and its construction in language. 'Gender' is often
used as a current coinage, a conventional key term whose signification is agreed upon, the way I myself—like others—have used it in
the preceding paragraphs. Nevertheless, 'gender' signifies a problematic concept. Even the most cursory survey of recent feminist publications on the gender question (for instance in Braidotti,[4] Showalter,[5]
Butler,[6] Haraway[7]) illustrates that there are many issues involved and
unresolved. Just how, in contemporary discourse, is 'gender' distin-
guishable from 'sex'? Epistemologically, since we all (women and men,
feminists and non feminists) operate from within a culture founded
on biological difference as well as similarity, can anyone say that the
notion 'gender' in patriarchal discourse, even for women thinkers, is
essentially (and I use this word advisedly) different from the notion
'sex'?[8] Can, are, 'men' and 'women', 'males' and 'females', gendered
symmetrically into two parallel social groups?[9] Is it important to
distinguish between the two notions, 'sex' and 'gender'? Is the theoretical distinction useful pragmatically and, if so, for whom and what
for?[10] How do sex and sexuality function as partial determinants of
gender? Is 'gender' a better concept than 'sex' for [re]constructing a

---

[3] P.R. Davies, *In Search of 'Ancient Israel'* (JSOTSup 148; Sheffield: Sheffield Academic Press, 1992), esp. pp. 11–48.
[4] R. Braidotti, 'What's Wrong with Gender', in F. van Dijk-Hemmes and
A. Brenner (eds.), *Reflections on Theology and Gender* (Kampen: Kok, 1994), pp. 41–79.
[5] E. Showalter (ed.), *Speaking of Gender* (London: Routledge, 1989).
[6] J. Butler, *Gender Trouble and the Subversion of Identity* (New York: Routledge, 1990).
[7] D. Haraway, 'Situated Knowledges: The Science Question in Feminism and
the Privilege of Partial Perspective', *Feminist Studies* 14.3 (1988), pp. 575–99; *Simians,
Cyborgs and Women: The Reinvention of Nature* (New York: Routledge, 1991).
[8] For a collection of articles on the issue of 'essentialism' see T. Brener (ed.),
Feminism and Psychoanalysis (London: Routledge, 1989).
[9] Braidotti, 'Gender'.
[10] See, for instance, the critique of Butler and Haraway's position from a Marxist-
theological perspective in M.A. Hewlett, 'Cyborgs, Drag Queens, and Goddesses:
Emancipatory-Regressive Paths in Feminist Theory', *Method and Theory in the Study of
Religion* 5.2 (1993), pp. 135–54.

new, less oppressive, bi-gender world of social (including literary) discourse? Conversely, is the whole point of feminism to try and transcend sex/gender differences?

It is difficult not to be quite aware of the problems created by the theoretical concept/term 'gender'. And yet, I find the term indispensable for reading biblical texts. It is a meta-term that allows a discussion of physical [sex] characteristics in separation from, as well as in tandem with, socio-psychological images that are attributed to the bearers of the sex characteristics. It enables a principal distinction between physicality and social categorization precisely because it links the two together. In short, the term is convenient shorthand for differentiating sex identities from social identities—and for assessing when and how the two 'identities' are conceived of as indistinguishable or interchangeable.

My tentative answers to the questions I set for myself, with regard to the Hebrew Bible and in dialogue with current feminist discourse about gender and sex, are certainly not comprehensive—nor are they intended to be. They are linked to the deceptively simple conviction that, in biblical texts as authored and read by ancient through to modern readers, gender differences are created out of sex differences in a variety of ways, means and devices, with a variety of social ends in mind. These ends, means and so on are complex and at times inconsistent and contradictory. In addition, they are sometimes erased and even obliterated by the almost universal M bent of the HB. Therefore, the [re]construction of a bi-gendered picture for biblical texts requires a mixed methodology to suit the complexities and inconsistencies.

For a growing number of scholars, it has become inconceivable that social structure and social power relations are not in some ways be bound up with, and reflected by, conceptualizations of desire, sex and sexuality.[11] My own position is strongly anchored in this recognition.

---

[11] For instance: D. Biale, *Eros and the Jews* (New York: xxx, 1992; also in Heb. translation), esp. ch. 1. D. Boyarin, *Carnal Israel: Reading Sex in Talmudic Culture* (Berkeley: University of California Press, 1993); *A Radical Jew: Paul and the Politics of Identity* (Berkeley: University of California Press, 1994); 'Are There Any Jews in "The History of Sexuality"?', *Journal of the History of Sexuality* 5.3 (1995), pp. 333–55. Howard Eilberg-Schwartz, 'The Problem of the Body for the People of the Body' in H. Eilberg-Schwartz (ed.), *People of the Body: Jews and Judaism from an Embodied Perspective* (New York: University of New York at Stony Brook, 1992), pp. 17–46; and *The Savage in Judaism* (Bloomington: University of Indiana Press, 1990). S. Olyan, '"And with a Male You Shall Not Lie the Lying Down of a Woman": On the

In the HB—and once again, if its evidence be adopted, also in at least some times and places of the conventionally labelled 'ancient Israel[s]'—the socialized classification into 'gender' (and class) supersedes the psycho-social concept that we moderns call 'sexuality' and, also, categorizes it. 'Gender' genders sexuality, defines and formulates it. As Daniel Boyarin convincingly argues,

> Perhaps the most solid conclusion of Michel Foucault's last research and the scholarship that has followed in its wake has been that there was no autonomous realm of 'sexuality' within classical cultures at all; desire and pleasure were inextricably bound up with the relations of power and domination that structured the entire society. Permitted and taboo sexual behaviour was completely a function of status. The world was divided into the screwers—all male—and the screwed—both male and female.[12]

What remains to be seen is how this subordination of love, desire and 'sexuality' to social domination is achieved in and by the HB texts.

This is a highly personal book. To begin with, I am very much aware of factors of my personal life, circumstances and beliefs that affect—probably even determine—my readings and interpretations. Undoubtedly, there are factors affecting my work that I am not aware of too. I am a feminist (after my own personal fashion), which entails a bias towards the neglected areas of female lives in ancient Israel and the HB rather than a more naive interest in male lives as representative of human life, a subject which has been interpreted as gender inclusive for centuries. This study is personal also in the sense that I chose to discuss exclusively issues that I found of relevance and of interest to me. No attempt was made to write about all aspects of love and sex in the HB; I certainly did not set out to compose an extensive tome about biblical love and desire. For instance, I felt that studies of marriage, motherhood, menstruation and birth are so widely available in the fast-growing corpus of biblical interpretation (including feminist interpretation) that there was not much I wanted to or could add to what other scholars have written. Similarly, the concept of 'jealousy' or 'mimetic desire' has been dealt with exten-

---

Meaning and Significance of Leviticus 18:22 and 20:13', *Journal of the History of Sexuality* 5.2 (1994), pp. 179–206.

[12] D. Boyarin, 'Are There Any Jews', p. 333.

sively in recent publications, as provoked by Girard's work.[13] I limited my quest to my initial question, deciding to discuss issues of direct bearing on the social construction of gendered love and desire which, according to my knowledge, have been relatively neglected in biblical scholarship until recent years. Some of the topics were chosen because of their general relevance, like a general survey of linguistic terms in the field of love/desire; others because of their status as signifiers of 'deviant' sexual phenomena (like incest or prostitution), since what a society thinks about deviations from the norms it sets for itself is clearly significant for understanding that same society's attitudes and boundaries; and others still, like contraception and abortion, because their almost total absence from the HB intrigued me. My choice is a personal choice: it does not imply that phenomena related to sexual behaviour and human desire other than the ones I chose to discuss are not as worthy of study.

While I was writing, I found myself drawn more and more to a substantial use of post-biblical Judaic sources. I use these materials— Apocrypha, Dead Sea Scrolls, Mishna, Midrash, Talmuds, medieval commentaries, Maimonides and others, not to mention secondary literature relating to them—throughout for clarification of, analogies to and support for understanding the HB. This praxis does not signify that I consider the 'Judaisms'-in-emergence of the last two centuries BCE or the Judaisms of the first centuries CE and later as either direct descendants of biblical literature or as privileged, know-best commentaries. I hope that I have not privileged Judaic/Jewish interpretations over cognate materials from the ANE, the Hellenistic and Graeco-Roman world, or from archaeological studies. I appealed so extensively to Jewish sources chiefly for the following reasons: they constitute M voices which seem preoccupied with women and female bodies; they contain many sharp textual observations and formulations of problems—formulations that I found, time and time again, more relevant for my quest than the answers they offer, while the information obtainable in them can be collated with other extrabiblical sources; and I find studies of these materials illuminating for biblical materials. On the other hand, I used relevant New Testament (NT)

---

[13] R. Girard, *Things Hidden since the Foundation of the World* (Stanford: Stanford University Press, 1987); *To Double Business Bound* (Baltimore: Johns Hopkins University Press, 1978); *Violence and the Sacred* (Baltimore: Johns Hopkins University Press, 1977).

materials rarely and no early Christian Church materials; in these
fields, I feel, I am no match for the pioneering work recently published, for instance by Boyarin[14] and Eilberg-Schwartz;[15] I lack the
expertise to approach a gendering of NT/early Christian 'sexuality'.

A short description of the chapters to follow seems to be in order
at this point.

Chapter 2 is an attempt to construct a loosely-described semantic
field for terms of desire, love and sexual activity in BH, then to
classify the linguistic and semantic data according to its textual usage
and to allocate it to the gendered emotions and activities signified.

Chapter 3 constitutes a preliminary exploration of biblical terms
for female and male body parts, as well as terms signifying male and
female beauty and—to a lesser extent—ugliness. The relevance of
these visual and corporeal terms for gendering 'sexuality' is evaluated and discussed. It is found that whereas, somewhat surprisingly,
body parts (especially male body parts) are obscured by the language,
beauty is firmly differentiated and gendered functionally if not necessarily visually.

Chapter 4 is a discussion of sex, procreation, fertility and contraception. A review of anthropological-archaeological data on human
life expectancy leads to the conclusion that women died earlier
than men because of pregnancies and child-rearing related problems.
A survey of pertinent ANE, Judaic and Mediterranean data on
contraception and abortion points to the plausibility of anti-fertility
knowledge in ancient Israel, a subject about which the HB is almost
completely silent.

Incest, with blood and marriage kin, is considered a serious deviation from social norms in law texts and in the prophetic books (Chapter 5). The addressee of incest prohibition lists is male, the object a
class of females, the penalty extreme. The category of father-daughter
incest is completely absent from the law codes. In most narrative
sources, however, the picture is different: daughter-father incest obtains; women are initiators but the moral tone is less severe. The
insistent law/prophecy taboo is rendered interesting by the differently focused biblical narrative on incest, as well as by modern—
biological, sociological, anthropological and psychological—theories.
The significance of incest to the understanding of societal boundaries

---

[14] In *Carnal Israel; A Radical Jew*; 'Are There Any Jews', and other articles.
[15] In 'The Problem of the Body' and *The Savage in Judaism*.

and the gendering of sexuality is considerable, hence the relatively lengthy treatment of it.

Chapter 6 too deals with sexual phenomena labelled as deviations from the accepted socio-sexual mores: adultery, rape, prostitution, 'homosexuality'[16] and bestiality.[17] Descriptions and prohibitions of these phenomena, and the penalties prescribed for them, are found to be gendered to a very wide extent (apart from in the matter of bestiality), with different roles and penalties envisaged for males and for females within such sexual modes of conduct.

Chapter 7 is a discussion of what I call 'pornoprophetics', passages in the Latter Prophets which contain the twin image of the divine husband (Yhwh) and his errant, promiscuous wife (the land, the people, Jerusalem and Samaria). It is concluded that the image, or metaphor, is a propaganda device which is pornographic in nature because of the female exposure and sexual violence against women that it builds on and even advocates, and because of its methods of persuasion.

Finally, in Chapter 8 a short discussion of the gendered body, 'sexuality' as knowledge, 'soul', the theologies of love (of humans and of the divine) is embarked upon. The Priestly account of the creation—of the male? male and female? both primordial humans?—'in god's image' (Gen. 1.26-27; 5.1) is as problematic for gender relations as it is for biblical theology, as is the narrative account (chs. 2–3) and other sources. The husband/wife image or metaphor is, once more, problematic in both fields. The same applies to the apparent view of [chiefly male] sexual activity as 'knowledge'. A few reflections on this cluster of issues are offered in this concluding Chapter.

---

[16] I have retained the traditional term 'homosexuality', here used without further gendering or activity specification, rather than opting for more detailed or politically correct modern equivalents (such as 'homoerotics'). Further specifications, including the question of what is meant by HB 'homosexuality', will be discussed in the Chapter itself.

[17] It is questionable whether masturbation is considered a category of 'negative' sexual activity in the HB. The sin of Onan (Gen. 38) is not necessarily that of masturbation; otherwise, oblique references to seminal emission, like 'and a man, when an emission of semen comes out of him' (Lev. 15.16), refers to the emission rather than its circumstances; and female masturbation is never mentioned in the HB. Hence, this category will not be discussed separately but only under the heading of incest (Chapter 5).

CHAPTER TWO

LOVE, DESIRE AND SEXUAL ACTIVITY: ON THE CLASSIFICATION AND GENDERING OF THE LINGUISTIC AND SEMANTIC DATA

Preliminary remarks

For the purpose of semantic inquiry, the linguistic data of HB terms for love and desire may be schematically classified into five preliminary categories. The criteria for this preliminary categorization are not unified. Rather, the formulation is guided simultaneously by the twin criteria of formal features and content features, as befits (in my view) a semantic inquiry. The categories are:

• *Terms for 'male' and 'female'*. These terms, strictly speaking, belong to the semantic field which constitutes the body (Chapter 3). They are discussed here because the HB semantic categorization into 'male' and 'female' clearly indicates a world view pertaining to the gendering, in/by the language, of love, desire and especially sexuality.[1]

• *Specific terms for 'love' or any emotional/physical aspect of 'love'*. These terms are mostly monolexemic. Several verb phrases (like, for instance, a verb phrase consisting of a verb followed by a preposition, i.e. ידע את, 'know' as a euphemism for 'have intercourse with') belong to this category too.

• *Similes and metaphors*.

• *Circumlocutions*, such as 'his [Jonathan's] soul was bound to his [David's] soul' (1 Sam. 18.1), because Jonathan's 'love' for David was as strong as his self-love (v. 3); or some instances of 'find favour in the eyes of',[2] in the more specialized sense of 'love'.

• *Terms for sexual pleasure*.

This preliminary categorization can serve as an artificial construct only, as rough guidelines. A linear description of linguistic stock and

---

[1] See also Boyarin, 'Are There Any Jews', p. 345.

[2] מצא חן בעיני—1 Sam. 20.3; Est. 5.8, 7.3 and a variation in 8.5; possibly also Ruth 2.10, 13.

its socio-semantic implications is an impossible task. In praxis, a certain seesaw movement between categories is necessary—among other things, because of the paucity of linguistic data but also because of the fact that linguistic expression is, by its very nature, fluid. Nevertheless, some mixed system of classification and organization into an imprecise hierarchy is deemed helpful for understanding the available data.

The specific HB terms for 'loving' as well as sexual desire are first and foremost אהב and its derivatives.[3] אהב is a general term with specific and non-specific, sexual and non-sexual significations, denotations and connotations. Some, albeit not all, of the other terms available are less well distributed, and display less general albeit more helpfully specific scopes and applicabilities. These secondary terms are—in alphabetical order and without any kind of hierarchic [formal or designatory] arrangement for the time being—the following consonantal sequences (roots): אוה and its derivatives, בוא אל (a person), בעל (in the Qal formation, with a person or a metaphorical person in the accusative), . . . דבק ב (Qal, 'cling, adhere to'), דו[ו]דים ('physical love') and דוד ('[male] lover'), חפץ with the preposition ב (followed by a 'human' object), (נפשו) חשק, ידע את, ענב (with or without the preposition על) and its derivatives, צחק (in the Pi. formation, followed by the prepositions עם or את, and a human indirect object), קרב אל (followed by an indirect object), several occurrences of רחם, שכב עם/את (male subject and female object), and תשוקה*.

A primary term is usually defined, among other things, by its usefulness for designating non-specific as well as specific notions. To illustrate: terms for 'wanting, desiring' may serve as general, wide-scope signifiers as well as for the narrower denotations of 'desire' sexually; or, the general notion of 'sexual pleasure' appears to be signified by 'love' and is also subsumed under the general notion of 'love', in its more specific sense. Hence in the compound אהבה בתענוגים, 'delectable love' (an M designation of a female lover in SoS 7.7), the element of 'pleasure' appears to be connoted by both constituents of the compound. The absence of sexual pleasure can be denoted simply by 'hate' (שנא Qal), the primary binary opposition of 'love' (אהב

---

[3] The binary oppositional term of which is שנא, 'hate', with a similar general character. Although the structuralist, Saussurean, reciprocal binary delineation of terms must be accepted as valid in any semantic analysis, here I've opted for discussing the 'loving' pole on its own rather than in conjunction with its relevant linguistic opposite.

Qal), as exemplified by the circumstantial contexts of 1 Sam. 13 and
Deuteronomy 22.13, 24.3: in all three instances, a male (respectively,
Amnon and a hypothetical husband) finds that he 'hates' a woman
after having intercourse and hastens to get rid of her.

'Love' as well as other emotions can be expressed by terms designating specific physical activities, like 'kiss' (נשק), or 'hug', 'hold' (חבק
Qal, חזק Hif.). Sexual pleasure can be connoted by euphemistic, non-
specific generalities such as 'find favour with', 'be right in the eyes
of', as narrated about Esther with regard to Ahasuerus, and Samson's
Timnite first wife (Judg. 14.3). Nevertheless, and not surprisingly,
the HB linguistic data for 'love' and desire, in their widest sense, is
covered by general terms that may serve as signifiers for other areas
of human experience as well.

Metaphors and similes for 'love', as undifferentiated for 'physical'
and other kinds of 'love', abound in the Song of Songs: love is an
orchard, garden and perfume garden; it is like death, fire, stronger
than water, as strong an emotion as קנאה, 'dedication' (SoS 8.6–7).
It is like a drink (Prov. 7.18), like wine and better than wine (SoS
1.2, 4.10, 5.1, 7.10, 8.2), like food (5.1; and in the case of Samson,
like honey),[4] an illness (SoS 2.5, 5.8), like an animal (Judg. 14; and
in the SoS by depicting lovers in terms of animals, especially female
lovers as associated with wild animals).[5] It can touch the heart[6] and
the soul (1 Sam. 18.1–3). It can be the love of parents for children,
of same-gender as well as transgender subjects and objects, between
the human and the divine, ever-lasting or subject to change.

My interest in this Chapter is, first and foremost and almost
exclusively, in specific—although, as stated above, not necessarily
monolexemic—terms for 'love', desire and love/sexual behaviour.
Metaphors, similes and unstable or idiosyncratic circumlocutions are
perhaps less significant for constructing a semantic, hence a socio-
linguistic, assessment of this area of human experience in the HB. In
other words, my interest is mainly in the first and second of the

---

[4] Cf. Mieke Bal's reading of Samson's riddle and its solution in Judg. 14: M. Bal,
Death and Dissymmetry: The Politics of Coherence in the Book of Judges (Bloomington: University of Indianapolis Press), ch. 5.

[5] For awe- and even terror-inspiring depictions of female lovers, hence by exten-
sion love, see Carol Meyers, 'Gender Imagery in the Song of Songs', originally in
HAR 10 (1986), pp. 209–23; repr. in A. Brenner (ed.), *A Feminist Companion to the
Song of Songs* (Sheffield: Sheffield Academic Press, 1993), pp. 197–212.

[6] If this is the designation of the twice-occurring לבבתיני (SoS 4.9), from לבב,
'heart' or, by contiguity, 'mind' or 'emotions'.

preliminary categories delineated. This interest is neither etymological nor lexicographical/lexicological per se: a brief survey of biblical dictionaries such as the BDB, the KBL or the new Sheffield dictionary[7] will be helpful for etymology, in the instance of the first two dictionaries cited, and/or general data in the case of all. My interest is in semantic ways and means of *gendering* linguistic coinage, especially in the *gendered* application of linguistic signifiers to the depiction of non-linguistic *sexed* signifieds. In other words, I would like to trace:

- How terms for love and desire are used in biblical texts, so that a loosely-defined 'semantic field' of love and desire can be constructed;
- the ways in which the ensuing, loosely defined, more specialized layer of the 'semantic field' construct and its constituents characterize gendered authorly and readerly attitudes to gendered sexuality in the HB;
- how an understanding of love and desire terms within the HB texts, as individual terms and as a cumulative whole, might be helpful for reading the individual texts in which they occur and, also, how such terms may serve as documentary reflections of cultural attitudes to socio-sexual mores in ancient Israel.

The methodology adopted, of organizing the relevant linguistic data into a loosely-defined semantic construct, is best explained by itself as well as by reference to my earlier work on two other semantic fields, those of colour and of humour.[8]

The terms: data and description

Male and female

The Hebrew word for 'male'—human (Gen. 1.27), animal (Deut. 15.19) or inanimate (of an image, Deut. 4.16)—is זכר, apparently

---

[7] D.J.A. Clines (ed.), *Dictionary of Classical Hebrew* (Sheffield: Sheffield Academic Press, 1993, 1996), vols. 1 and 2, letters *aleph* to *waw*.

[8] Cf. A. Brenner, *Colour Terms in the Old Testament* (Sheffield: *JSOT* Press, 1982), esp. pp. 1–59, with recurrent references to works by Avi Hurvitz, to whose methodology and good sense I owe so much. Also cf. A. Brenner, 'On the Semantic Field of Humour, Laughter and the Comic in the Hebrew Bible', in Y.T. Radday and

from a root denoting 'to remember'. An alternative and less frequent form is זכור, a passive participle Qal formation, 'remembered [one]'. The more general and superordinate term 'man', איש, can sometime serve in the narrower sense of '[human] male'—as for instance in Judg. 11.39, where Jephthah's daughter 'has never known[9] a man'.

A female, human (Gen. 1.27) or animal, is designated by נקבה, derived from a consonantal sequence designating 'pierce, make a hole' (Qal) and formally constituted as the grammatical F formation of נקב, 'hole', 'cavity', 'opening', 'orifice'. In places, the more general 'woman', אשה, has the narrower signification 'female' (cf. Gen. 2–3).

Is there a generic term for males and females together, an equivalent of the non-gendered and non-sexed 'humanity'? Whether the term אדם or האדם (Gen. 1–3) has a bi-sex or bi-gender undifferentiated signification, at least to begin with and as advocated by Trible, Bal and others,[10] is in my opinion highly doubtful. The term's form is grammatically masculine and its generic, bi-gender or bi-sexual (in the sense of non-sexual state) force far from established. It seems more probable that the 'ādām of Genesis 1–3, even though at times introduced by the definite article, is a male.

If we disregard the superordinate terms 'man' (איש and ה[אדם]) and 'woman' (אשה), we are left with the specific binary opposition זכר/נקבה (זכור). The conceptualization of each is of course different, as evidenced by the terms' etymological derivation and semantic cognates. A 'female' is sexed rather than gendered: she is an 'orifice'; orifices and holes require that they be filled. A 'male' is gendered: he is the carrier of memory, the one 'to be remembered', thus a social agent. The female is there to be penetrated and to be receptive; the term נקבה implies that, socially, there is no difference between her biological and social functions. The male agent carries the burden of social continuity, of culture ('remembrance'); he is there to 'give', that is, penetrate the female 'hole' or receptacle. In the course of culture's taming of nature, males—as their linguistic designation testifies—are the superior gender. In fact, they are the only gender: women are a sex, definable by a decisive physical characteristic. This attitude is

---

A. Brenner (eds.), *On Humour and the Comic in the Hebrew Bible* (Sheffield: *JSOT* and Almond Press, 1990), pp. 39–58.

[9] Heb. ידעה. On this passage and similar ones, where the subject of the verb 'know' is a female agent, see below.

[10] P. Trible, *Love and the Rhetoric of Sexuality* (Philadelphia: Fortress Press, 1978), pp. 144–65. M. Bal, *Lethal Love* (Indianapolis: University of Indiana Press, 1987), pp. 104–30.

clearly central also in the rest of the linguistic stock and discursive treatment of love and desire, as well as to the HB discourse on reproduction (Chapter 4). In other words, it follows from the choice of terms for 'female' and 'male' that the language of love and desire, linked as it must be to the language of reproduction by the contiguity of love, sexual activity and procreation, will reflect—more or less consistently—a social bias for presenting males as active subjects/agents and females as receptive/objectified agents, especially so within the realm of love/desire. What are the differences, then, between the ways women and men 'love' and 'desire' in the HB? In order to answer these question and related ones, a brief survey of the available terms needs to be undertaken.

אהב *and its derivatives*

The HB primary term for 'love' is the consonantal sequence אהב and its derivatives. אהב in the Qal formation is the principal verb form, 'to love' in all senses of the term and with many applications; אהבה, 'love' is the principal noun. The nominal forms נאהבים, 'loved ones' (2 Sam. 1.23) and מאהבים, '[male] sexual lovers' (restricted to Hosea, Jeremiah and Ezekiel; and see below) demonstrably derive from Nif. and Pi. verb formations respectively. The nominal plural אהבים (Hos. 8.9; Prov. 5.19, 7.18) is more restricted in semantic scope because it designates 'sexual activity' specifically, rather than 'love' in general.

The primariness of the sequence אהב (and most of its derivatives, excluding אהבים) is borne out by the extent of its distribution along axes of genre, time, place, quantity, scope and applicability. The designations and connotations of אהב are by no means restricted to either physical/sexual 'love' or else to non-physical/non-sexual 'love'. It is to be expected that no such distinction obtains in the usages of a primary term. Neither is there a discernible discrimination in this consonantal sequence's applicability to variations and shades of [not necessarily physical] 'loving'—'devotion', 'fondness', 'caring', 'affection', 'liking', 'attachment' and so on. A meaningful difference emerges, though, once an analysis of the specific verb formations and their nominal derivatives focuses on the grammatical subject-object relations they are structured into.

אהב (mainly in the Qal verb formation) designates the [subject] activity as well as [object] receptivity of 'loving' in the case of gods and humans alike. In other words, both the subject and the object of the 'loving' emotion or act may be either divine or human. In the case of divine/human reciprocal relations, the distribution of the verb's usage is more restricted to genre/text than to when the referential signifieds of both love-subject and love-object are human. Generally divine-human 'love' is a-sexual in scope (apart from the metaphor of the divine/human marriage, see below and in Ch. 7).[11] Yhwh may have the collective community as his love object,[12] or an individual like Solomon (2 Sam. 12.24) or the elusive 'servant' of deutero-Isaiah (for instance, Isa. 43.4).[13] Yhwh's love may be paternal or maternal.[14] The divine love object may be non-human, inanimate or abstract—like the concept of 'justice' (Isa. 61.8) or Jerusalem/Zion (Ps. 68.68). Within the context of the divine-human 'love and marriage' metaphor of chiefly Hosea, Jeremiah and Ezekiel, Yhwh 'loves' his female love-object. This love-object symbolizes a territory and/or community and/or city but remains, within the metaphor, a woman— that is, a sexed and sexual as well as a gendered object of Yhwh's [metaphorical] sexed, sexual and gendered 'love'.

The HB god may be the object as well as the subject of 'love'. Humans do and/or are commanded to 'love' (אהב) Yhwh, his commandments and his ways, that is, to regard him and his as a supreme love object.[15] Humans might also be accused of 'loving' other gods (1 Kgs. 11.2, of Solomon; also Jer. 8.2, 31). Both as subjects and objects of divine love, humans are addressed as males—unless their

---

[11] Within the present framework of a semantic discussion, I can see no reason to discuss whether passages such as 'and Yhwh opened her [Rachel's] womb' (Gen. 30.22), or the divine man/messenger who 'comes to' Samson's mother (Judg. 13), contain covert allusions or traces to sexual liaisons between divine [male] figures and human [female] partners. The only explicit exception to this, apart from the divine/human marriage metaphor, is the brief and cryptic narrative about the 'sons of god/the gods' who 'came to' (ויבאו אל) 'the daughters of the 'ādām' (Gen. 6.1–4).

[12] Deut. 7.8 and 13, 10.15, 23.6; 1 Kgs. 10.9; Isa. 48.14, 63.9; Hos. 3.1, 11.1 and 4, 14.5; Zeph. 3.17; Mal. 1.2; 2 Chron. 2.10, 9.8.

[13] Perhaps also Abraham, if 'my lover' (Qal active participle, in the defective spelling אֹהֲ[ו*]בִי) is to be emended into the Qal passive participle, אֹהֲ[ו]בִי* in Isa. 41.8.

[14] Hos. 11.1–4; cf. H. Schüngel-Straumann, 'God as Mother in Hosea 11', in A. Brenner (ed.), *A Feminist Companion to the Latter Prophets* (Sheffield: Sheffield Academic Press, 1995), pp. 194–218. For other examples see M. Gruber, 'The Motherhood of God in Second Isaiah', in M.I. Gruber, *The Motherhood of God and Other Studies* (Atlanta: Scholars Press, 1992), pp. 3–15.

[15] For instance: Exod. 20.5 = Deut. 5.9; Deut. 5.9, 6.5, 7.9, 10.12, 11.1 and 13 and 22; 13.4, 19.9, 30.6 and 16 and 20; Josh. 22.5, 23.11; Judg. 5.31; Isa. 58.6; Ps. 5.12, 31.24, 69.37, numerous times in Ps. 119; Prov. 3.12; Dan. 9.4; Neh. 1.5.

'love' for Yhwh is mentioned within the context of the 'marriage metaphor'.

The quantitatively prevalent gendering of both the divine-for-human and the human-for-divine 'love' as grammatically masculine is a conspicuous phenomenon. Whereas women have reputedly been and still are considered inherently religious, that wide-spread cultural view is hardly expressed in the HB's definitions of divine-human and human-divine 'love'.[16] This semantic and grammatical phenomenon can hardly be read as inclusive, bi-gender 'love' language in the religious sphere. Thus, the ability to generate and to act as both subjects and objects of religious 'love' is different for and by M and F constituent members in the envisaged reciprocal relationship between 'them' and their god. This gendered usage persists also in other spheres, as illustrated by the application of 'love' (אהב and other) terms to the [extra-linguistic] field of human-to-human 'love'.

HB women may love their children,[17] another woman,[18] or a man.[19] Nevertheless, no 'real' (to distinguish from metaphorical, collective) woman figure 'loves' a man figure apart from two notable exceptions—Michal and possibly Leah[20]—unless we are within the context of the Song of Songs. In the Song of Songs, the emotional and sexual thrust of the F love subject/object for the M love subject/object is unmistakable.[21] Indeed, the community or Jerusalem—as metaphorized into a woman—may 'love' Yhwh (Jer. 2.2, Lam. 1.19) or other gods and political allies (Jer. 2.25, 33), especially her 'lovers';[22] that 'love', however, is pejoratively depicted. All in all, from the survey of אהב terms it seems that Hebrew Bible F figures do not excel as 'loving'

---

[16] I can see no need, at this point, to substantiate this claim. Although women have by and large been excluded from the official cult in/by biblical literature and beyond it, their presence in it, and their religiosity, can hardly be doubted. Even within the HB, incidental passages bear witness to this state of affairs, such as the passage (1 Sam. 22–25) about the women who 'throng' or 'crowd' the entrance of the tabernacle. The Heb. word for 'gather', 'throng', הצבאות, is extremely strong—as is the implication of the women's sexual exploitation by the officiating priests, Eli's sons.

[17] Rebekah loves Jacob, Gen. 25.28.

[18] Ruth loves Naomi, Ruth 4.15.

[19] Michal loves David (1 Sam. 18.20, 28). The זרה woman (Prov. 7.18) as well as the wisdom figuration (8.17, 21) 'love' men.

[20] Perhaps Leah's words on the birth of Reuben (Gen. 29.32), 'now my man may love me' (יאהבני), are an indication of her love for Jacob.

[21] SoS 1.3, perhaps also v. 4, 5, 7; 2.4; 3.1, 2, 3, 4, 5, perhaps 10; 8.4, 6.

[22] The pejorative מאהבים, as in Jer. 22.20 and 22, 30.14; Ezek. 16.33, 36, 37 and 23.5, 9, 22; Hos. 2.9, 12, 14, 15.

agents—of the legitimate divine male figure (completely absent), their
children (rare), other women (apart from Ruth, who loves Naomi) or
men (rare outside the SoS, explicitly only Michal and, by implication,
Leah). The survey of אהב and other terms supports the notion that
women's subjectivity of/for 'loving' appears impaired by comparison
to male loving subjectivity in all but one area of human loving—
that is, within the realm of illicit desire, as signified by the applicability and distribution also of other subordinate or more specialized
terms in the field.

It appears, therefore, that if scope and number of occurrences are
reliable indications, then males' capacity to be loving subjects/agents
is much better documented, perhaps also better recognized, than
females' capacity to be loving subjects. Some more examples seem
to support this contention. Males 'love' (אהב) their sons: Abraham
loves Isaac (Gen. 22.2), Isaac loves Esau (25.28), Jacob loves Joseph
(37.3, 4; 44.20), a slave might love his sons more than his personal
freedom (Exod. 21.5). A father loves his son (Prov. 13.24). A male
may love another male: Saul loves David (1 Sam. 16.21), as does
Jonathan (18.1, 3; 20.17; 2 Sam. 1.26); perhaps David loves them
both in return (2 Sam. 1.23); Hiram loves David (1 Kgs. 5.15). Pashur
(Jer. 20.4, 6), Haman (Esth. 5.10, 14; 6.13) and David (1 Sam. 18.16,
22) are the love objects of their related communities, presumably
male (grammatically masculine) communities. The male slave might
love his [male] master above his personal freedom (Exod. 21.5; Deut.
15.16). Males (grammatically masculine) are entreated to 'love' other
people, that is, other males, be they social equals (Lev. 19.18) or
foreigners.[23] Males are capable of 'loving' conceptual objects, objects
of moral and intellectual knowledge such as truth and peace (Zech.
8.19), cult (Am. 4.5), goodness (Am. 5.15, Mic. 6.8) or injustice and
evil (Isa. 1.23; Hos. 12.8).[24] Males have appetites: they may love food,
as in the case of Isaac (Gen. 27.4, 9, 14), or wine (Prov. 21.17), or
sleep (Isa. 56.10, 57.8). But, above all, they are the subjective agents

---

[23] Heb. גר, as in Lev. 19.34; Deut. 10.18, 19.

[24] It is possible, of course, to treat the grammatical/semantic masculine subject of
certain 'lovers' as inclusive designations for male 'lovers' and also for female ones,
as subsumed under the gendered heading 'masculine'. However, the HB contains specific instances of inclusive language, such as the specific 'man or woman'
(Exod. 21.29; Num. 5.2, 6; Deut. 17.2, 29.17) or 'male or female' (Deut. 4.16) of
some Law texts. The praxis of interpreting grammatically masculine language as
designating bi-gender inclusivity points, at the very least, to the androcentric bias of
the interpreters.

who 'love' or 'hate' the object *woman*, so much so that their 'love' serves as motivation and has implications for their social and even political behaviour. Isaac 'loves' Rebekah (Gen. 24.67), Jacob loves Rachel (29.18, 20, 30) but 'hates' (שׂנא) Leah. Shechem 'loves' Dinah (34.3). A slave might love his wife, as well as his children and master, above his personal freedom (Exod. 21.5). A man might 'love' or else 'hate' his newly-acquired wife (Deut. 21.15, 16). Samson 'loves' Delilah (Judg. 16.1), and is blackmailed into demonstrating his love for a nameless Philistine woman and for Delilah (14.16; 16.4, 15). Elkanah loves his wife Hannah (1 Sam. 1.5). Amnon loves his half-sister Tamar (2 Sam. 13.1, 4, 15), although his 'love' turns to 'hate' or 'aversion' after he rapes her.[25] Solomon loves many ethnically and culturally foreign women (1 Kgs. 11.1). Rehoboam loves Maacah (2 Chron. 11.21). Hosea is commanded to love a fornicating woman (3.1). The best, says the author of Qoheleth, is to love your wife and enjoy life with her (Qoh. 9.9). Ahasuerus loves Esther (Esth. 2.17). Wisdom can be embraced by its [male] disciples like a female lover (Prov. 4.6, 5.19); [male] love for a woman may be mocked but is nevertheless powerful (SoS 7.7).

Within the divine/human marriage metaphor, the metaphorized woman has 'lovers', מאהבים. The sexual connotations of this Pi'el-derived lexeme are unmistakable: while an active formation designating [masculine, male] love-subjects, it is a pejorative term that conjures, by its plurality, promiscuity of the female.

When a man 'loves' a woman in the HB it is emotional as well as sexual love he is narrated as feeling. Unfortunately more often than not, but with the emphatic exclusion of the Song of Songs texts and implied world, a male's female love-object fails to reciprocate in kind. Thus Rebekah 'loves' her son Jacob, not her husband Isaac. Rachel is nowhere depicted as loving Jacob. Dinah has no narrated emotions for or against Shechem; neither are Samson's beloved women de-picted as reciprocating his feelings. Hannah prefers a son to her hus-band's declared love. Tamar does not reciprocate Amnon's 'love' or 'hatred'. The emotions of Hosea's woman (Hos. 3) are not disclosed. The wisdom figure and the זרה figures (Proverbs 1–9) recommend that their clients 'love' them but, for their part, never give their own emotions away. The wonderment concerning heterosexual sexual love

---

[25] Cf. also Deut. 22.13, 16 and 24.3, where a male's aversion towards a female is considered a ground for divorce.

in Proverbs 30.18–20 is androcentric in the extreme. The apparent
awe expressed for the mystery of the 'the way of a man in a [young]
woman' is directed at the mystery of male love and sexuality rather
than at the miracle of reciprocal man/woman emotions.[26]

It would seem, therefore, that the linguistic data presented by the
textual occurrences of אהב and its derivatives is valuable for a *gendered*
understanding of *gendered* 'love' in the HB. Males are certainly and
by far the more frequent subjects of אהב, be the object of their 'love'
human or divine, sexual or otherwise. They are grammatically active
'lovers', pejoratively or positively referred to as the case might be, of
a variety of objects: divine, human, non-animate. Human females
appear to have a diminished or lesser capacity than human males
for general, active, subjective 'loving', especially but not only for
reciprocating male love towards them. Whether this picture—again,
not applicable to the Song of Songs, where the reverse seems to
be the rule—is reflective of an androcentric world view, or of value
judgment on female loving, or of accidental transmission, or of a
relative lack of authorly interest in female emotion, should be left
hanging for the time being and until other terms for 'love' are
discussed.

Lower-hierarchy love and desire terms

We have already seen that some formations derived from אהב, 'love'
(with general applicability) serve as more *specific* terms for sexual desire,
such as אהבים ('sexual activity') and מאהבים ('[male] sexual lovers'). It
remains to be seen how other, less general terms from the perspectives
of distribution, scope and applicability, function within the semantic
realm of love and desire. In this section, I shall describe some terms
whose denotations as well as connotations sometimes fall within the
realm of sexual 'love' but, at others, transcend it. No precise struc-
turing will be attempted here; rather, an alphabetical order of the
terms will be adhered to. In the next section of this Chapter, specific
terms and idioms for sexual intercourse will be discussed.

Terms that signify 'want, desire' may at times—although not
necessarily—serve, in 'love' contexts, in the partly overlapping but
narrower sense of 'love-motivated desire'. אוה, '[to] desire'—in the

---

[26] Brenner in Brenner and van Dijk Hemmes, *On Gendering Texts*, pp. 133–63.

Pi'el formation (usually with נפש, 'being' as its grammatical subject), Hith. or in the noun תאוה, 'desire'[27]—has in several contexts 'love' connotations. However, such connotations are nowhere sexual connotations. Apart from in Genesis 3.6, where the woman sees that the fruit of the tree is 'desirable to behold', the grammatical or implied subject of the verb is always masculine/male. The object is either inanimate or abstract.[28] The distribution of אוה-derived terms is either in the Pentateuch or else in the so-called wisdom books and the psalms. Their usage is of little substantial assistance for the present inquiry. An apparent variation of אוה, the phonetically and sense-wise similar אבה ('want', in the sense of 'be willing'; Gen. 24.5, 8 and elsewhere), also the noun formation תאבה (Ps. 119.20) and perhaps also the similar but differently arranged sequence תאב ('long for', from the context of Ps. 119.40, 164),[29] are again borderline cases between 'want', 'desire' and 'love', with no sexual connotations.

The term חפץ, in the Qal verb formation, and the nominal חפץ, usually lie within the 'wish', 'want', 'be interested in' field. However, in some instances—especially of the noun phrase ... + ב [נפש] חפצה, when the situational context thus indicates, the implied (to distinguish from the grammatical) subject is a male and the object is either a human female, or male, or inanimate—at least the connotation is that of 'love, desire'. Thus, Shechem loves Dinah and 'cleaves unto her' (דבק and אהב, Gen. 34.3); he does what Dinah's brothers require of him כי חפץ בבת יעקב (v. 19), 'because he desired (= loved) Jacob's daughter'; this is, in my view, as good a translation of this phrase as 'because he *wanted* Jacob's daughter'. Similarly, no woman may 'come' to the king unless he 'desires her' (חפץ בה) and expresses his choice by name (Esth. 2.14); and a man may desire or not desire a woman to be his sexual partner in legal texts.[30] Saul's love for David, documented by the verb אהב, is also signified by the compound

---

[27] Also a Nif. participle in the sense of 'attractive,' hence 'desirable and also appropriate'—concretely (SoS 1.5, 2.14, 4.3, 6.4) as well as in the abstract (Ps. 93.5, 147.1; Prov. 17.7, 19.10).

[28] Like food and drink, several times in Num. 11 (cf. Ps. 106.14), Deut. 14.26, 2 Sam. 23.15, Job 33.20; or material possessions, Deut. 5.17, Qoh. 6.2. Otherwise, abstract concepts are the objects of desire, like 'the day of Yhwh', Am. 5.18.

[29] To distinguish from the homophonic (and perhaps etymologically homonymic) תאב of i.e. Am. 6.8 ('abhor'), which looks like an alternative form of תעב—'abhor', 'be disgusted by'.

[30] Deut. 21.14, 25.7 and 8 (here חפץ is followed by לקחתה, 'to take her [as sexual partner]', rather than by נפש and the preposition ב + [female] object).

... ב חפץ.[31] Other examples, even with Yhwh as subject, are in evidence.[32] In short, at least some occurrences of the HB verb חפץ and its derivatives should be re-examined for a 'love' signification.[33]

The usage of חשק is similar to that of חפץ. Again, an apparent import from another semantic field serves to signify '[to] love, desire', sexually and otherwise. Again, the verb in the Qal formation may appear with the preposition ב, 'in'.[34] Again, the structure חשקה נפשו ... ב, 'his being desired [an object]', may occur with the masculine/male subject and a feminine/female object of desire.[35] Again, the noun חשק—similar in denotation and form to the noun חפץ—may signify non-sexual 'wish' or 'desire'.[36]

The term ... ב דבק, 'cling to', may signify 'love, affection, loyalty'. It affords a good example of how words for various manifestations and measures of 'love' are loaned from other semantic fields. Because the term basically and tangibly has a primarily concrete physical reference ('be in very close proximity to'), it could have been expected that its signification within the 'love' realm will be 'sexual intercourse'. This is certainly not so in the case of Ruth, who 'loves' Naomi (Ruth 4.15) hence 'clings to' her (1.14), or the 'clinging' of most subjects to David (2 Sam. 20.2), or the deuteronomic and psalmist exhortations to cling to Yhwh,[37] or the statement that [a] 'loving [friend] might be closer [דבק] than a brother' (Prov. 18.24). A sexual connotation might be appropriate for the primordial man's departure from his parents in order to 'cling to' his wife (Gen. 2.24), or Shechem's 'being' [נפש] that 'clings to Dinah', for he 'loves' her (34.3). Perhaps a play on both meanings obtains in Joshua 24.24, where the speaker exhorts his audience not to 'cling to' other nations and not to intermarry with them.[38] The secondary, metaphoric nature of דבק in any

---

[31] 1 Sam. 18.22, 19.1.

[32] With a human figure as the object of the divine loving: 2 Sam. 22.20, 1 Kgs. 10.9 (Solomon as object), Isa. 62.4 (with the F territory/community as object).

[33] Including the recurrent refrain of the SoS (2.7, 3.5, 8.4), אם [מה] תעירו ואם [מה] תעוררו את האהבה עד שתחפץ; or the Esther idiom (6.6, 7, 9.11), אשר המלך חפץ ביקרו.

[34] Deut. 21.11, where the subject is an Israelite male and the object a good-looking foreign prisoner of war; or Deut. 10.15, with Yhwh as subject, the Israelite patriarchs as the objects of his love.

[35] Shechem is again the subject, Dinah the object: Gen. 34.8, as in Deut. 21.11.

[36] As expressly concerning Solomon's desire for building constructions, such as in 1 Kgs. 9.1, 19 and 2 Chron. 8.6.

[37] Like in Deut. 10.20, 11, 22, 13.5, 30.20; Josh. 22.5, 23.8; Ps. 63.9, 119.31.

[38] For another tenuous connection between 'sexual love' and 'cling to' cf. the deuteronomistic account of Solomon's failings, 1 Kgs. 11 (esp. v. 2).

sense of 'love' is transparent. Its distribution is largely within well-defined genres or texts (Dtr., hymns) in the general sense of 'love', specific for 'sexual love' or 'intercourse' only in a handful of passages. Therefore, the latter occurrences are here considered as idiosyncratic usages.

Finally, two terms—restricted in scope as they are—have feminine/female agents as their regular subjects. The verb sequence רחם (in the Pi'el formation), probably etymologically akin to the noun רחם ('uterus'), occurs once with the signification 'love', with a woman subject 'loving' her son (Isa. 49.15). Whether this singular occurrence means that the noun רחמים signifies 'love' (especially divine love), remains questionable in spite of the Pu'al form, [לא] רחמה, 'unloved', applied as a name to Hosea's narrated daughter.[39] Last but not least, there obtains a direct term for 'desire' in the HB. The term, תשוקה, is direct and explicit, although it occurs only three times in the entire HB (Gen. 3.16, 4.7; SoS 7.11). At least in Gen. 3.16 and SoS 7.11, the term seems to refer to *sexual or loving desire* (in the unclear Gen. 4.7 passage, the 'desire' appears to be directed towards 'sin' in general): respectively, the desire of a female subject for a male object; and of a male subject for a female object although, in the latter case, the male desire is 'quoted', thus embedded, within an F speech.

Explicit terms for sexual intercourse

Explicit terms for sexual intercourse are grouped below in the following order: first, terms that are more common (that is, have a wider textual distribution); then, terms whose textual locations are more restricted. In other words, rather than adhering to an alphabetical order (as in the previous sections), a construction of a hierarchy based on considerations of distribution and, to a lesser extent, quantity is attempted.

The problem with most of the relevant terms is that they are rare and/or peculiar to a certain text or genre. For instance, the consonantal sequence בעל (see below) has a specific, exclusive signification of 'perform penetration' (in the active mode) or 'be sexually penetrated' (in the passive mode). By right, it should be considered a head-term in the field of 'actualizing sexual desire' or 'sexual consummation' on this count. And yet, its scope and quantity are less

---

[39] Hos. 1.6, 8; 2.3, 25.

than those exhibited—for instance—by the compound בוא אל, 'come
[on]to, penetrate'. Thus, most of the terms signifying sexual activity
are compound terms, that is, expressions compounded of terms used
for other significations too but which acquire a 'sexual' meaning
once they are paired off with certain prepositions within a 'sexual'
circumstantial context. Furthermore, even when it is quite clear that
a verb or verb phrase have penetration/being penetrated as their
signifieds, it is mostly impossible to surmise which kind of 'penetration' they refer to—vaginal, anal, oral or otherwise. We assume, given
the HB preoccupation with procreation, that mostly vaginal intercourse is thus designated. This, however, is an argument from context which might not fit all contexts. This same difficulty pertains to
the more versatile and better attested terms for 'have sexual intercourse' that are described below.

These more frequent idioms which refer specifically and almost
exclusively to 'sexually penetrate', are: בוא אל, (lit. 'come to/onto'),
ידע את ('know' + an accusative marker), קרב אל ('come near to') and
שכב עם/את ('lie with').[40] All four are euphemisms. All four are verb
phrases rather than single verb lexemes. As such, their idiomatic
(euphemistic) signification and usage are different from those of 'come',
'know', 'come near' and 'lie' on their own, without the attached prepositions, or when the verb is not linked tightly and idiomatically
with the preposition following it. Nevertheless, and because in many
cases the prepositions are only loosely attached to the verbs as location markers rather than bound constituents which carry the (euphemistically expressed) meaning—in some non-prepositional and/or
ostensibly non-'sexual' contexts, the verbs will have a dual meaning
or merely introduce ambiguity and 'sexual' insinuations, especially
when clustered together in great density. Thus, for instance, in Ruth 3
'know', 'come to' and 'lie' occur abundantly, without the customary
prepositions, together with 'feet' and the verb 'to expose',[41] within a
potential seduction context; consequently, it is up to the reader to

---

[40] The *ketib* has another root sequence, שגל ('violate', 'ravish'—BDB, p. 993). The
four occurrences—Qal with a female object, Deut. 28.30; Qal pass. with a female
subject, Jer. 3.2; and Nif. with female subject, Isa. 13.16 and Zech. 14.2—are substituted in the *Qere* system by שכב, apparently for being too obscene. The late שגל,
'king's consort' (Ps. 45.10, Neh. 2.6) is probably different etymologically. See also
the occurrences within a biblical Aramaic text, in Dan. 5.2, 3, 23.
[41] For the euphemistic significations of 'feet', 'legs' and so on see Chapter 3, 'A
Body of Difference'.

decide what in fact happens between Ruth and Boaz on the thresh-ing floor.[42] When Joab says to David about Abner, 'You *know* Abner son of Ner; he has come to *seduce* you, to *know* your *ins and outs*, and to *know* all that you do' (2 Sam. 3.25), the 'sexual' innuendo is well-marked. So also when the Israelite spies 'come to' (Jos. 2.2, 3) the prostitute Rahab, literally 'the wide [one, opening]', and 'lie' in her place (v. 2).[43] In all three cases the sly insinuations are more than merely suggestive, even if the regular prepositions are missing or grammatically function as location markers.

Usually and prominently—at least from the perspective of quan-tity and distribution across genres—a man 'comes onto' (בוא אל) a woman:[44] she is the object of the action, he is the subject.[45] A man 'knows' (ידע, followed by את or the accusative) a woman sexually; it may be inferred that vaginal penetration is thus designated, since a virgin is defined as one who has 'not known' a man.[46] A woman or female figuration might be in the subject position of such 'knowing' or 'experiencing' penetration if she is Yhwh's re-educated wife (Hos. 2.22), or might not 'know' if she is 'a virgin that has not known a man'.[47] A woman-subject who 'comes near' (קרב אל) an animal to 'have sex with'[48] will be sentenced to death; in other cases of 'come near' the acting subject is a male, the acted-upon object is a woman—

---

[42] See also Ch. 3, 'A Body of Difference'.

[43] P. Bird, 'The Harlot as Heroine: Narrative Art and Social Presupposition in Three Old Testament Texts', *Semeia* 46 (1989), pp. 127–28. For a humorous inter-pretation of the Rahab story see also Y. Zakovitch, 'Humor and Theology, or the Successful Failure of the Israelite Intelligence (Josh. 2): A Literary-Folklorist Ap-proach', in S. Niditch (ed.), *Text and Tradition: The Hebrew Bible and Folklore* (Atlanta: Scholars Press, 1990), pp. 75–98.

[44] Gen. 16.4, 29.23, 30.3, 4; 38.2, 8, 9, 16; 39.14, 17; Deut. 21.13, 22.13; Judg. 15.1, 16.1; 2 Sam. 16.21, 17.25; Ezek. 16.33 and 23.17, 44; Ps. 51.2; Ruth 4.13. Puns on the compound 'come to', with the regular as well as the specialized, euphemistic 'sexual' meaning are possibly to be read in Josh. 2.3; Judg. 3.20, 4.21, 13.6, 19.22; 2 Sam. 11.4; SoS 2.4, 5.1; Esth. 2.12, 13, 15 and 4.11, 16.

[45] The only possible exception is Bath Sheba after David sends for her: '. . . and she came to him [ותבוא אליו] and he lay with her [וישכב עמה] . . .' (2 Sam. 11.4), if we read reciprocity into their actions. Otherwise, Bath Sheba 'comes to' David in the non-euphemistic sense, so that he can have sex with her. In so far as the girls 'coming to' Ahasuerus in Esther are concerned, the wordplay is just that, a word-play based on the dual usage of the term.

[46] Cf. Olyan, '"And with a Male"', p. 184. Other examples are Gen. 4.1, 24.16 cf. 19.8; Judg. 11.39, 19.22, 21.12; 1 Kgs. 1.4; Hos. 2.10.

[47] Jephthah's daughter, Judg. 11.39; and the girls from Jabesh Gilead, 21.11, 12. For the specific usage of 'a woman who has known [ידעה] the lying of a man' (Num. 31.17, 18, 35), see below.

[48] Heb. לרבעה, apparently 'to have sex with her [the animal, hence "it"]' (Lev.

as illustrated by Moses' decree for the real [male] members of the covenant community just before they witness the theophany on Sinai, 'do not come near a woman' (Exod. 19.15). Although the term here employed is נגש אל rather than קרב אל, the concept as well as the intention are identical. Independent, legally-condoned sexual agency is first and foremost, although not entirely and exclusively, the prerogative of males; this attitude is etched into the linguistic usage which, in its turn, fosters the attitude and perpetrates it.[49]

One of the regular expressions for denoting 'to have sexual intercourse' is שכב את/עם, 'lie with'. This expression appears approximately forty times with this denotation in the HB. In the majority of cases, a male is the verb's subject, a woman its object.[50] The only clear inversion of roles into female subject, male object of the action, occurs in the case of Lot's daughters who, as the plot dictates, initiate the incestuous sex with their father.[51] In a few other cases the implied subject is a male but the object of the action is an animal.[52] A male agent (of penetration) and a male object (of penetration) are indicated by Leviticus 18.22, 20.13.

The nominal משכב, 'lying' in the sense of 'experience intercourse', is used of male as well as female agents; however, the linguistic usage in each case is slightly different. Men, according to the Holiness code, are proscribed from 'lying with a man the *lying of a woman*', משכבי אשה (in the plural)—whereas women are defined as virgins or non-virgins by 'knowing' a man (איש) from the aspect of 'lying with a male' (משכב זכר, in the singular), or simply as 'knowing/not knowing' [the lying of] a male. Olyan rightly asks whether the two concepts,

---

20.16). See also 18.23, 'and a woman will not *stand in front of an animal to have sex with it*', with the same word; and the Hif. form, 19.19.

[49] Other examples of קרב אל are: Lev. 18.6, 14, 19; Isa. 8.3. See also variations on this usage in Num. 25.6 (in the Hif.: 'a man' 'brings his brother [a male object] closer' to a Midianite woman [a grammatically indirect, female object]; the purpose is clearly sexual), Prov. 5.8.

[50] Gen. 30.15, 16 (Jacob with Leah); 34.2, 7 (Shechem with Dinah); 35.22 (Reuben with Bilhah); 39. 7, 12, 14 (Potiphar's wife asking Joseph to 'lie with her'); Exod. 22.15; Lev. 15.33, 19.20; 20.11, 12, 13, 18, 20; Deut. 22.22, 23, 25, 28, 29 and 27.20, 22, 23; 1 Sam. 2.22; 2 Sam. 11.4, 11; 12.11, 24; 13.11, 14.

[51] Gen. 19.32, 33, 34, 35; and see Chapter 5. Olyan, '"And with a Male"', p. 185 n. 16, implies that a woman is the subject of sexually 'lying' in Gen. 39.7, 12 and 2 Sam. 13.11—which seems to me strange for Gen. 39.

[52] Exod. 22.18 and Deut. 27.21 (animal); Lev. 18.22, 20.13 (human male). See Ch. 5.

'lying of a male' and 'lying of a woman', are a true pair, given the difference in number (plural as against the singular) and the binary opposition male/woman instead of male/female (נקבה); and what each of these signifies. The issue of uneven terminology, singular/plural formations and male/woman, is not easy to solve. It is made easier, perhaps, by interrelating our passages to Leviticus 19.20, 'when a *man* (איש) lies with a woman שכבת זרע'. This construct form of שכבה is defined by the dictionaries (cf. *BDB*) as the regular 'layer'. שכבה, however, can be read as a polysemic equivalent of משכב, a different formation but with the same sense. In 19.20, then, a 'man lies with a woman a lying of seed'; this is probably the meaning of 'the lying of a male'. This passage, situated as it is between the two occurrences of משכבי אשה, is helpful. And indeed, on the question of extralinguistic signification Olyan is quite direct:

> If *miškab zākār* means specifically 'male vaginal penetration', its ana-
> logue *miškĕbē 'iššâ* should mean something like 'the act of condition of
> a woman's being penetrated' or, more simply, 'vaginal receptivity', the
> opposite of vaginal penetration . . . Thus, in vaginal intercourse, a woman
> experiences (idiomatically 'knows' or 'lies') *miškab zākār* (male penetra-
> tion) while, presumably, she offers her partner *miškĕbē 'iššâ* (vaginal
> receptivity), which he experiences ('knows' or 'lies').[53]

While I wholly agree with Olyan's conclusion that, in spite of the linguistic difficulties involved, vaginal penetration (for the male; cf. 19.20) and reception (for the female) are implied by משכב, I cannot agree with his evaluation of the verb sequence שכב as designating equal agent/subject positions for females as well as males. In the HB and *contra* Olyan, a woman cannot '"lie" with a man' just as a man can '"lie" with a woman'.[54] The reasons for objecting to Olyan's position here are several. Quantitatively, as has been shown here, the occurrences of females 'knowing', 'coming to', 'coming near to' and 'lying with' as agents are very few in comparison to similar male activity; and females never 'master' (בעל) male partners (see below). Within the Holiness code itself, only 'men' are the subjects of 'lying with', and females are the verb's object. Furthermore their 'knowl-edge' or 'lying' as subjects, if it occurs, is either pejoratively depicted or else denotes lack of 'knowledge'. There are no negative connotations

---

[53] Olyan, '"And with a Male"', p. 185.
[54] Olyan, '"And with a Male"', p. 185 n. 16.

attached to the nominal phrase משכב זכר wherever it occurs; there is obviously a negative evaluation, a proscription, attached to משכבי אשה. As their forms indicate, the two expressions are not fully analogous: while the male version is active, the female version is receptive/passive.

The single lexeme בעל ('have sexual intercourse'), from the same sequence as the term for 'master' (בעלים) and the god Ba'al, always has a male as its subject, a female as its object when in the Qal formation.[55] The female is the בעולה (Qal participle) or בעו[ל]ת בעל,[56] the one who has been 'mastered', that is penetrated (by a 'husband'); or the grammatical—albeit not the actual—subject of the sexual action is in the Nif. formation.[57] No BH female figuration actually 'masters' a male.

The Qal formation of צחק displays a basic meaning of 'laugh', as in the name יצחק (Isaac) and in the etymologically close and semantically homologous sequence שחק. The Pi. formation of צחק and, statistically even more so, of שחק, signifies 'to play, sport', especially in the contexts of visual performance in front of an audience,[58] dancing and music.[59] In some passages צחק Pi. implies by connotation, if not by more direct designation, 'to have sexual activity'. Thus Abimelek watches Isaac (יצחק) have sexual play (מצחק) with his wife Rebekah (Gen. 26.8); Potiphar's wife accuses her husband of bringing Joseph to 'sexually play with' her (39.17); Sarah sees Yishmael 'play' (מצחק; no object), perhaps sexually aroused or playing with Isaac, hence demands his expulsion (21.9); the Israelites construct the golden calf, then eat and drink, then proceed to 'play [sexually]' (Exod. 32.6). A similar usage of שחק Pi. is evident in postbiblical Hebrew, for example in b. Nid. 13b, which quotes tannaitic sources: in a discussion of this passage, Boyarin states that the term 'is used as an explicit term for sexual interaction'.[60] It would therefore seem that, while the sexual connotation of צחק Pi. is evident, its distribution is somewhat limited to specific narrative sources. Moreover, in at least two of the

---

[55] Deut. 21.13, 24.1; Isa. 62.5 (twice).
[56] Gen. 20.3; Deut. 22.22; Isa. 54.1, 62.4.
[57] Isa. 62.4; Prov. 30.23.
[58] Like Samson in front of the Philistines, Judg. 16.25 (צחק Pi.) and 27 (שחק Pi.); Or the representative combatants of Abner and Joab, 2 Sam. 2.14.
[59] For instance 1 Sam. 18.7; 2 Sam. 6.5, 21; Jer. 15.17, 31.4; Job 40.29; 1 Chron. 13.8.
[60] Boyarin, 'Are There Any Jews', p. 438.

four instances recorded a pun on the name Isaac is undoubtedly intended.[61] Thus, the notional reference—at least for the HB occurrences of this term—is elusive and remains general. Nevertheless, it would seem that this term too is constructed as a signifier of male active sexual agency: its grammatical subject is always male, or an implied collective male subject (as in Exod. 32.6); its object, when available, may be either a female (Rebekah, Potiphar's wife) or another male (Yishmael and Isaac).

Apart from אהבים, sexual love/intercourse is referred to by the term ד[ו]דים, although the reference is opaque or perhaps non-specific. This term occurs in Ezekiel (16.8, 23.17), Proverbs (7.18) and the Song of Songs (1.2, 4; 7.13; 4.10[62]). A male lover in the Song of Songs is designated דוד, exclusively in F speech.[63] ד[ו]דים, [sexual love] as well as דוד, '[male] lover' appear to be a loan from the kinship field: the primary signification of דוד is 'uncle', much like the functioning of אחות, 'sister' as '[female] lover' in M speech.[64] The female equivalent of the male דוד, 'lover', seems to be רעיה, 'friend', once again a loan from a close semantic field and—apart from one occurrence (5.16)—always an F voice designation of 'his' female lover.[65]

Another monolexeme, עגב and also עגב על,[66] with noun derivatives (עגבים, Ezek. 33.31, 32;[67] עגבה, 23.11), probably denotes 'make sexual advances' and 'court', 'play sexual games', perhaps 'courtship, sexual teasing' for the nominal lexemes. Apart from the instance in Jeremiah, all the verb occurrences have a female or female figuration as a subject, males or male figurations as objects of the action. The

---

[61] Y. Zakovitch, 'Dual Name Play', MA dissertation, The Hebrew University (1971, Heb.), pp. 14–15, 59–61.

[62] If this instance is not to be read as דדיך, 'your [female] breasts'.

[63] 1.13, 14, 16; 2.3, 8, 9, 10, 16, 17; 4.16; 5.2, 4, 8, 9, 10, 16; 6.1, 2; 7.10, 11, 12, 14; 8.14. Perhaps an undifferentiated usage gender-wise is indicated by the M voice address of 5.1, 'eat and drink [wine]', *lovers* (= דודים).

[64] SoS 4.9, 10, 12; 5.1 and 2 (the latter a 'quotation' of M speech embedded in F discourse). When F discourse refers to 'brothers' in the SoS, it is to actual kin brothers (1.5–6, 8.8–10), apart from the single wishful statement of 8.1, 'I wish that you were my brother . . .'. I doubt whether much can be deduced from the seemingly incestuous contents of such terms of endearment, although the term 'sister' is coupled with the term כלה, 'bride'—see Chapter 5 of this book.

[65] 1.9, 15; 2.2, 10, 13; 4.1, 7; 6.4.

[66] The verb forms in Jer. 4.30; Ezek. 23.5, 7, 9, 12, 16.

[67] This apparently plural formation functions much like אהבים and ד[ו]דים, that is, as a designation for [physical, sexual] love; cf. Rashi and RaDaK for occurrences of עגב verb and noun formations in the verses quoted.

term is certainly pejorative, as gleaned from the situational and verbal contexts.[68] At any rate, the narrow distribution precludes further
conclusions.

The idiom נלה ערוה, 'expose nakedness = sexual organs', occurs
quite a number of times. However, most if not all of these occurrences are within the circumstantial contexts of incest and within the
law codes. Therefore, it would seem preferable to discuss this noun
phrase together with other incest terms (Chap. 5). Nevertheless, it
undoubtedly has a sufficiently broad semantic scope to have func-
tioned as a wide-ranging denotation of 'sexual games'. Like in the
case of most of the other terms, the subject of the verb is almost
always male, whereas the 'nakedness' exposed belongs to a female. A
situation of total male subjectivity holds also for the idiom נתן שכבת
... ב [זרע], 'put seed in', a truly specific M term restricted to the
priestly literature.[69]

Assessment and conclusions

The assessment of BH semantic data is always problematic. The
Hebrew Bible is a small, finite, limited corpus. So many terms are
either *hapax legomena*, rare (probably about half if not more of the
linguistic stock), or genre-specific. Etymology and cognates are not
necessarily of reliable value. We know too little of the history of
ancient Hebrew and of its development. We know too little of the
societies that produced the HB, about their times and locations. We
know next to nothing about biblical authors, compilers and editors,
and about their motivations. Our acts of interpretation are conditioned by our readerly locations and by ideologies, whatever they
are. And so on. Keeping all these reservations in mind, the time has
come to assess the 'evidence' of the primary-layer terms for 'love', as
they are presented here.

My principal concerns were to list the available terms, in an
attempt to organize them into some kind of a coherent semantic
construction; to examine their usage, especially as influenced by
and illustrating gendered [textual, grammatical and extra-linguistic]

---

[68] See Rashi and RaDaK for these passages.
[69] Lev. 18.20 and 23, 20.25; Num. 5.20; cf. also Lev. 19.20, discussed above.

applications; and to draw tentative conclusions concerning gender [social] practice and sexual conventions in ancient Israel.

The conclusions are not uniform. In the language of all strands of HB literature, males are designated agents and subjects of 'love' and 'loving' much more frequently and much more positively than females. This holds true for all kinds of 'loving' in all spectrums of intensity, from an emotion felt for peers, children, the divine, inanimate objects, concepts, women, to being designated almost exclusively as the active partners in sexual intercourse. Women are designated mostly as love objects or recipients, especially so in the sphere of sexual activity.

Nevertheless, in the Song of Songs female figures are subjects as well as objects of love and sex. In the 'marriage' metaphor, divine loving is metaphorized into male [sexual and otherwise] love for a symbolic female. This 'female' object, in her turn, is narrated as capable of feeling and pursuing love and sex as a subject; nonetheless, the objects of her desire are depicted as negative, and so is 'her' sexual behaviour. The 'love' language of the 'marriage' metaphor has much in common with the love language of the Song of Songs; however, its gendered usage is so diametrically opposed as to render female subjectivity in 'loving' into nothing but [im]pure lust.[70]

Thus, semantically love, desire, lust, sexual intercourse and 'sexuality' are differently constructed for males and for females. In the language, males have a greater capacity for love and desire on all levels. They may lust and covet,[71] they may rape before or after claiming to 'love' their female victim (as in the cases of Shechem and Amnon). Male 'loving' is not always what it perhaps should be, certainly it is not always legitimate. But, on the whole and in general, males can be subjective and active agents of desire. Furthermore, and with few exceptions, men are the *knowing* subjects of the supreme act of knowledge, the sexual act. Women are, by comparison and—again—outside the Song of Songs (and the prophetic marriage metaphor), more passive, less knowing and less discerning in their 'love', from love for children to sexual desire. Consequently,

---

[70] As shown, for instance, by F. van Dijk-Hemmes for correspondences by reversal between the SoS and Hosea: 'The Imagination of Power and the Power of Imagination: An Intertextual Analysis of Two Biblical Love Songs—The Song of Songs and Hosea 2', *JSOT* 44 (1989), pp. 75–88; repr. in A. Brenner (ed.), *A Feminist Companion to the Song of Songs* (Sheffield: *JSOT* Press, 1993), pp. 156–70.
[71] As, for instance, in Exod. 20.17 = Deut. 5.21.

while male sexual pleasure as well as displeasure is mentioned in passing in several genres—in the Deuteronomic law, in narratives—female desire and sexual pleasure is celebrated only in the Song of Songs;[72] in the prophetic metaphor it is acknowledged but judged promiscuous.

In the last Chapter of this book (Chapter 8) a more detailed discussion of HB 'knowledge' and sexuality will be broached. Meanwhile, suffice it to claim that, in the light of linguistic evidence, in most of the HB both female capacity for general 'loving' and female desire (including sexual desire) are suspect and need regulating by a knowing, that is, male agent. This attitude will be found consistent with the investigation of other sets of related terms (Chapter 3, for instance). It will also be found (particularly in Chapter 7) that female sexuality, not only desire, is suspect. Love and lust are according to the HB experienced and acted upon by members of both genders, but in different ways.

---

[72] Unless we understand the injunction to a newly-married man to 'make his wife joyous' (ושמח את אשתו, Deut. 24.5), instead of going to war, as an indirect allusion to *her* sexual pleasure.

CHAPTER THREE

A BODY OF DIFFERENCE? THE CONSTRUCTION OF MALE AND FEMALE BODIES IN LANGUAGE AND IDEOLOGIES[1]

How are sexual, in the sense of biological-anatomical, differences between females and males conveyed in the language of the HB? How are visual and affective sex differences conveyed by the language? How does the semantic data reflect and perpetuate gender differences and social norms? How is the gendered body constructed as sexually appealing or, on the contrary, repulsive? What is perceived as human, physical, male and female beauty?; and how do perceptions of human beauty serve as motivations and justifications: first and foremost in the context of sexuality and desire but also in other social and political contexts?

A male sexual body may be primarily recognizable by its penis and ability to produce semen; a woman's sexual body is primarily defined by virginity (or its lack) and then menstruation. But penis and semen, virginity and menstruation and other sex-specific bodily attributes are not immediately apparent. They can be disguised or obliterated by clothing. 'There should not be a man's outfit[2] on a woman, and a man should not wear a woman's garment,[3] for all this is an abomination for Yhwh your god' (Deut. 22.5). This short passage betrays a concern, perhaps an anxiety, about visible differences between the clothed male and female bodies: they should be clear-cut. The insistence on easily recognizable boundaries often signifies uncertainty about those same boundaries.[4] In the present

---

[1] This Chapter contains short descriptions of biblical semantic stock for body organs. Z. Zevit delivered a somewhat similar linguistic analysis of biblical terms for body parts in the AAR/SBL meeting in Chicago (1994). Unfortunately, I have not been able to consult his work although, as I have been told, it contains points similar to mine. Each of our two analyses, needless to say, was conducted independently.

[2] Heb. כלי, in the HB usually 'vessel' but, as amply attested in the Mishna and in other postbiblical Hebrew (MH) sources, also and specifically 'garment'.

[3] Hebrew שמלה, the usual term for 'garment'.

[4] M. Douglas, *Purity and Danger* (London: Routledge & Kegan Paul, 1966), p. 53; and *Implicit Meanings* (London and Boston: Routledge & Kegan Paul, 1975).

case, *visible* difference appears to be at stake. But, as usual, the visual is an aspect of the social. In other words, the instruction that sex (anatomy-biology) should correspond in appearance to gender (the social), and that the boundaries in both cases be unequivocal at all times, suggests uncertainties on the social as well as the corporeal level.[5] This uncertainty about the clothed body, together with the insistence that the body be clothed (thus more gendered than sexed), apparently promotes physical difference, hence gender difference. However, and paradoxically, biblical language is not consistent in this respect: the naked body is not similarly and unequivocally differentiated into female and male.

By and large, the Bible is reticent about physical descriptions. This is well in keeping with the prevalent narrative and/or editorial preferences for brevity and economy,[6] perhaps also with the somewhat deficient capabilities for plastic representations of living and especially human forms (as also evidenced by material culture remains of ancient Israel). This austerity may also represent socio-sexual mores and conventions. Therefore, it seems, biblical designations of human erogenous zones, primary and secondary and of both sexes, are in general euphemistic—even in the Song of Songs, this quite unique of biblical books. Norms or, perhaps, ideals of sexual modesty are possibly reflected by and in the semantic-literary usage. However, as we shall see, circumspection and prudence obtain especially in relation to the [naked] male body. Less discretion is applied to descriptions of the female body, which is regarded in and by the language as relatively public, in contrast to the relative privacy of the male sexual body.

The linguistic inventory of reproductive and sexual body parts embodies a tension between two tendencies. On the one hand, the relative exposure of the female sexual body—and, especially, the linguistic/textual preoccupation with female breasts as a locus of sexual attraction—are noticeable. On the other hand, what seems like ideomoral reticence results in a hardly differentiated language for females' and males' genitalia and reproductive organs. This in effect camouflages, within the language, obvious referential differences. For in-

---

[5] It is therefore not surprising that the Jewish sages expanded the prescription beyond appearance, to include gendered occupations and gendered behaviour in general: see *b. Naz.* 59a and Rashi for the passage.

[6] Cf. for instance S. Bar-Efrat, *The Art of Narrative in the Hebrew Bible* (trans. from Hebrew; Sheffield: *JSOT* Press, 1992), Part II.

stance, 'children' are sometimes designated by the poetic, metaphoric idiom פרי בטן; how is בטן to be understood? In several passages the term refers to 'stomach' as digestive organ, but these occurrences seem to be mostly concentrated in wisdom literature.[7] 'Stomach' or 'belly' are an appropriate euphemism for the womb inside it. Therefore, in the case of Rachel, 'fruit of the *womb*' seems an appropriate translation for פרי בטן (Gen. 30.2), as it is in Job's statement, 'naked I came forth *from my mother's* womb' (מבטן אמי, Job 1.21); or his lament that he would have preferred his 'womb' (בטן), that is, the one that gave him birth, to have been closed (Job 3.10)—as it is in the address of Lemuel's mother to her son as 'son of my womb', בר בטני (Prov. 31.2).[8] We understand that the word בטן is linked to a female subject, hence it coyly and poetically designates 'womb'; also, its parallelism with 'thigh' in at least one passage (Num. 5.22, 27) indicates that (and see below). However, פרי בטן is even more frequent when no gender marker obtains for the parent or, better still, when the addressed parents are male parents.[9] The shift from the general ('stomach') to a part thereof ('male reproductive organ'?) is not easily explained. Similarly, the use of the more frequent term for 'belly, bowels', מעים,[10] as designating 'womb' appears to be self-understood.[11] 'Bowels' as the locus of male procreation, at times in parallelism to other euphemistic terms like 'thigh' and 'stomach', are more problematic.[12] Obviously, outside language children cannot be and are not men's 'fruit of the belly' in the way they are women's 'fruit of the belly'. Female and male 'bellies' are differently constructed. Be the semantic processes that blur such sex differences in/by the language what they may, the result is odd. Sex differences are not adequately signified in/by the language because the distinction is only sketchily applied

---

[7] Ezek. 3.3; Ps. 44.26; and six times in Job.

[8] Cf. M. Stol, *Zwangerschap en geboorte bij de Babyloniers en in de bijbel* (Leiden: Ex Oriente Lux, 1983), pp. 7–9, also about the 'full belly > womb' (בטן מלאה*) of Qoh. 11.5.

[9] Deut. 7.13; 28.4, 18, 53; Mic. 1.7; Ps. 132.11. A similar expression occurs in Hos. 9.16.

[10] 2 Sam. 20.10; Ezek. 3.3; Job 20.19; Ps. 22.15, 40.9; Jon. 2.2; 2 Chron. 21.15, 32.21. For the 'belly' as the locus of extreme emotion: Jer. 4.19, 31.19; Lam. 1.20; Job 30.27.

[11] Gen. 25.23 (Rebekah); Ruth 1.11; Ps. 71.6; perhaps also SoS 5.4, where sexual excitement may be signified by the phrase ומעי המו עליו, 'and my innards were disturbed for/because of him'.

[12] Gen. 15.4 (Abraham); 2 Sam. 7.12 (David); Isa. 48.19.

to the sexual body. And yet, while distinction is camouflaged in sexual
and procreational matters, it continues to exist socially and morally.

The narrative coyness and/or compactness do not indicate that
corporeality, appearances and physical beauty are not recognized as
sexually meaningful. On the contrary. Beauty may be irrelevant to
or redundant in a wife (Prov. 31.30), but is a fundamental requirement in a lover (SoS). Male beauty is important, especially in a political
leader (see below). Depictions of desirable, non-erogenous physical
beauty features are for the most part conventionalized and similar
for males and females. In males physical strength, stature and height
are at times cited as added attractions; so does hair. In females, evo-
cations of gentleness[13] through metaphors are more frequent than of
power. Indeed and not surprisingly, physical beauty appears to underlie sexual desirability in both females and males.

In the following remarks, I shall proceed from a short discussion
of human erogenous zones, to nudity in general, to considerations
concerning physical beauty and its lack.

Male and undifferentiated sexual organs

The culture reflected in the Bible appears to have been particularly
and vigorously dedicated to protecting the human penis and its physical
environs.[14] This zealous protection is extended by the language or
rather, I should say, by the lack of specific relevant terminology for
designating the penis as well as by scanty usage of the few, euphemistic recorded terms.

This state of affairs is paradoxical, because the society that created
biblical literature is an undoubtedly phallic, phallocentric society.
Characterizing biblical Israel/ancient Israel as a phallocentric society
is by no means an empty generalization. Such a characterization
does not imply a mere reduction of the data to a socio-psychological,
gendered state: it does not imply simply that males, because they
have penises, are the owners of the phallus. The society thus referred
to posits the human penis as the explicit, emblematic and exclusive

---

[13] As for instance in Isa. 47.1, where 'soft and gentle' (רכה וענגה) seem like typical lady-like qualities, to be taken away from the metaphorized 'daughter of Babylon'.
[14] The graphically explicit references of Jer. 5.8 and Ezek. 23.20 are exceptions
which highlight normal linguistic, hence social, conventions.

symbol of religious identity and membership of the communal order. The penis symbolizes the special link between this society's god and the members of the community. It serves as a physical reminder of both inclusion in the community and exclusion from it. Circumcision, taken over from other cultures and re-interpreted, defines males and males only as the full members of the covenant community.[15] No wonder that Christianity did not separate itself from Judaism— from carnal Israel, physical Israel, the Israel of the flesh—until the connection between the penis and the divine was severed.[16] By this same token, women are excluded a-priori from that communal and symbolic order. The bonding with the [male] god is stamped on the [male] body: the anti-woman bias is built into physicalities, whereby it is transposed to the sphere of symbolic order. By contiguity of signifier (circumcised penis) and referent (phallus), by substituting gendered body for gendered sexuality and vice versa, the link between male sexuality and the divine is established through and by the male body. Furthermore the penis, not only the phallus, acquires spiritual significance. This significance is enhanced, for instance, by the Priestly injunction about human procreation: the penis is the *instrument* of divinely ordained work. No symmetrical view of female sexuality obtains: the uterus is the *vessel*. Thus, it becomes culturally easier to devalue female sexuality while upholding male sexuality.

The identification of, or link between, the human circumcised penis and the divine phallus is far from theologically unproblematic. It relates to questions about the Hebrew god's gender; and to the general problem of humanity's [dis]similarities to that god. These issues, although related to the present topic, will be discussed in the final Chapter of this book (Chapter 8).

---

[15] For psychological and literary aspects of biblical circumcision, its connections with the perception of female sexuality as a threat to males and, particularly, its castration contents, cf. I.N. Rashkow, *The Phallacy of Genesis: A Feminist-Psychoanalytic Approach* (Louisville, KY: Westminster/John Knox, 1993), pp. 91–109. References to secondary literature can be found there and in the Notes, pp. 125–28.

[16] In the following analysis I am deeply and gratefully indebted to Daniel Boyarin (*Carnal Israel: Reading Sex in Talmudic Culture* [Berkeley: University of California Press, 1993], esp. ch. 1, pp. 31–60; and *A Radical Jew: Paul and the Politics of Identity* [Berkeley: University of California Press, 1994]); and Howard Eilberg-Schwartz ('The Problem of the Body for the People of the Body' in H. Eilberg-Schwartz [ed.], *People of the Body: Jews and Judaism from an Embodied Perspective* [New York: NYU in Stony Brook, 1992]), pp. 17–46.

To return from ideology to the language that expresses it. Not surprisingly, the 'foreskin', עָרְלָה, designating the part removed from the penis and dedicated to the divine, is a specific term mentioned sixteen times in contexts of circumcision; its only other contexts are either agricultural or martial. Yet, the penis itself is simply and politely 'flesh' or 'meat', בָּשָׂר;[17] and 'flesh' also has many other denotations. The evasion is highlighted by postbiblical MH.[18] MH has more specific terms for designating the penis, like זַיִן (also and transparently 'weapon') and אֵבֶר ('limb', '[physical] organ'). These MH terms are euphemisms too, but with a difference: the euphemism is loaned from another semantic field. When זַיִן designates a weapon, it usually appears within the noun-phrase כְּלִי זַיִן, literally 'weapon, weaponry'. אֵבֶר, 'limb' may be understood as an ellipsis for 'the limb' par excellence. Thus, the non-sexual extralinguistic referents of the euphemistic linguistic signifiers for 'penis' in MH are different and more varied than the referential scope of the BH term בָּשָׂר, 'flesh' and also 'meat'.

Reticence about male genitalia is to be surmised from the rarity of occurrences as well as the nature of the euphemisms employed. The specific term 'testicle' (אֶשֶׁךְ) occurs only once (Lev. 21.20).[19] Another euphemism for male genitals is the single occurrence of מְבֻשָׁיו (Deut. 25.11), 'his shameful', hence private, parts. The single occurrences of the singular form שֵׁת (Isa. 20.4) and the plural שְׁתוֹתֵיהֶם (2 Sam. 10.4) perhaps designate 'genitalia' in general; otherwise, they designate 'backside' or both front and back 'nakedness'.[20] That the term was hardly used is evidenced by the substitution of מִפְשָׂעָה, from a root meaning 'walk', for the obscure plural שְׁתוֹתֵיהֶם in I Chronicles

---

[17] Notably in Gen. 17, in the compound בְּשַׂר עָרְלָה, and in Ezek. 16.26 (quoted above).

[18] Mishnaic Hebrew or, rather, Middle Hebrew: the linguistic traditions of Hebrew preserved in the Mishna, Tosephta, Talmuds, Midrash, early *piyyut* and so on. 'MH' is clearly an inaccurate, generalized construct. It is here used in that sense, without taking into account variations of time and place, in as much as BH (Biblical Hebrew) is regarded, inaccurately and consciously, as a literary unity for the purpose of the present discussion.

[19] In this reference, a man with a ruptured testicle, like any other male of marked physical defect, cannot officiate as an Aaronide priest before God. MH has another euphemism, בֵּיצָה (also 'egg'), which has passed on into colloquial Modern Hebrew usage.

[20] At least in the case of the Chron. term, מִפְשָׂעָה, it is clear that it is, once more, a euphemism. And see below for 'leg/foot/', 'thigh' and so on as euphemisms for 'penis'.

19.4 (the parallel of 2 Sam. 10.4); that its designation was far from certain is evidenced not only by the interpretations of medieval Jewish commentators[21] but also by the English translations, for instance the RSV and NRSV which simply and vaguely have both terms rendered as 'hips'. מרגלות (literally, 'the place of the legs/feet') derives from רגלים ('legs/feet'),[22] as possibly in Ruth 3 (vv. 4, 7, 8, and 14).[23] רגל or רגלים, 'leg/s' may serve as a similar euphemism in compounds referring to sexual activity and physical relief for both males and females although, once more, the statistical bias (for whatever it is worth) is in favour of male bodily representation.[24]

A crude reference to 'penis' is perhaps obtained in the young advisers' words to Rehoboam (1 Kgs. 12.10 = 2 Chron. 10.11). The young advisers suggest that Rehoboam refuse the people, who ask that the oppressive measures decreed by his father Solomon be lifted, and answer them thus: קטני עבה ממתני אבי. Although the words מתן (singular) or מתנים (dual) usually signify 'waist', 'hip[s]',[25] it is here and perhaps also elsewhere[26] probably a reference to the royal penis. Rehoboam is probably advised to say, 'my small [finger] is thicker than my father's penis'; which makes much more sense than the rendering, 'my small [finger] is thicker than my father's *waist*'. No wonder that, as the story unfolds, this part of the advice is omitted from Rehoboam's public reply to the people (1 Kgs. 12.14 = 2 Chron. 10.14), although he certainly refuses to comply with their demand. Elsewhere, the same word is linked with female sex/procreation organs through a birth metaphor (Isa. 21.3, cf. Nah. 2.11).

Similarly, the dual term חלצים, 'sides' or 'loins' may also signify 'waist' or 'genitals', as girdled (Isa. 5.27, 11.5, 32.11). Or, in the

---

[21] See Rashi, RaDaK and RaLBaG for 2 Sam. 10.4, Isa. 20.4, 1 Chron. 19.4. Also RaDaK for Judg. 5.15, Isa. 19.9 and 47.2, Jer. 4.17, Am. 7.1, Mic. 1.11, Zec. 14.5 and Rashi for Ps. 73.6.

[22] Perhaps by analogy to מראשות ('place of the head', 'where the head is put', as in Gen. 28.11) from ראש, 'head'.

[23] The sexual connotation, perhaps even denotation, of מרגלות was already recognized in Jewish midrash. Cf. *Ruth Rab.* and *Yalkut Shimeoni* for Ruth 3.

[24] As in Deut. 28.57; Judg. 3.24; 1 Sam. 24.3; 2 Kgs. 18.27 = Isa. 36.12; Isa. 7.20; Ezek. 16.25.

[25] As for instance in Exod. 28.22, where the priests are ordered to wear pants 'from waist to thigh' [!] while officiating at the alter.

[26] As in the case of Jeremiah, who wears a 'linen girdle' on his 'waist', according to the translations (Jer. 13.1, 2). A rendering of מתנים* here as 'genitals, loins' will make Jeremiah's gesture more impressive visually. The translation 'genitals', 'loins' is perhaps also more fitting for Deut. 33.11 than simply 'waist'.

interesting metaphor of Jer. 30.6, translated by the NEB as 'Why then do I see every man gripping *his sides like a woman in labour*' (my italics). Clearly, other translations apart from 'sides' are possible here.

יָרֵךְ, 'thigh',[27] is another euphemism for genitalia. Like 'legs/feet', 'thigh' for 'genital organs' operates by physical contiguity.[28] 'Thigh', as well as 'flesh', may indeed designate female sexual organs too; admittedly, however, such applications are less frequent than to male sexual organs. Thus we find a woman's בָּשָׂר ('flesh') in the sense of 'genitalia' in Lev. 6.20, 15.19; and a female 'thigh', יָרֵךְ—in Num. 5.22, 21, 27.[29] It is interesting, then, that apart from the specific terms for 'testicle' and 'foreskin' hardly any differentiation is made in HB language between male and female genitals.

So far, it has been noticed that human genitalia of males and females are protected in biblical language by euphemisms. There are no specific, exclusive terms; or, perhaps, there is no evidence for such terms in biblical texts. When an exclusive term seemingly obtains in the language, as in the case of אֶשֶׁךְ, 'testicle', it is a *hapax legomenon*. This is not surprising, given the *literary* and elite nature of the Bible, a written (as opposed to oral), polished, socially-conscious product. And yet, it is surprising, since that same culture that produced the Bible valorizes the circumcised human penis as a symbolic marker of the [male] link with the divine. The designation for the missing part, the foreskin, is relatively frequent; the whole, the penis itself, is linguistically and conspicuously absent. This omission amounts to a textual spiritualization of the penis, to its transformation into a phallus. Since, outside language, the penis continue to exist as such, tension obtains in the ideological system.[30] In other words, the penis is privileged and privatized by textual omission: it cannot be viewed by readers. Eventually, after discussing female sexual body parts, this

---

[27] Gen. 24.2 and 9, 32.25 and 32, 46.26, 47.29; Exod. 1.5; Judg. 8.30. Cf. N. Sarna, *Understanding* Genesis (New York: Schocken, 1970), pp. 170–71; and Rashkow, *Phallacy of Genesis*, p. 125 n. 13.

[28] See *SoS Rab.* for SoS 7.2 where it is stated briefly that 'thighs' is an implicit reference to the circumcised penis placed between them.

[29] Given the ribald tone of SoS 7.1–7, perhaps the mention of 'thighs' in v. 2 should be understood as a euphemistic reference to female genitalia too. On the general tone of the passage see A. Brenner, '"Come Back, Come Back the Shulammite"', in Y.T. Radday and A. Brenner (eds.), *On Humour and the Comic in the Hebrew Bible* (Sheffield: *JSOT*/Almond Press, 1990), pp. 251–76. Repr. In A. Brenner (ed.), *A Feminist Companion to the Song of Songs* (Sheffield: Sheffield Academic Press, 1993), pp. 234–57.

[30] Cf. the discussion in Eilberg-Schwartz, 'People of the Body'.

linguistic distinction between the private vs. the public domain will lead us to the question of viewing, of the gendered biblical descriptions of human nakedness.

The female sexual body

To the best of my knowledge, the only HB specific term for female genitals, 'vagina' or 'vulva' occurs in Isaiah 3.17. In a violent passage on the 'daughters of Jerusalem' as a symbolic mirror of the city itself (3.16–4.1), the same fate is predicted for both. Zion will be devastated in war and its 'openings' (פתחיה) will lament (3.26); similarly, in v. 17, Yhwh will 'expose' its women's 'genitals' (פתהן יערה). That 'female genitals' is implied by the *hapax* פתהן is supported by early Jewish sources.[31] Medieval Jewish commentators concur, viewing the term as a euphemism related to the Aramaic for 'breadth'.[32] The term is explained by the MH idiom בית הרהם,[33] 'house/place of the womb' (Rashi); or בית הערוה, 'place/house of nakedness' (RaDaK). It is equated with the phonetically similar פתח, 'opening' (v. 26) as well as the פתיניל (v. 24), read as two words: the 'joyful [female] genitals'.[34] The admittedly oblique reference to female genitalia as 'opening' or 'wide opening' reminds us of the prostitute Rahab, literally '[the] spacious' or, better still, '[the] broad'. Thus female genitalia are gendered by the [male] analogy drawn between the 'exposed genitals' and 'opening[s]' first in the Isaiah text itself, then in the decoding of the difficult term by later Jewish commentators. At any rate and unlike the penis, the female 'opening' is exposed in the language as well as by it, by the threat of exposure it promises metaphorical and other females.[35]

---

[31] *b. Shab.* 62b. Also in the largely parallel narratives of *Lev. Rab.* 16.1, *Lam. Zut.* 1.19, *Pes. Kah.* 17.6 and *Pes. Rabbati* 31.

[32] As, for instance, in Ezr. 6.3.

[33] *Kal.* 1.7, *Kal. Rabbati* 1.10; cf. Rashi to this verse, 3.24 and Num. 31.50.

[34] *b. Shab.* 62b and Rashi to the passage; Rashi, RaDaK, *Mez. Zion* and *Mez. David* for Isa. 3, although the last three also consider פתיניל also as a compound of 'cord' (פתיל) and 'joy' (ניל).

[35] My thanks to Yuval Warshai who, in an e-mail message, alerted me to the possibility that the term פתח, 'opening' in Genesis 38.14 is an allusion to female genitals. According to Warshai, the possibility that 'opening' here is a sly reference for female genitals, and Judah's 'stick' (cf. also the blessing to Judah, Gen. 49.10) and other personal paraphernalia also function—on at least one level—as signifiers of male genitals, should be entertained.

'Womb', an innard unlike the penis, is freely mentioned in various contexts. It is public property, much the same as female reproduction capabilities are.[36] 'Uterus' even defines 'woman' (Judges 5.30) somewhat like 'foreskin' defines despised non-community [male] members, such as the Philistines whom David kills (1 Sam. 18.25, 27); hardly a complimentary reference, and one that substitutes the anatomical (uterus or foreskin) part of the cultural Other (woman or male foreign enemy) for the whole in much the same fashion for both social categories. Indeed, the reference to woman as 'womb' is attributed to a foreign (Canaanite) female speaker-in-the-text within a 'female' poem in Judges 5.30. This attribution, however, does not necessarily imply a female voice underlying the usage.[37] It does imply, though, an analogous status for male uncircumcised bodies and female bodies, that is, for male 'outsiders' and female 'insiders'. And is the phrase שָׁרְרֵךְ כְּאַגַּן הַסַּהַר (SoS 7.3) to be translated, 'your navel is like the bowl of the moon'; or, with Pope[38] and others, 'your vulva/ uterus is like a [generous] bowl'? The second reading cannot be adopted unless it is understood that greater liberties are exercised in the depiction, that is exposure, of the naked female body than in that of the male body. This practice of exposing females in/by language appears in disparate types of biblical literature and within different contexts, from the physical exposure prescribed for a wife suspected of adultery (Num. 5) to love poetry (as in the SoS).[39] The praxis of exposure extends to genitalia and womb as well as to breasts, to normally clothed as well as normally covered female limbs.

Female breasts (דַּדִּים, שָׁדַיִם) are much on view, that is, verbally, in biblical literature. This is perhaps to be accepted, given the great emphasis on reproduction, female fertility and motherhood in all strata of biblical literature.[40] Nonetheless, I counted more occurrences of

---

[36] See Chapter 4, 'Sex, Procreation and Contraception'.

[37] For grounds for and against the gendering of Deborah's song as a woman's poem see F. van Dijk-Hemmes, *On Gendering Texts*, pp. 42–3, with additional literature cited; and in more detail in her Dutch dissertation, *Sporen van vrouwenteksten in de Hebreeuwse bijbel* (Utrecht: Faculteit der Godsgeleerdheid, 1992), pp. 175–242.

[38] M.V. Pope, *The Song of Songs* (AB; Garden City, NY: Doubleday, 1977), pp. 617–19.

[39] I have demonstrated elsewhere (in Brenner, '"Come Back"') how, even in the SoS, a male lover's body is hardly specifically described from the neck down (5.10–16). Instead, the literary trope of a statue (cf. Pope for the passage) is reverted to. This is very different from depictions of female corporeality in the SoS which, at the very least, proceed beyond the neck to the breasts.

[40] Chapter 4 below.

'female breasts' as erogenous zones than as fertility symbols or life-sustaining apparatus. And this leads us directly to the issue of 'gendered nakedness/being clothed' in the HB.

Gendered human nakedness

Clothing distinguishes man from woman (Deut. 22.5) and culture from nature (as Susan Griffin asserts time and time again).[41] It is easy to accept that in films and other modern representations, for instance, images of females [un]willingly undressed are stripped of their cultural identity; they become, literally and figuratively, more 'natural'. The same applies to male images, only that their stripping in art is much less frequent and follows different rules.

Such a universe of habitual female exposure is indeed portrayed in the Bible and in related literature. Alice Bach has demonstrated how the subjective/collective male gaze, in the biblical text and of the reader, zeroes in on the biblical female object.[42] Jennifer Glancy[43] and Amy-Jill Levine[44] show how the male-gazing-and-female-gazed-at principle operates in Susanna. Mieke Bal discusses the gaze as knowledge in a new article on Judith and some of 'her' representations in visual arts.[45] Susan Durber writes about the difficulty for women to switch from being-looked-at-ness into looking, that is, reading—in her case, into reading the NT parables of the lost.[46]

Indeed, clothing in the Bible does symbolize culture: let us remember Genesis 2 and 3 to begin with. As soon as the two gendered

---

[41] S. Griffin, *Pornography and Silence*.

[42] Alice Bach, 'Mirror, Mirror in the Text: Reflections on Reading and Rereading', in A. Brenner (ed.), *A Feminist Companion to Esther, Judith and Susanna* (Sheffield: Sheffield Academic Press, 1995), pp. 81–6.

[43] Jennifer Glancy, 'The Accused: Susanna and her Readers', *JSOT* 58 (1993), pp. 103–16. Reprinted in Brenner (ed.), *A Feminist Companion to Esther, Judith and Susanna*, pp. 288–302.

[44] A.-J. Levine, '"Hemmed in on Every Side": Jews and Women in the Book of Susanna', in F. Segovia and M.A. Tolbert (eds.), *Reading from This Place* (Philadelphia: Fortress, forthcoming). Reprinted in Brenner (ed.), *A Feminist Companion to Esther, Judith and Susanna*, pp. 303–23.

[45] M. Bal, 'Head Hunting: "Judith" on the Cutting Edge', *JSOT* 63 (1994), pp. 3–34. Reprinted in Brenner, *A Feminist Companion to Esther, Judith and Susanna*, pp. 253–85.

[46] S. Durber, 'The Female Reader of the Parables of the Lost', in G.J. Brooke (ed.), *Women in the Biblical Tradition* (Studies in Women and Religion, 31; Lewiston/Queenston/Lampeter: Edwin Mellen Press, 1992), pp. 187–207.

humans eat from the tree, they improvise a coverup for their nakedness (Gen. 3.7). It is therefore worth noting that, in the Bible, female
figurations are much more easily exposed, that is, presented as naked,
than male figurations. Nakedness is a shameful state in culture. Thus
representatives of culture should be especially careful about their
clothing: this, presumably, is why [male] priests' clothing are prescribed with elaboration (Exodus 28 and 39); and they should wear
linen pants while climbing the altar stairs to officiate so that their
genitals, their 'nakedness' (ערוה) is not exposed (Exod. 28.42). How
then should we evaluate the representation of females as naked, as
being punished by being stripped naked, by having even their genitals exposed to the collective gaze of textual figures and readers of
both genders—like in Isa. 3.17–24, Ezek. 16.37 and 23.26, Hos. 2.5,
all within highly religious contexts?

Where nakedness is concerned, the number of depictions of female
nakedness far outstrips those of male nakedness in BH. ערוה, 'nakedness', unlike its more general twin term עירם, refers in numerous
instances specifically to exposed genitalia. A polite, *pars pro toto* term.
A simple survey of the term results in a straightforward picture. In
most cases a woman's ערוה, 'nakedness > genitalia' is thus implied in
and by the text.[47] The technical term for incest with both blood kin
and marriage kin is לגלות ערוה or לראות ערות, decorously and literally translated as 'to see, uncover nakedness'.[48] Let us remember that
the object of biblical incest taboos is always a female, as she is categorized by blood and marriage affinities; whereas the law itself is
always addressed to males (Lev. 18 and 20, Deut. 27 and elsewhere).
Therefore the object of the incest taboo, the objectified 'nakedness'
which is put on view in order to be avoided, is female nakedness. This
euphemism becomes even more opaque in David's case (2 Sam. 6).
David dances in front of the ark while wearing a short garment. In
so doing he 'uncovers' (נלה Pi.) simply *himself*, not his own 'nakedness' (ערוה), although his indecent exposure is the axis the story hinges
on; Michal's punishment for mocking him, and the care taken in
1 Chron. 15.27–29 to dress David up in decent, long clothing, constitute further indications of the general linguistic practice. It is clear
that, in David's case, the secondary text (Chronicles) must hide his
genitals. Male genitalia must be protected from view; hence, refer-

---

[47] Notable exceptions are Gen. 9; Exod. 20.23, 28.42; Isa. 20.4.
[48] Cf. Chapter 5.

ences to it in the language are, at the very least, opaque. This does not symmetrically apply to women's nakedness-in-the-text. Thus, even a mother's 'nakedness' can be conjured up by a curse (1 Sam. 20.30) that, incidentally, is preserved also in modern Hebrew usage.

Where does this survey take us? Let us have a look at the available objects. Where can we view, so to speak, female breasts and genitalia in the HB? In the Song of Songs, of course; there is a density of presentation there. We can also turn to the books of the prophets: there we can view, touch, feel and handle female breasts. In Hosea (ch. 2) and Ezekiel (chs. 16, 21.8, and 23), for instance, we can share in the textual/sexual violent excitement while so doing. There female nakedness is highly visible and doubly vulnerable, for it is both explicit as well as repeatedly threatened. There is a veritable mass of female breasts and total or near-total nudity: there is no *symmetrical* image of male nudity. Nudity in a woman is attractive albeit immodest, appealing if also condemned. The male figure remains, by and large, as fully clothed as possible.

The body beautiful: female and male

It is quite clear that, in the HB, physical appearance and physical beauty matter. And so does the lack of beauty. Understanding what is 'beautiful', hence sexually 'attractive', or 'not beautiful, ugly', is largely a matter of readerly construction. However, even the little material there is points to conceptions of beauty that are only partially gendered. On the other hand, it would appear that physical beauty is not only sexually relevant but also politically and socially relevant, since it is often equated with wholesomeness and health. It would also seem that whereas female beauty determines private socio-sexual behaviour, thus may have political consequences, male beauty may and does at times have political significance in and by itself. It can function as either sexual motivation and/or a symbolic mark of social and political excellence.

Basic semantic terms for beauty: a survey

The primary term for 'beauty' is יפ׳. It refers to a wo/man's (like the זרה woman in Prov. 6.25) and, more specifically, a young

wo/man's beauty as such, also by various verbal derivatives in the
Qal and Hith. formations (Jer. 4.30; Ezek. 15.14, 25; 27.3, 4, 11;
28.12, 17;[49] 31.3;[50] SoS 7.7). The beauty of a king (Jer. 33.17) is
mentioned too.

The primary adjectives for 'beautiful' are יפה[51] and טוב,[52] especially—but not only—in the bound noun-phrases יפת/ת יפה/ת תאר,
מראה (app. 'beautiful-looking') or תאר חן/ת טוב, ת מראה/ת טוב and טוב ראי
(app. 'good-looking'). The binary opposition seems to be רע מראה or
רע תאר, although these terms appear in one text only and are
applied to 'cows',[53] not persons. A superlative is expressed by either
the addition of מאד ('very'), or by a tautology (variants of two
compounds together).

Tamar, sister to Amnon and Absalom, is simply יפה, 'beautiful'
(2 Sam. 13.1), like Job's second set of daughters (Job 42.15) and
female lovers in the Song of Songs;[54] so is Tamar's brother Absalom
(14.25) and, once, a male lover in the Song of Songs (1.16). Rebekah
(Gen. 26.7; cf. 'very good-looking', 24.16), Vashti (Esth. 1.11) and
the virgins collected for Ahasuerus (2.2, 3), as well as the young Daniel
and his friends (Dan. 1.4), are all 'good-looking'. Sarah (Gen. 12.11;
'very beautiful' in v. 14), the ethnically foreign female prisoner of
war (Deut. 21.11), Abigail (1 Sam. 25.3) and Tamar daughter of
Absalom (2 Sam. 14.27),[55] as well as the young David (1 Sam. 17.42),

---

[49] In Ezek. 27 and 28 the 'beauty' is that of Tyre, a city metaphorized into a
woman figure.

[50] Of Assyria, also metaphorized into a woman figure.

[51] See also the partially doubled form יפהפיה (Jer. 46.20; and the verb form in
Ps. 45.3), similar to formations like ירקרק or אדמדם from ירק ('green, yellow') and
אדם ('red', 'pink', 'brown'). Whether the partially duplicated form in all these cases
and others denoted intensification of attributes or, on the contrary, their dilution in
relation to the parent term remains difficult to determine. Cf. A. Brenner, *Colour
Terms in the Old Testament* (Sheffield: JSOT Press, 1982), pp. 106–10.

[52] While טוב is typically translated as 'good' or 'proper', 'appropriate', that is, as
denoting ethics, in numerous instances its scope seems to incorporate aesthetics as
well. The two understandings do not seem mutually contradictory or exclusive in
quite a few texts. For instance: Gen. 1.4, 12, 18, 21, 25 (about god's creative activities); 3.6 (the fruit of the tree in the garden); Exod. 2.2 (the infant Moses); Qoh.
5.17 (a difficult text, perhaps a gloss: 'good, that is, beautiful' [טוב אשר יפה]); Hos.
10.11 (טוב צואָרה, 'her beautiful neck'). The 'daughters of man' are טבת, 'beautiful',
right > 'attractive' for the sons of [the] god[s] (Gen. 1.2). King Saul is defined as
בחור וטוב, 'young and beautiful' (1 Sam. 9.2). See also the verb form, as in Esth. 2.4
(ותיטב בעיני המלך), lit. 'and she was beautiful in the king's eyes').

[53] Gen. 41.3, 4, 19; as against the 'beautiful-looking' (vv. 2, 4, 18) or simply
'good' [טוב] cows (vv. 5, 22, 26).

[54] SoS 1.8, 15 (x2); 2.10.13; 4.1, 7, 10; 5.9; 6.1, 4; 7.2, 7.

[55] But see for the daughter's name the traditions of the LXX and V translations;

are 'beautiful looking'. David is elsewhere 'good-looking' (1 Sam. 16.12). Of superlative beauty, 'very good-looking', are Bath Sheba (2 Sam. 11.2) and Adonijah (1 Kgs. 1.6). So are Rachel (Gen. 29.27) and also Rachel's son Joseph (39.6), whose supreme good looks are conveyed by the repetitious יפה/ת תאר ויפה/ת מראה. Similarly, Esther is יפת תאר וטובת מראה (Esth. 2.7).

The sequence נאה/ו, and the apparently related nominal נאוה (SoS 1.6, 10; 6.4), also denote physical beauty. Another root sequence which might, at least in some contexts, denote 'be beautiful', 'beauty' or 'be pleasant', 'pleasantness' is נעם and its derivatives. When יפה occurs in parallelism with נעים (SoS 1.16, of a male lover; 7.7 in the Qal formation for both sequences, of a female lover), or when 'looking upon the נעם of god' is the topic (Ps. 27.4, 90.17), 'beauty' seems to be referred to.[56]

The survey of basic/general terms for human beauty reveals that, in so far as these terms are concerned, there is no marked distinction between references to female or to male beauty. While female beauty is referred to more often, most of the available terms serve to depict both genders. The gendered differences are contained in other data: the actual descriptions of body parts (rare but sometimes available), and the metaphors used for illustration or description.

Ideals/norms of beauty

What are the extra-linguistic references of physical beauty in the HB? In other words, how does a beautiful person—be that person male of female—come to be defined as such? What does a Sarah look like, so that Egyptians recognize her beauty so easily (Gen. 12)? What does a Joseph look like, so that his looks move Potiphar's wife to attempts of seduction (39.6)? The blanket terms 'beautiful', 'good-looking' or 'very good-looking' are not informative. They neither allow

---

not to mention the discrepancy of the verse, which cites three sons and a daughter for Absalom, with 18.18, which has him die without sons, at least.

[56] See also the parallelism with טוב in Ps. 133.1, הנה מה טוב ומה נעים שבת אחים גם יחד; cf. the parallelism of טוב and נאוה in Ps. 147.1. Since the sequence נעם primarily denotes '[be] pleasant', also 'tasty' and perhaps 'sweet' (Prov. 3.17, 9.17, 16.24 and more), its status in the semantic field of 'beauty' appears to be subsidiary. At any rate, the denotation or connotation 'beautiful' enriches the significations of proper nouns like Naomi, Na'aman and Na'ama, together with David's definition of נעים זמירות ישראל (2 Sam. 23.1), 'the beautiful[?] singer of Israel'.

us to visualize, at least approximately, most of the physical features
of the textual figures thus portrayed, nor to form an approximate
idea of ideals or norms of beauty in the HB and in ancient Israel. It
therefore seems appropriate that, in order to explain Sarah's great
charms and fatal appeal, her numerous charms must be elaborated
upon. But, even as they are catalogued in the Genesis Apocryphon,
for instance, not much can be gleaned from the description; everything
about her is repeatedly 'beautiful' and 'dainty'; visual details are not
much in evidence.[57] As we shall see, biblical description is conventionalized and, as such, a direct descendant of HB conventional models.

The descriptions of physical appeal in the Song of Songs are helpful. Some *wasf*-type poems[58] are dedicated to physical descriptions of
female and male lovers, in addition to generalized attributions of
beauty to the beloved person.

A female lover is described as having eyes like doves (4.1, also
1.15): symmetry, shape, perhaps a dark colour are invoked. She has
long, curly or wavy dark hair, like a herd of goats sliding down a
mountain (4.1, 6.5). She has all her teeth; they are symmetrical
and white like a flock of sheep (4.2, 6.6). Her lips are red, her
complexion a healthy pink (4.3, 6.7)—like crimson, like a pomegranate. Her neck is long and stately like the 'tower of David',
enhanced by the jewelry she wears (4.4). Her breasts are like 'twin
gazelles' (v. 5, also 7.4): it is not clear whether the metaphor implies
colour, symmetry, size, movement, softness or—preferably—all of
these. The rest of her body is shrouded by decorous references to
smell and sexual intent (v. 6). The closing line is circular (cf. v. 1)
and also emphasizes that the woman described is totally beautiful
(v. 7), that is, her beauty is without blemish.

The *wasf* of 7.1–7 shares a few points of reference with that of
4.1—the long neck (7.5), the twin-gazelle breasts (v. 4; also v. 8), the
long hair (v. 6)—but is apparently a humorous depiction in which
the aesthetic gives way to desire-laden ambiguity.[59] Therefore the
full body (vv. 2b, 3), turbulent eyes (v. 5b) and towering nose (v. 5c)

---

[57] J.A. Fitzmyer (ed.), *The Genesis Apocryphon* (Rome: Biblical Institute Press, 1971),
col. xx, p. 63.

[58] Poem of praise for physical appearance. For the term (loaned from Arabic), other
*wasf*s in the SoS and the following discussion see Pope, *Song of Songs*, pp. 55–6, 67,
142–4.

[59] Brenner, '"Come Back, Come Back"'. For an early recognition, albeit with a
totally different interpretation, of the impossibility of understanding some of the
terms in this passage as praise for physical features, see Rashi's commentary.

can hardly constitute a beauty ideal, although the desire is apparent in the description and explicitly stated at its end (vv. 7–10). Vv. 8–9 add another element: the dancing woman is apparently tall and straight, since her stature is compared to a palm tree.

Moving on to the SoS *wasf* (5.10–16) where a female textual speaker describes her male lover's physical charms, quite a few features resemble those of women's. His complexion is pinkish too (5.10).[60] His hair glows[61] and is dark, wavy or curly (v. 11). The eyes are, again and with some elaboration, like doves (v. 12). The cheeks and lips are not visualized; rather, they are referred to by smell imagery (v. 13). The rest of his body is imaged as a statue, built of precious materials (vv. 14–16).[62] It is however clear that he is tall and stately, like the cedars of the Lebanon (v. 15b).

A pinkish complexion is attributed to David too (1 Sam. 16.12, 17.42).[63] The convention of 'peaches and cream', white-and-red complexion for male as well as female beauty is present also in Lamentations 4. Before the city's destruction, the sons of Zion had that complexion (Lam. 4.7);[64] as a result of the siege and conquest, they became dark and thin (v. 8). Perhaps the red-and-white convention is an urban one, as against the defiant insistence of a female pastoral voice that she is dark-complexioned as a result of open-air occupations but, still, beautiful (SoS 1.5–6).

Metaphors are meaningful for understanding the emotive value of references to physicality. In the SoS women are imaged as or associated with animals, wild and domesticated (mare, 1.9; dove; once with lions and leopards, 4.8), flowers, a palm tree, a garden, a vineyard, aromatic plants. Female body parts are imaged as or associated with fauna (twin gazelles, sheep, goats, doves), fruit (pomegranate), food (honey, wheat), drink (milk, wine) and a garden. Males are imaged as or associated with trees (2.3), a gazelle (2.8–9, 8.14), wine. Male body parts are once a dove and once a perfume garden (ch. 5), but no more; otherwise, they are associated with precious materials. Both

---

[60] צח ואדום, often translated as 'white and ruddy', refers in my opinion to a mixture of the two colour elements. See Brenner, *Colour Terms*, pp. 118–20.

[61] כתם פז, 'gold', is probably a signifier of sheen rather than colour, since the hair colour is explicitly stated in the next stich.

[62] Pope, *Song of Songs*, pp. 542–548.

[63] For reading אדמ[ו]ני as signifying skin instead of hair colour, also in the case of Esau (Gen. 25.25), see Brenner, *Colour Terms*, pp. 127–29.

[64] The element of 'glow, sheen', which in the SoS passage is applied to male hair, serves in Lam. 4.2 as a metaphor for the young males' general appearance, or worth.

males and females are associated at times with military artifacts, fortifications and architecture (4.4, 7.5 and 8.8–10 as female imagery; 3.7–11 for male imagery).[65] While stock imagery seems to be applicable in both female and male descriptions, subtle differences obtain in the overall balance as well as in details. Females are, finally and on balance, more a domesticated garden than threatening fortifications; males, finally, are more wild (a forest tree, 2.3) than domesticated (the 'female' palm tree, 7.8–9), more free to escape, less earth-bound. SoS female figures are energetic and dynamic; nevertheless, the metaphors that describe them convey (on the balance) a beauty that is gentler and more domesticated than the males'.[66]

An important token of male beauty is, in addition to strength and tallness, hair—and lots of it. Absalom's beauty is praiseworthy and exceptional, with no blemish from foot to head (2 Sam. 14.25). He also has an abundance of hair (v. 26). The hair is necessary for the unfolding of Absalom's story: he hangs by it from a tree, thus becomes a helpless target for Joab to kill (18.6–17). Absalom's hair is his downfall—as is Samson's hair (Judg. 13–16). Although Samson is never described as 'good-looking', his hair, strength and the sun imagery attached to his figure are indicative of his physical attractions. This feature should probably be connected to the utilization of uncut hair in the *nazir* prescription (Num. 6), as well as to modern discussions of hair as the symbolic locus of male strength and virility.[67]

What about ugliness? I have not found any specific term, an individual lexeme, in the HB which denotes 'ugly', 'ugliness' and similar concepts, although such terms exist in MH.[68] Lack of ugliness is referred to as such, as 'absence of blemish'. However, in at least two contexts human obesity is referred to pejoratively. Eglon (lit. 'big calf') king of Moab (Judges 3) is a very fat man, which hastens his end and is something to sneer at.[69] The elite women attacked in

---

[65] For a detailed discussion see C. Meyers, 'Gender Imagery in the Song of Songs', *HAR* 10 (1986), pp. 209–23; repr. in Brenner (ed.), *A Feminist Companion to the Song of Songs*, pp. 197–212.

[66] See also Leah's eyes, which are designated 'soft' (רכות, Gen. 29.17). There is hardly a linguistic/semantic basis for understanding 'soft' or 'gentle' here or elsewhere as 'ugly'. Rather, the passage probably implies that, in contradistinction to the overall beautiful Rachel, Leah's eyes are her only beautiful feature.

[67] See Mieke Bal, *Death and Dissymmetry in the Book of Judges* (Bloomington: Indiana University Press, 1988).

[68] From the root כער: כעור, מכוער ('ugly'), כיעור ('ugliness') in the Mishna, the minor tractates, the midrash and the Babylonian Talmud. The wide distribution perhaps points to an accidental absence in BH stock.

[69] R. Alter, *The Art of Biblical Narrative* (New York: Basic Books, 1981), pp. 36–41.

Amos 4.1 are addressed as 'cows of the Bashan'. Obesity is appropriate, hence beautiful, in cattle but—*contra* RaDaK[70] and commentators who imagine that the obviously corpulent Shulammite is praised for her fat appearance[71]—there is no basis for assuming that in HB usage fat is considered beautiful for either men or women.

Physical appearance as motivation

Textual female beauty is part of female attractiveness. As such, it explicitly or implicitly motivates male desire and is functional in numerous stories of seduction and/or love (Sarah, Rebekah, Rachel, Tamar daughter of David, the זרה woman, Vashti, Esther). In places, this is the function of textual male beauty—as in the case of Joseph and Potiphar's wife or, at least implicitly, in the case of David the attractive womanizer. In other places, though, male beauty has another function altogether which is not shared by female beauty.

It seems that the attributes of physical beauty or strength, or both, are integral to at least some early political leaders, as imaged in biblical literature. This is especially relevant to the descriptions of several kings or royal heirs, although not restricted to them. Moses is a beautiful baby. Joseph is 'doubly beautiful'. Perhaps Samson is too, a physical brute with long hair. King Saul is young, beautiful and taller than any other Israelite (1 Sam. 9.2); he is also strong (ch. 11). David is beautiful. Absalom is beautiful, with very special hair. So is the king addressed in the wedding poem of Ps. 45, whose beauty surpasses that of any other human (v. 3).

The story of David's relationship with Mephibosheth (2 Sam. 4.4; ch. 9; 16.1–4; 19.25–31), the last remaining member of the Saulide house, indicates that a crippled male could not be considered a claimant to the throne. Whether that was motivated by the king's position as military chief, or by cultic considerations of wholeness,[72] or by an ideology that saw humans as a reflection of god, hardly matters.

---

[70] For Am. 4.1 and Jer. 46.20.

[71] For a convenient summary see Pope, *Song of Songs*, for SoS 7.4.

[72] As in the case of the Aaronide priests. In this office that, like the kingship, eventually became hereditary, individuals with bodily defects are barred from officiating. A list in Lev. 21.17–23 covers the ground from physical imperfections and blemishes to serious defects. The reason given is because the priests are made sanctified by Yhwh. This reason may be applicable to kings too, since they are also anointed into office, like the priests; and, perhaps, by extension to other leaders.

Absalom's body was free of physical blemish; but this is hardly enough. A physical beauty was attributed to early leaders, by way of extension of the physical wholeness principle.

The result of this apparent imaging is interesting for the gendered approach. Physical beauty is appreciated in males and females alike. The body beautiful is the body attractive, the body approved-of. This principle is trans-gender. In the case of women, their beauty determines their individual history and fate by confining their essence to the sexual [personal, private] domain. This is so for the female figures concerned even when their fate has public implications that far outreach their own, individual destiny. But in the case of males, their physical beauty—especially tallness and hair, and also of eyes (David, 1 Sam. 16.12)—is a signifier of their socio-political destiny in the public domain. Beauty is one of the features that lends their governing credibility. According to this model (whose applicability is not universal), the leader is perfect in every respect, corporeal as well as spiritual.

Concluding remarks

While discussing the sexual body in this Chapter, I referred mainly to body parts, metaphors and descriptions that were directly relevant to the gendering of sexual bodies. I found that, at least from the perspective of the conventional and ideal, HB males are defined physically and socially by a triple lack: of the circumcised foreskin, of the penis (so protected that it disappears from view), and of the [naked] body. Females are defined physically and socially by a triple presence: of breasts, womb and nakedness. If the blessing of/by 'breasts-and-womb' (Gen. 49.25) is a trace and reflection of an early goddess,[73] 'she' indeed symbolized not only the fertile aspect of the female body but also its sexual essence.

The body sexual is, ideally, the body beautiful and therefore attractive. Notions of physical beauty were found to be conventional if vague, hence difficult to visualize. They were also found to be largely non-gendered. The gendering resides in the understanding of male beauty as requisite for a political career (in certain cases of

---

[73] B. Becking in B. Becking, P.W. van der Horst and K. van der Toorn, *Dictionary of Deities and Demons* (Leiden: Brill, 1995), pp. 336–37.

founding leaders), whereas female beauty is narrated as state and cause for action rather than a property which contributes to the establishment of sociopolitical self-authority.

A certain mingling or overlap of sexual, aesthetic, ethic and spiritual categories of beauty is perhaps indicated, among other things, by the semantic interchangeability of 'good' (טוב) and 'beautiful' (יפה). Beauty is equated with wholesomeness which, in the case of males, facilitates their serving in a public office like kingship or priesthood.

Claus Westermann[74] writes about beauty as a theological concept: his primary occupation is the question, Does beauty pass between God and humanity? Westermann draws a distinction between 'beauty as object' and 'beauty as event'. According to him, beauty-as-being entails an objective attitude towards it; it requires viewers and consumers for it to exist. Beauty-as-event requires more than that: it requires active participation and reciprocity if it is to materialize. In Westermann's description, therefore, beauty-as-being has a minor role in life; beauty-as-event is much more significant. Ultimately, he classifies material beauty—including human physical beauty—as 'being' and the beauty of god's blessings as beauty 'events'.

Westermann's model of a binary opposition between two kinds of beauty can be usefully reapplied to the human/corporeal sphere even though, originally, it applied to the human/divine spheres and transcends the physical. If 'beauty as object' is equated with 'beauty as gazed at and motivational' and 'beauty as in the private domain', and 'beauty as event' is equated with 'beauty as a dynamic force' and 'beauty in the public domain', then Westermann's distinctions may be translated into gendered distinctions. Although the basic beauty terminology and physiognomic stereotypes are identical or very similar for females and for males, and although cases of gender-bender do obtain,[75] the essential stereotypes are: activating[76]/objective/private for women's beauty, dynamic/subjective/public for men's beauty.

---

[74] C. Westermann, 'Das Schöne im Altem Testament', in H. Donner, R. Hanhart and R. Smend (eds.), *Beiträge zur alttestamentlichen Theologie: Festschrift für Walther Zimmerli zum 70. Geburtstag* (Gottingen: Vandenhoeck & Ruprecht, 1977), pp. 479–97; repr. in C. Westermann (R. Albertz, ed.), *Erträge der Forschung am Alten Testament: Gesammelte Studien III* (München: Chr. Kaiser Verlag, 1984), pp. 119–37.

[75] As in the case of Joseph who, precisely like his mother Rachel, is 'doubly beautiful'. Some Jewish sages were quick to understand this gender-bender, hence portrayed Joseph as an effeminate dandy: see for instance *Gen. Rab.* 84 and *Yalk. Shim.* for Gen. 39.

[76] To be distinguished from 'active'.

CHAPTER FOUR

SEX, PROCREATION AND CONTRACEPTION: IDEOLOGIES AND PRAXIS

Procreation is introduced in the Bible's first chapter as a blessing. פרו ורבו: 'be fruitful and multiply' is the divine gift and blessing meted out to creatures of the higher orders—animals (Gen. 1.22) and humankind (v. 28)—upon their creation, as well as to the land (and especially the land designated for the Israelites, which will become evident later).[1] No gender differentiation is made in the blessing; no sexual activity is mentioned, although it can be assumed: why, otherwise, should male and female—in that order—be created together as a primeval couple?[2] Far be it from me to suspect that the so-called priestly writers, to whom this scheme is attributed by scholarly consensus, were unaware of the fact that sexual activity precedes procreation. If they chose to mention multiplication without reference to its vehicle, this can only mean that social ideology—monogamous liaisons, regulated procreation—rather than biology is on their agendas. And in their religious ideopicture,[3] sexuality is secondary to the higher status of procreation—for both males and females, in that order.

The 'priestly' authors are not the only ones to express an ideopicture concerning the genesis of procreation and desire. Sex and procreation do get to be closely linked with monogamous desire in the Garden story (Gen. 2.4b–3): in fact desire is mentioned first, at least

---

[1] I. Fischer, '". . . und sie war unfruchtbar": Zur Stellung kinderloser Frauen in der Literatur Alt-Israels', in G. Pauritsch *et al.* (eds.), *Kinder Machen: Strategien der Kontrolle weiblicher Fruchtbarkeit* (Vienna: Wiener Frauenverlag, 1988), pp. 116–126 (p. 117).

[2] Some feminist thinkers deduce from this passage that the vision of creation in Gen. 1 is egalitarian insofar as gender issues are present. See, for instance, P. Trible, *God and the Rhetoric of Sexuality* (Philadelphia: Fortress, 1978). However, contemporaneous creation does not necessarily imply gender equality. Neither does the powers of government over the world, given to both male and female at the creation, necessarily signify symmetrical gender responsibilities.

[3] Bal, *Lethal Love*, esp. the 'Introduction', pp. 1–9, but also see the Index under 'Ideology'.

as the male's 'cleaving' unto his woman (2.24).[4] But the female's 'desire' for her man (3.16b) is linked to procreation in a linear-spatial rather than causal manner. In her case the natural order of things is reversed, from procreation (3.16a) to desire instead of the other way around. And the divine blessing of the potential to reproduce becomes somewhat modified and certainly gendered. Yhwh Elohim says to the woman, 'I shall multiply your suffering[5] and your pregnancy [pregnancies]; with pain[6] you shall give birth to sons;[7] and your desire shall be unto your husband, and he shall rule over you' (3.16). Any interpretation of this utterance—as a curse, aetiological statement of fact, blessing or otherwise—is largely dependent on the reader's gender position and may vary considerably. Be that as it may, it cannot be overlooked that, for the first woman and by default for her successors, procreation is closely linked with desire. In fact, for women procreation precedes desire (and logic be hanged), at least socially.

Within the first three chapters of the Bible, then, we are informed that,

- the primal condition of humans is to be socially organised in heterosexual couples (chs. 1 and 2–3);
- procreation is a value bestowed by divine blessing (ch. 1);
- males and females share in the blessing (ch. 1);
- procreation is superordinate to desire, although the two are closely linked somehow (for both genders in ch. 1; for the female in ch. 3)—for the male, desire comes first (2.24);
- procreation depends on women's fertility, but

---

[4] See also Prov. 5.17–18, 18.22 and the discussion in T. Frymer-Kensky, 'Law and Philosophy: The Case of Sex in the Bible', *Semeia* 49 (1989), pp. 92–3.

[5] Heb. עצבונך.

[6] Heb. עצב; 'pain', 'sorrow' or 'suffering'.

[7] Here the Heb. has בנים, literally 'sons'. Most Bible commentators tend to read the Heb. בן or בנים, 'son/s' as inclusive language designating both 'sons' and 'daughters', that is, children (Heb. ילד/ים)—like also in Gen. 30.1, when Rachel says to Jacob: 'give me בנים [sons] or else I will die'. In my opinion this practice testifies to the phallocentric, pro-male prejudice of biblical text and commentators alike. The Jacob-Rachel dialogue is instructive in this regard: Jacob's answer, 'Am I like God, who withheld from you fruit of the womb', can be read both ways. Either he understands 'sons' as inclusive of daughters, or else he extends his answer in relation to her complaint to include children of both genders, so that the sarcasm is even more pronounced. I would suggest that equating 'sons' and 'children' in text and interpretation amounts to obliteration of gender ideology in both.

- this entails suffering (3.16)—hence, the extension of the blessing to females is somewhat qualified; and
- in desire there is a hierarchy (chs. 2–3): the primal order of things has been reversed by divine statement or punishment so that the woman's desire is for the man.

In spite of the differences between the two accounts about the genesis of procreation, the stage is already set for understanding biblical views on sex and reproduction. Sexual activity and desire are certainly not negated but neither are they idealised.[8] Ultimately, sexual desire holds second place to the divinely pronounced blessing for or statement of multiplication. This basic attitude is presented as the binding supernatural, to distinguish from the natural, order of things. I use 'supernatural order' here in the sense of social, religious, ideological order. Of course the privileging of this supernatural order over the natural order can be explained by the social motivation of the community to survive, a strong and valid rationale.[9] This rationale may in turn explain why in time, certainly so already in early rabbinic Judaism, procreation became a primary commandment.[10] However, the roots of the process by which a blessing/statement became an asymmetrical duty/commandment for males or females[11]

---

[8] This is always valid, even when no link between sexual desire or love on the one hand and procreation on the other hand is made in a biblical text. A good example is the Song of Songs. Although no procreation features there, it hardly furnishes an idealized picture of heterosexual desire. Cf. F. Landy, *Paradoxes of Paradise* (Bible and Literature, 7; Sheffield: Almond Press, 1983).

[9] The survival rationale does not necessarily imply that the society which holds it is a child-centred society. No group-oriented ideology in the HB is child-centred in the modern sense, that is, so that the welfare of infants is ideologically and materially preferable to adult welfare. For the predominant group-oriented ideologies reflected in the HB see L. Bechtel, 'Genesis 2.4b–3.24: A Myth of Human Maturation', *JSOT* 67 (1995), pp. 3–26, esp. pp. 5–9.

[10] In early and later rabbinic Judaism, a Jewish male's duty to procreate is established beyond question. The only problems are a male convert's duty and whether the commandment is extended to non-Jewish males as well. On the other hand, it is clear that women's duty to procreate is not anchored in the same law but in her duty towards her husband. See D.M. Feldman, *Birth Control in Jewish Law* (New York: New York University Press, 1968), pp. 46–59.

[11] Again, in early Judaism in an asymmetrical manner genderwise. In *Mish. Yeb.* 6.6, *b. Yeb.* 61b, the commandment of procreation is minimally fulfilled by a man if he has two sons according to the house of Shammai, a son and daughter (cf. Gen. 1.27) according to the house of Hillel. In the Tosefta there are also other versions: Shammai scholars consider a son *and* a daughter as sufficient, Hillel scholars—a son *or* a daughter; or: Shammai scholars prescribe two sons and two daughters, Hillel scholars one son and one daughter. The law follows the house of

is to be found already in biblical narrative, although not explicitly so in biblical law-prescribing texts. It is therefore important to stress that, since the blessing/burden of continuity is highly gendered from the very start and recognized as such in the primal history, biblical texts that deal with aspects of procreation, sexual activity and hetero-sexual desire can and should be read in the light of this asymmetrical gendering and asymmetrical ideological preferences.

The case of infertile women figurations

Biblical men wish for children, preferably sons and the more the better.[12] Job initially has ten of them, seven sons and three daughters, which is one measure of his social status (Job 1–2). Sturdy sons, beautifully curved daughters, food and property—in that order—are the indexes of individual and communal prosperity (Ps. 144.12–13). And who is a truly happy man?

> Your Wife is like a fertile vine . . .
> Your sons like olive plants around your table
> This is how a god-fearing male is blessed . . .
> And may you see sons to your sons . . . (Ps. 128.3–6).

It would seem, then, that like in the rest of the ANE,[13] a man needs sons more than daughters: the incidental mention of Dinah's birth after the detailed story of her brothers' birth is instructive (Gen. 30.21).[14] Male wish for posterity is depicted as basic and intrinsic, but nothing is mentioned about an *instinct* for fatherhood. The preference for male children, it is understood, is motivated by and propagates the patrimonial order.

Hillel's ruling (the married couple must reproduce themselves). Although the final ruling opts for at least one child of each gender in the interest of further procreation, the discussion shows a preference for male children.

[12] This in no way implies that the culture[s] reflected in biblical literature is [are] paedocentric. The biblical stereotype of wisdom as a property of older people (a good example is 1 Kgs. 12.1–15 = 2 Chron. 10.1–15), together with details about parents' and especially fathers' authority over their children, precludes any notion of children's social centricity.

[13] Cf. the beginning of the Ugaritic epic about KRT. KRT, apparently a king, once had a numerous family that perished. The action starts with KRT's divinely supported attempt to obtain a suitable new wife and procreate new children.

[14] For the problematic relationships between fathers and daughters cf. Ch. 5, and literature cited there.

The description becomes somewhat more complex with regard
to women. Reproduction is the most essential wish of everywoman;
everywoman wants, desires, needs to become a mother; there is
nothing worse for a woman than to be infertile (that is, sonless),
especially when her husband is not.[15] At the very least, this is one
of the lessons to be gleaned from the numerous narratives about
mothers of future leaders and heroes,[16] whose stories are set up as
instructive examples. Interestingly, the Bible introduces this maternal
desire explicitly as a social motive. In several texts this desire is indeed
presented as deriving from the necessity to propagate the social group:
Lot's daughters (Gen. 19.30–38) err in assuming that humanity
will be extinguished if they do not propagate it; Tamar continues
her dead husband's line (Gen. 38). Implicitly, this motivation
might also be ascribed to Ruth. Otherwise, women's motivation for
becoming mothers is [re]presented as inherent, intrinsic, innate, inborn,
instinctive, congenital—in short, women *desire* children. They are
prepared to go to great lengths in order to achieve this purpose. For
instance, Hannah gives Samuel to god in return for receiving him
(1 Sam. 1–2); and Rachel dies at childbirth (Gen. 35.16–20), an event
that is ironically foreshadowed in her complaint to Jacob about her
innate lack and resultant death wish (30.1).

It is tempting to accept this literary picture of gendered female
motivation for reproduction. If women desire parenthood more than
men (who desire it too), since their desire is as instinctual as it is
social, since motherhood is essential to their nature, this makes them
into custodians of social survival in social ideology as well as in

[15] Thus Abraham, although old, sires a son with Hagar; there is no difficulty,
while Sarah is old and infertile. Jacob is certainly fertile. The question of male
infertility is hardly even acknowledged, although eunuchs are certainly known and,
furthermore, the possibility of male sterility is mentioned in passing in Deut. 7.14—
cf. Fischer, 'Zur Stellung kinderloser Frauen', p. 118. In postbiblical Judaic sources,
although a man is allowed to divorce an infertile wife after a ten-year barren union
(*b. Yeb.* 64a and Rashi in his commentary on this talmudic passage; *b. Ket.* 77a; *Tos.
Yeb.* 8; after the example of Sarah, who waits ten years before giving Hagar to
Abraham, Gen. 16.3. See also Feldman, *Birth Control,* pp. 36–45 for more sources
and details) in order to remarry and procreate, the possibility of male infertility is
broached.
[16] The list of such mothers includes: Hagar, Sarah, Rebekah, Lot's daughters,
Leah, Rachel, Zilpah, Bilhah, Tamar, Moses' mother, Samson's mother, Hannah,
and the Lucan account of Elizabeth and Mary. Cf. A. Brenner, 'Female Social
Behaviour within the "Birth of the Hero" Paradigm', in A. Brenner (ed.), *A Feminist
Companion to Genesis* (Sheffield: Sheffield Academic Press, 1993), pp. 204–21.

physicality. However, there are a few difficulties in embracing this biblical picture uncritically. To begin with, biblical women's desire is to be the mothers of *sons*, not daughters.[17] In that, they are not different from the men. Such a desire is socially motivated, whereas a desire for just a *child* would have been more credibly essential.[18] Much depends, of course, on the interpretation of the Hebrew בנים, as mentioned earlier: does it signify 'sons', or 'children' of both genders, as for instance also in the poem attributed to Hannah:

> ... until a barren [woman] gives birth to seven [m.]
> and [a woman] with seven sons [בנים] is distressed ... (1 Sam. 2.5b);

or this poem's close parallel in Ps. 113.9,[19]

> [Yhwh who] establishes the barren [woman] of the house,
> the mother of sons [בנים] is joyful.

If בנים here and elsewhere be understood in the limited sense of 'male offspring', then the case for ideal[ized] motherhood is somewhat limited: ideal[ized] motherhood then becomes the mothering of a son. This understanding is corroborated by the complete absence of daughters' birth stories in the HB, as against the numerous examples of sons' birth stories; and the lack of information on mothers/daughters relationships apart from the scanty clues in the Song of Songs.[20]

And yet, no woman in the HB is described as resisting motherhood. On the contrary. Mothers are indispensable to patriarchy (especially for Yhwh-oriented patriarchy and its literature, since it furnishes Yhwh with a chance to interfere and prove his ability to change the situation). It remains to be asked why, if motherhood is 'natural' to women, it has to be foregrounded in such an emphatic manner. Why, assuming that the recurrent paradigm of the infertile

---

[17] See R. Kraemer, 'Jewish Mothers and Daughters in the Greco-Roman World', in S.J.D. Cohen (ed.), *The Jewish Family in Antiquity* (Atlanta: Scholars Press, 1993), pp. 89–112, esp. pp. 89–91.

[18] It might be argued that Hannah, who desires 'human seed' (Heb. זרע אנשים, 1 Sam. 1.11), wishes for any offspring, regardless of gender. However, her willingness to dedicate the child to the temple service, a male occupation, and the male language she uses, belie this interpretation.

[19] The subject matter—Yhwh's ability to reverse fates—is similar; also cf. vv. 7–8 to 1 Sam. 2.7–8.

[20] C. Meyers, 'Returning Home: Ruth 1.8 and the Gendering of the Book of Ruth', in Brenner (ed.), *A Feminist Companion to the Book of Ruth* (Sheffield: Sheffield Academic Press, 1993), pp. 85–114.

(older or husbandless) matriarch is a literary device rather than reflections of historical facts, is that paradigm or model used so often
in Genesis and beyond it? If women concur with this assessment of
their nature, the repetition and emphasis might be redundant. The
repetition, then, sounds like too much of a protest. It sounds problematic. Perhaps it points to a need to socialize women into internal-
izing the requirements of community survival in terms of personal
desire. In short, the portrayal of motherhood as an ideal, not only a
necessity, requires some more investigation. This investigation must
perforce go out of the biblical text, because the latter contains hardly
any other option for sexually mature women but an internal[ized]
urge for motherhood.

Kunin[21] argues that, paradoxically, it becomes apparent that the
first Hebrew families cannot multiply naturally, without god's assistance. Human seed needs divine seed in order to procreate. *Both*
natural parents are denied spontaneous capabilities to procreate,
according to Kunin, and he continues:

> Barrenness (denial of sexual role) should not be seen as the sole pre-
> serve of women in the biblical text since the role of the father is also
> denied. In these texts both the father and the mother are unable to
> produce the chosen line without divine intervention. *Although it is women
> who are called 'barren'*,[22] the sexual potency of the father is also denied:
> his age is emphasized, he is symbolically castrated. The structural logic
> of the myth is the denial of the human element in Israelite birth.[23]

The structural opposition between humanity's potential for natural
reproduction and the infertility of some patriarchs and matriarchs is
beyond question. Nonetheless, Kunin's attempt to de-gender the
procreative paradox seems to me unsuccessful although it might prove
more comfortable for womanly readers. Female barrenness is claimed
directly; male infertility is either implied or non-existent (as in the
case of Jacob). Males require heirs as much as women do; however,
the men are not depicted as having the same *emotional* motivation as
women do: males' desire for sons is always social, never essential.
Neither do males go to such great lengths in order to acquire the
'right' son or any sons: let us note, for instance, that Abraham would

---

[21] S.D. Kunin, *The Logic of Incest: A Structuralist Analysis of Hebrew Mythology* (JSOTSup,
185; Sheffield: Sheffield Academic Press, 1995), pp. 259–60.
[22] My italics.
[23] Kunin, *Logic of Incest*, p. 259.

make do with Yishmael as his licit heir (Gen. 17.18). The initiative for producing sons is the women's.[24] When Isaac implores Yhwh he does so, expressly, 'for his wife, because she is barren' (25.21), not for himself. In short, barrenness is gendered in the HB. While both partners may be infertile or fruitless, the burden of transforming the condition as well as its causal background are the women's. The divine intervention too affects the woman physically—Yhwh has to 'open the womb'—while the man is affected socially. Whereas the structural significance of the barrenness mytheme is indeed to be accepted, the issue remains: how is this mytheme gendered, and what are the social functions of that gendering?

Before this cluster of questions can be discussed further, and before extra biblical data can be weighed, another factor has to be taken into account. Female fertility may carry hazards, immediate and long-term, for female physical well-being and even life. Pregnancy and birth are dangerous. This is perhaps hinted at already by the divine word to the first woman concerning birth (Gen. 3.16). This is not a risk shared by males. How does biblical literature deal with such hazards?

Women's lot in the Hebrew Bible: literary depictions of women's life span and death at childbirth

In contemporary western societies, the life expectancy of women is higher than men's. This is borne out by a cursory survey of the official statistics for almost all westernized societies[25] although, to be sure, differences of ethnicity, class, life style (rural or urban) and economic circumstances are relevant and influential. While the life span of both females and males is on the increase, the differential between women and men is widening in favour of the former. Statistically, a western woman today can expect to outlive a man of similar age and circumstances by some years. The chief reasons for male death are cardiac, circulatory, cerebral and capillary disorders, then cancer; for women the chief reasons for mortality are malignancies

---

[24] Sarai's (Gen. 16), Rachel and Leah's (ch. 30).
[25] For instance, in Israel of the mid-1990's women's life expectancy is almost seventy-seven years, while men's is a little under seventy-five. The relevant data is published annually in the official (government) *Statistical Survey*. Readers are invited to compare this to the data in their own countries.

of the reproductive system (including breast cancer), which outnumber cardiac-circulatory-cerebral-capillary illnesses. The implications
and ramifications of the data are numerous and diverse. For the
present discussion, it is worth noting that western[ized] female Bible
readers tend to outlive men; and that their reproductive system,
in spite of the great advances of modern medicine in matters of
obstetrics and female maladies, still remains their most vulnerable
physical locus.

It would be unwise, however, to learn from this modern situation
anything about 'ancient Israel'. In the HB women's life span as
narrated is shorter than men's life span. Sarah dies before Abraham,
at one hundred and twenty-seven years of age (Gen. 23.1) to his
hundred and seventy-five (25.7–8). Rebekah disappears from the scene
before Isaac, who manages to be blind and senile for ages, dies at a
hundred and eighty years (36.28–29). Jacob buries Rachel who dies
at childbirth (35.19–20), Rebekah's nurse Deborah (35.8), and Leah
(49.31). Bath-Shua, Judah's wife, dies when he is still potent and
fertile (38.12). Rebekah, Dinah, Bilhah, Zilpah and Tamar disappear
without death or burial before the males they are linked to die. Since
daughters do not have birth stories, it is hardly surprising that women
do not have death stories either, unless their death serves to highlight
a patriarch's life journey (as in the cases of Abraham and Jacob).
Wherever available, the pattern is consistent. Prominent women somehow tend to die *after* their spouses. There are exceptions, of course:
Naomi, Orpah, Ruth and all the nameless 'widows' mentioned in
the BH as objects for special societal support; beyond the HB, Judith
is a widow who lives long after her husband dies. The insistence on
the earlier death of matriarchs and other prominent women can
therefore be read as an ideologically slanted picture: since men are
presented as more significant in patriarchy, their longer life span may
function as a literary and ideo-social marker of their more blessed
state. And yet, the longer life span attributed to males may also be
read as a reflection of 'real' life conditions if and when external
corroboration can be found.

One of the reasons indicated for women's early death is childbirth or, rather, son-birth. This happens to Pinehas' wife (1 Sam.
4.19–22) and also to Rachel.

Interestingly, the dying Rachel is encouraged by the midwife
thus, 'Do not fear, this is a son too' (Gen. 35.17); Pinehas's wife is
told by the helping women, 'Do not fear, you are giving birth to a

son' (1 Sam. 4.20). Is the birth of a son to be regarded as consolation upon a woman's deathbed? No wonder that Pinehas' wife does not pay heed and does not answer. Both women die after giving their sons names. Their last act is symbolic of their social duties and function,[26] as is their death at this particular juncture in their career. Significantly, both women are presented by the [implied] narrator, through the female speech of the woman or women assisting at the birth, as almost resigned to their fate. Their F[27] protest, feeble as it may be, is restricted to their silence or to the name-giving itself. Rachel pointedly names her son בֶּן אוֹנִי, 'son of my strength'. The narrator dryly observes that Jacob changes the boy's name to Benjamin, 'son of right [hand?]' (Gen. 35.18).[28] The nameless wife of Pinehas names her son אִי־כָבוֹד, 'no glory'; the name, as explained by the narrator, does not refer to her personal circumstances at all but to the national catastrophe the birth scene seals (1 Sam. 4.22).[29]

Such fortitude as exhibited by the unfortunate priest's wife, such annihilation of the self in favour of the social good seem, much as the all-embracing desire for a son attributed to certain female figurations, like a propagandistic device aimed at women's socialization into motherhood. Such a device should be considered—together with its twin brother, the 'barren woman' device—against the evidence furnished by archaeological and anthropological data.

Motherhood, women's life span and child mortality: archaeological and socio-anthropological considerations

The logical place to look for information about life span and mortality is reports on burial grounds (and, for later periods, burial inscriptions). Elizabeth Bloch-Smith, who discusses Judahite burial practices of the first half of the first millennium BCE, shows that

---

[26] For women's naming of their sons see I. Pardes, *Countertraditions in the Bible: A Feminist Approach* (Cambridge, MASS.: Harvard University Press, 1992), pp. 39–59.

[27] For the concepts of F (Feminine/Female) and M (Masculine/Male) voices in biblical texts cf. Brenner and van Dijk-Hemmes, *On Gendering Texts*, esp. pp. 1–11 ('Introduction').

[28] On Rachel see Pardes, 'Rachel's Dream' in *Countertraditions*, pp. 60–78.

[29] Although there is a reference to the death of the woman's father-in-law and husband (v. 21), the emphasis is on the national calamity (v. 22). Furthermore, she is presented as not paying any attention to her own physical plight (v. 20), although the shock of the news caused her to go into premature labour (v. 19).

burial was customary and communal. This is borne out by biblical
as well as archaeological data. Bloch-Smith writes:

> Infants, children, adolescents and adults were buried together. The
> patrimony with tombs as the physical claim to the land was maintained
> by the *bēt 'āb* (lineage) and its constituent elements, extended or multi-
> plied families . . . most undisturbed burials housed from 15 to 30 individ-
> uals of varying ages, which would represent two to four generations.[30]

In medical-anthropological analyses, samples of buried human remains
are usually individualized, aged and sexed in so far as this is possible
given the character of the burial, the condition, the types of bones
found and other circumstances. There is one explicit exception:
buried children's sex is hardly ever given.[31] The question is whether
the methodologies and implications of sexing remains are taken seriously enough, so that they would furnish results that are interesting
for the link between women's mortality and child-bearing.

I have chosen one burial ground, the 'En Gedi tombs, in order to
illustrate the point in detail. My source is an article by B. Arensburg
and A. Belfer-Cohen, 'Preliminary Report on the Skeletal Remains
from the 'En Gedi Tombs'.[32] The 'En Gedi site is dated as late, in
the early Roman period. Similar reports on other and earlier tombs
are available.[33] I assume that the 'En Gedi findings are indicative
also for the earlier (properly 'biblical') period precisely because the

---

[30] E. Bloch-Smith, *Judahite Burial Practices and Beliefs about the Dead* (JSOTSup, 123;
Sheffield: Sheffield Academic Press, 1992), p. 148.

[31] This lack of sex discrimination for infant remains excludes, for instance, any
discussion of the possibility of female infanticide, a practice still prevalent in south-
east Asia and certain Third World countries nowadays. The castaway, metaphorical
female infant whom Yhwh chances to find 'in the field' (Ezek. 16) might, perhaps,
be imagined as a victim of female infanticide. And since female infanticide was
practised in the Graeco-Roman world, perhaps also in ancient Mesopotamia [see
K. van der Toorn, *From Her Cradle to Her Grave: The Role of Religion in the Life of the
Israelite and the Babylonian Woman* [Biblical Seminar, 23; *JSOT* Press, 1994, p. 77, with
a bibliographical source cited in n. 1]], this is a valid image. On the other hand,
female abandoning and/or explicit infanticide does not seem to have been practised
in Egypt, for instance, at least as presented by J. Tyldesley, *Daughters of Isis: Women
of Ancient Egypt* (London: Penguin Books, 1994), p. 69. For infanticide as demographic
regulator see also J.M. Riddle, *Contraception and Abortion from the Ancient World to the
Renaissance* (Cambridge, MASS/London: Harvard University Press, 1992), pp. 10–15.

[32] In *'Atiqot* 26 (1994), pp. 12*–14* (English section).

[33] For this article and the materials to be mentioned shortly I am greatly
indebted to my colleague Dr. Karel Vriezen, of the Faculty of Theology, Utrecht
University. A chance conversation on this topic resulted in Dr. Vriezen's voluntary
search for materials. I am deeply grateful to him for his kind help and for his efforts
on my behalf.

situation they represent with regard to climate, diet, surroundings, technology and, subsequently, human well-being and life expectancy might be superior to that of earlier times. At any rate, within a 'long duration' analysis, the finds are applicable to 'biblical' times, the somewhat late date notwithstanding. In fact, the relevant finds at Megiddo, an admittedly small sample of skeletal remains from the chalcolitic through to the Iron Age,[34] do not substantially contradict the findings of the 'En Gedi tombs. Neither do other reports, as we shall see presently.[34a]

The 'En Gedi report covers remains of 164 individuals from five tombs, all of which are communal. The male/female ratio given is 55.5:45.5 for adults, 51:49 for infants. This ratio, which the authors call 'normal demographic distribution of gender [*sic!*] and age',[35] raises speculation about the mortality rates for infant girls,[36] which are appreciably higher than those for boys'. Another methodological problem that is immediately apparent is the question, How is the sexing operation conducted?

An answer can be worked out, at least in part, in the Tell el Mazar report.[37] Methods of archaeological as against anthropological sexing depend on preconceived notions; either of these two methods, or approaches, may furnish mutually contradictory results. Archaeological notions, such as assigning crouched or extended burial positions to either females or males, have proven less reliable than one might desire.[38] The preferred methods, of medical-anthropological bone sexing, are in general much more accurate. But when the bones are not pelvic bones, their sexing often depends on stereotypic notions of size (women are usually considered[39] smaller than men). However,

---

[34] A. Hrdlicka, 'Skeletal Remains', in P.L.O. Guy and R.M. Engberg (eds.), *The Megiddo Tombs* (Oriental Institute Publications, 33; Chicago: University of Chicago Press, 1938), pp. 192–95.

[34a] So also in later times. Cf. evidence for life span in later times in P.W. van der Horst, *Ancient Jewish Epitaphs* (Kampen: Pharos, 1991), pp. 73–84, esp. 83–4.

[35] 'Preliminary Report', p. 12*.

[36] See also, but with some questions about the gender distribution, Riddle, *Contraception and Abortion*, pp. 12–13 for populations of some European cities from the 15th to the 20th centuries CE, together with instances of a reversed (higher mortality for male children) picture resulting from better female infant care.

[37] K. Yassine (ed.), *Tel el Mazar: I. Cemetery A* (Amman: 1985): A. Disi, W. Henke and J. Wahle, ch. vi ('Human Skeletal Remains'), esp. pp. 137–139. The site is defined as an Iron Age site.

[38] Disi, Henke and Wahle, 'Remains', esp. pp. 181–85.

[39] For instance, the often-quoted study by D.L. Risdon, 'A Study of the Cranial

when the height of female-male population appears to be similar, then the decisive criterion seems to be bone volume, or, to use the current coinage, how 'gracile' the bones are. 'Gracile' bones are assigned to females, as in the Gezer V report.[40] Studies of measurements and population types are obtainable; statistic data of life expectancy for the buried population is often computed—but without distinction between males and females. Skeletal pathologies, like those caused by arthritis,[41] are discussed because their worth for reconstructing work and life style is considerable. However, the pathologies as well as the life span are neither sexed nor gendered. Why are bones studied?

> . . . human skeletal remains are no less fruitful subject of research than pottery, metals, architecture, or any field of historical and prehistoric study. The 'biological remains' may have information for answering the questions concerning the past human population (i.e.) with respect of [sic] morphology, racial affinities and ethnic relationships, diachronic changes in geographical region, their mortality rate, life expectancy and their diseases.[42]

Indeed, it cannot even be argued that the medical-anthropological studies are confined to the biological/chemical side of the inquiry: all the articles cited and referred to contain larger or smaller sections not only on the anthropological implications of their analyzed data but also on the historical implications. But, apparently, gender relations are not a worthy subject of such investigations. No wonder that the singular lack of interest, together with the problems of methodology, yield neither fresh questions nor new results on that score.

---

and Other Human Remains from Palestine Excavated at Tell Deweir (Lachish) by the Wellcome-Marston Archaeological Research Expedition', *Biometrika* 31 (1939), pp. 99–161, for Lachish around 700 BCE; or N. Haas, 'Human Skeletal Remains in Two Burial Caves', *Israel Exploration Journal* 13 (1963), pp. 93–96, for Jerusalem around 700 BCE; *idem*, 'Anthropological Observations on the Skeletal Remains from Giv'at ha-Mivtar', *Israel Exploration Journal* 20 (1970), pp. 38–59, from the early Roman period (with one crucified individual, male); P. Smith and J. Zias, 'Skeletal Remains from the Late Hellenistic French Hill Tomb', *IEJ* 30 (1980), 109–15 (with additional bibliography for other sites); B. Arensburg, 'The Skeletal Remains', *'Atiqot* 12 (1977; English series), pp. 81–83, for Akko, 14th cent. BCE.

[40] D.J. Finkel, '2. Human Skeletal Remains', in J.D. Seger and H.D. Hance (eds.), *Gezer V* (Jerusalem: Annual of the Nelson Glueck Institute, 1988), pp. 129–45. The discussion concerns human skeletal remains of cave I.10A that is identified as 'a well defined sequence of transitional LB I and LB IIA deposits'. (J.D. Seger in the same volume, pp. 60–72; quote is from p. 60).

[41] Smith and Zias, 'French Hill tomb'.

[42] Disi, Henke and Wahle, 'Human Skeletal Remains', pp. 135–36. For literature on methodologies see there, pp. 136–37.

To come back to the 'En Gedi report. Given this scholarly climate, it is hardly surprising that it conforms to the general pattern.[43] Admittedly, the 'En Gedi report is a preliminary report only. However, like most other reports,[44] it lacks real interest in the implications of sex/gender issues—as if the anatomical burden of being a fertile woman is of less import than other life and death factors. The authors seem to be more interested in comparisons to other sites[45] than in a sex/gender study of the local human remains. This approach is highly surprising in the light of the effort made to sex the skeletal remains and the observation made, significantly under the subheading 'Results', that 'Estimates of age at death, especially in tomb 2, point to greater average life span among males'.[46]

Table 1 (p. 13* of the article) contains 'Distribution of Remains by Sex and Age' in the five tombs excavated. The numbers are perhaps more eloquent than the dry statement made in the 'Results' section. Most buried males seem to have died between the ages 25 and 40; at least 3 were more than 55 years old when they were buried. This in effect means that, for the individual males whose remains are part of the sample, the plausible life span was relatively high. For females, on the other hand, the situation was different. The most common age of mortality is set by the analysis at 20–25; very few females lived to be 35+; no female remains indicate that their female owners reached the ripe old age of 50+. Similar sex differentials obtain in several of the studies mentioned above, for various periods.[47] Arensburg and Belfer-Cohen state that 'All in all,

---

[43] 'Preliminary Report', pp. 12*–14*.

[44] Of the reports I read, only Disi, Henke and Wahle remark ('Human Skeletal Remains', p. 186): 'As the sample was too small, we did not establish sex-differentiated life tables, though it is well known from the literature that the average life span of women was apparently shorter in prehistoric times [sic!] than that of men, which means the sex ratio influences the results'. But, they continue to assert that '... in our opinion, this method can give us valuable demographic information though the basis is *not quite correct in the sense of palaeodemography*' [my italics]. No reasons are given for the qualification. Non-differentiated life expectancy at Tell-el Mazar was computed as 33–43 years.

[45] 'Preliminary Report', p. 14*.

[46] 'Preliminary Report', p. 12*.

[47] In Gezer V, for instance; see Finkel, 'Skeletal Human Remains', where 'Based on the 45 *adults* for whom age could be ascertained, the average age at death is 27.5 years, and the median and mode are both 24 ... the average life span was in fact extremely low, ranging in *adult* individuals from 14 to 56 with a definite skew toward the lower end of the scale' (p. 130; my italics). So also in the exceptional Herodian family tomb described by R. Hachlili and P. Smith, 'The Genealogy of

the "health status" of the 'En Gedi population described here was relatively good'. Why, then, such a difference between the life span of women and men, a difference which remains inexplicable by the report itself?

It would seem that the most common age of female mortality, a distinctive age of high fertility, is indicative of the most common reasons for female mortality. One assumes that both females and males shared the same climate, diet and creature comforts.[48] Child-bearing and child-nurturing, then, must be the culprits. Death at childbirth must have taken its toll, as did recurrent pregnancies (and see below) and the feeding of the young. These same factors must have contributed to the lower life expectancy of all females by causing severe depletion of physical resources. It seems strange that no comment is made in the report about this greater depletion of body resources which must have caused earlier female death. Until today, women's reproductive systems remain their most vulnerable physical locus. The longer life span and higher life expectancy women now enjoy in the western world, so much so that the gender differentials are completely inverted, can be linked closely to the demographic trend of having fewer children and better options for birth control (as much as to better diet, health care, and so on, which are shared by members of both genders).

Granted, the report by Arensburg and Belfer-Cohen is a preliminary report only. But, in view of the modern reality in which they operate, does the lack of investigation point to a lack of curiosity about the implications of the medical-anthropological findings for the largely socio-historical problem of female well-being in ancient Israel?

Another interesting cluster of information has to do with infant and child mortality (Table 1, p. 13*). 77 [unsexed] individuals of the 164 whose remains were found in the tombs, approximately 47%, were infants and children up to the age 12+ (*sic!*). 35 of these 77 were between fetus and three years old upon their death (app. 45.5%),

---

the Goliath Family', *BASOR* 235 (1979), pp. 67–70, with an 'Appendix' by M. Rimon, pp. 73.

[48] It is possible that males were given preference in matters of diet and physical comforts for material (their greater strength as providers of sustenance) as well as ideological reasons. Adult males might have received preferential treatment at the expense of children, perhaps more so at the expense of girls than boys. However, there is no evidence of that in biblical texts. I proceed here from the assumption that basic commodities, when and where available, were shared, at least after a fashion.

and 21 were between three and six (27.2%). In other words, 72.7%
of the dead children were under the age of six. We have no way of
knowing, of course, either what the rate of infant and child mortality
in that community was or how it compared with other contemporaneous communities (although other medical-anthropological
reports again confirm a similar picture for other times and different
sites). Nor can we compare female early death with male early death
because the young dead were not sexed, although that could have
been helpful for the present project. We can, however, get the
general impression that infant and young child mortality was extremely
high by modern western standards. This must have presented an
added physical burden for females of child-bearing age. Even if
they did manage to get through the risks of pregnancy and delivery
successfully, they could and often did find themselves embarking on
the same project soon afterwards because of the child's early death.[49]
Emotional distress upon losing a child was probably not experienced by women only and will not be discussed here. The need to
replenish in order to supply continuity and community survival,
however, was incumbent upon the all too often bereaved mother.
Disi *et al.* write:

> ... prehistoric populations existed under conditions which are comparable
> with those in underdeveloped countries, due to a high mortality rate in
> the youngest group and a high death rate of early adults by traumatic
> diseases in males and death in association with childbirth in females.[50]

This conclusion seems to fit in well with the situation Arensburg and
Belfer-Cohen report, at least for rural areas and perhaps in contradistinction to urban, more privileged lifestyles, as described by
Hachlili and Smith for the same period.[51] *Qal va-Homer*, then, that
the gendered interpretation I attempted to derive from the data can be
cautiously applied to earlier times, with the knowledge gleaned from
modern archaeology that most of even the sedentary population in
the second and first millennium was not affluent and lived—and
died—in rural areas.

---

[49] Early infant and child deaths are occasionally reported in the HB, for instance
in the case of the prostitute's son and Solomon's judgement (1 Kgs. 3.16–28). At
other times it is announced by prophets and interpreted as divine punishment—so
in the cases of David and Bath Sheba's first son (2 Sam. 11.14–23), or Jeroboam's
son Abijah (2 Kgs. 14.1–18).
[50] Disi, Henke and Wahle, 'Human Skeletal Remains', p. 189.
[51] Hachlili and Smith, 'The Goliath Family'.

Women's lot in ancient Israel of the second and first millennia BCE—especially in rural, predominantly agricultural and labour-intensive areas—was far from easy. Carol Meyers[52] has shown that the division into domestic and public domains did not obtain in their case, at least from the perspective of participation in [manual] labour, economic activity and management of family resources. That meant, among other things, that pregnancies, child-nurturing and child-rearing had to be fitted in with other, physically tasking activities, much like the situation in many so-called developing countries today.[53] The societal ideology of 'be fruitful and multiply' makes sense, given such factors of harsh conditions and child mortality. The societal pressure to procreate must have had an edge for women. If they complied with it, they enhanced their social status and thereby also contributed to their family's and their own security, prosperity and labour power. At the same time, frequent pregnancies must have diminished their biological well-being, to the extent of early death. If they chose to prefer health and long life to their own social and society's physical survival interest, they stood to lose security and even basic life support in old age. A complicated predicament. Women, at least some of them, were undoubtedly aware of this predicament.[54] A mixed blessing, indeed, 'Be fruitful and multiply' was for women.

The Hebrew Bible will have us believe that the choice exercised by ancient Israelite women was exclusively and consciously pro-life [of children and society at large], to use a current slogan; this in effect meant that, for themselves, that was a pro-early death choice. No biblical texts explicitly discuss the other option theoretically open to women—that is, to use contraception of any kind in order to prolong their lives, although long life is considered a supreme blessing in as much as children are. But the emphasis on the

---

[52] C. Meyers, *Discovering Eve: Ancient Israelite Women in Context* (New York: Oxford Press, 1989).

[53] See also C. Meyers, 'Gender Roles and Genesis 3.16 Revisited', in A. Brenner (ed.), *A Feminist Companion to Genesis* (Sheffield: Sheffield Academic Press, 1993), pp. 118–41.

[54] Savina Teubal raises the possibility that some matriarchs, notably Sarah, self-consciously delayed conception and birth for a later stage in their lives—although the reasons she surmises for the decision are religious-cultic rather than pragmatic. Their motivation, Teubal surmises, was later co-opted by biblical writers and incorporated into the fertility propaganda. See S. Teubal, *Sarah the Priestess: The First Matriarch of Genesis* (Athens, OH: Swallow Press, 1984), *Hagar the Egyptian: The Lost Traditions of the Matriarchs* (San Francisco: Harper & Row, 1990); and a summary of her position in Teubal, 'Sarah and Hagar: Matriarchs and Visionaries', in Brenner (ed.), *A Feminist Companion to Genesis*, pp. 235–50.

'distressed barren woman' woman figure raises questions as to its motivation and thus provides an opening for further discussion.

Birth control in the HB: meagre traces and how to fill the biblical lacuna

The only place in the HB which perhaps contains an oblique reference to male birth control is the passage about Onan (Gen. 38.8–10), which was taken up later by both Judaism and Christianity as the basis for their official, though in varying degrees, objection to birth control.[55] Whatever the method employed might have been, and whatever the motivation for Onan's reported 'destruction of seed',[56] it clearly constitutes an act of contraception. Whether *coitus interruptus* or another method is implied cannot be ascertained. As we have seen, female contraception is never mentioned. It would seem, on the basis of biblical literature alone, that an ancient Israelite/Judahite woman neither imagined nor had knowledge of birth control in any form, be it preventive or abortive.

The notion of abortion is perhaps present in the passage about the jealous husband and the wife suspected of adultery, usually referred to as *sôṭâ* (Num. 5).[57] Although he has no evidence, the husband may act on his suspicion and bring his wife to the priest for public trial. One component of the ceremonious ritual calls for the woman to swallow a concoction, mixed in an earthenware vessel by the priest, which includes holy water, holy earth and holy words (vv. 18–26), after repeating the priest's curse. The effect of drinking is to determine whether the woman is guilty. If she has been made 'impure' by sexual relations with another man, 'her stomach will distend and her thigh will fall'; if not, she is clean and can be fertilized by her husband (vv. 26–28).[58] This version of trial by water for suspected

---

[55] Feldman, *Birth Control in Jewish Law*, pp. 144–67 for both Judaism and Christianity, including citations of the relevant sources.

[56] Heb. הַשְׁחָתַת זֶרַע, the squandering of male seed instead of using it for the proper procreative function, became a principle informing subsequent rabbinical rulings on procreation and bans of male contraception. For the gradual development of the concept in rabbinic thought see M. Satlow, '"Wasted Seed": The History of a Rabbinic Idea', *HUCA* 65 (1994), pp. 137–75. Also to be found on the Internet, and can be downloaded from ftp://ftp.lehigh.edu/pub/listserv/ioudaios-l/Articles/msseed.

[57] Cf. *m. Soṭ., b. Soṭ.*

[58] But cf. van der Toorn in *From Her Cradle*, who interprets the ordeal as punish-

adultery[59] is clearly aimed at uncovering the missing evidence. If the evidence is a pregnancy (the logical outcome of a sexual liaison), then the distension of the body and the loosening or slackening of the 'thigh'[60] is expected to produce a decisive result in the form of an aborted fetus.[61] This reading of the *sôṭâ* ordeal[62] makes sense of the trial. It also points to the possibility that abortion, although unacknowledged as female voluntary praxis, can be induced orally (even though, in this case, divine intervention is assumed).

Similarly and again obliquely, involuntary miscarriage is mentioned in the Law, Exodus 21.22–23. In a hypothetical case, a pregnant woman might be hurt accidentally in a fight; she may then go into premature labour. 'If the fetus[63] comes out', there are two possibilities: no damage is incurred, or a miscarriage occurs and some damage is incurred.[64] In the first instance, the husband is reimbursed by the aggressor for the damage done to his property. In the second instance, the *talion* principle is to be activated. It is not clear who is hurt—the pregnant woman, the embryos, or all. All three readings are plausible, since woman and fetus[es] alike are the husband's legal property. It is at the very least implied that miscarriage because of external reasons—man-induced, like the *sôṭâ*'s abortion procedure— is known.[65]

These traces are simply inadequate. And yet, given the conditions of ancient Israelite societies, it is unthinkable that contraceptives and abortion techniques were unknown—especially to and by women, whose chief interest must have been to regulate their productivity

---

ment: the adulterous woman will remain childless (p. 79), within the general belief that barrenness indicates sin in its bearers (pp. 78–82).

[59] Cf. par. 129 of the Hammurabi code, where both suspected adulterers are bound and thrown into the water to determine their guilt or lack of guilt. The husband may forgive the woman if he wishes; cf. the same suggestion made in *Sif. Deut.* 218, but rejected. Cf. also par. 130–132, esp. 132.

[60] For 'belly' and 'thigh' as euphemisms for sexual/reproductive organs see Chapter 3.

[61] Cf. Frymer-Kensky, 'Law and Philosophy', pp. 97–8; also Frymer-Kensky, 'The Strange Case of the Suspected Sotah (Numbers v 11–31)', *VT* 34 (1984), pp. 11–26.

[62] Although later Judaism prescribed the ceremony and expanded on the passage, its performance was far from welcome. Cf. *m. Soṭ.* 9.9; and *b. Soṭ.* 47a.

[63] In the singular, after the Samaritan and the LXX; cf. BHS. The HB has a plural here (ויצאו ילדיה).

[64] Stol, *Zwangerschap en geboorte*, pp. 14–17, discusses Mesopotamian and other parallels.

[65] See the discussions in *m. Bab. Qam.* 5; *Tos. Bab. Qam.* 9.20; *b. Ket.* 33a, *Bab. Qam.* 42b, 48b, 49a; *yer. Bab. Qam.* 5; *Mek. de-Rashbi* 21.22; and more.

by the cheapest, most readily available means that could be found. In order to reconstruct a plausible, even if unverifiable, picture of gendered birth control in ancient Israel, extra biblical material has to be considered.

Looking for evidence of birth control knowledge, I started from the praxis often used in mainstream Bible studies. Extra biblical data can be arranged along the twin grids of time—before, during and after the time of 'ancient Israel';[66] and place—of lands surrounding the area[s] known during those times as Judah/Israel. If an element necessary for reconstructing a missing component in ancient Israelite sociology is found, along the time line, before and after the time of ancient Israel, not to mention during that time, then it is plausible to assume with a high degree of certainty that the component was present in ancient Israelite culture, even though it is not mentioned in the Bible itself. If, in addition, the same element is to be found also in the texts of cultures and locations surrounding ancient Israel geopolitically, then plausibility might turn into probability. The only question that remains is, Why is the plausibly available data missing in or suppressed out of the Bible itself.

A survey of ancient southern Levant and Mediterranean cultures, from the second millennium BCE and until the end of the first millennium CE (an extended period, as a precaution against too hasty conclusions), yields unsurprising results. Various male birth control techniques are well known but seldom practised. The gender motivation or religious ideology for that will be referred to below. Female birth control by contraception is widely known. The techniques usually involve consumption of chemical substances, mostly plants, taken orally or otherwise. Mechanical prevention of pregnancy by tampons is well-attested.[67] Knowledge about abortion in various early stages of pregnancy, including the inducement of premature labour, is available. The substances used are ordinary, easily accessible and

---

[66] For the purpose of the present discussion, from the middle of the second millennium BCE to the beginning of the second century BCE.

[67] As also in Islamic literature: '. . . some women practised contraception. Furthermore, in Arabic medicine, references to female contraceptives in the form of intra-vaginal suppositories outnumber by four to one references to male contraceptives.': B.F. Musallam, *Sex and Society in Islam: Birth Control before the Nineteenth Century* (London: Cambridge University Press, 1983), p. 37; and n. 60 (p. 132, with reference to a table on p. 80). See also pp. 62–3, for the use of tampons soaked in oil or honey.

convenient to obtain. The textual sources are in general disapproving male sources which retell female techniques: rarely is their tone prescriptive. The texts are of diverse backgrounds: medical, cultic, juridical, theological, narrative and so on. Practices persist for millennia and across spatial and chronological boundaries. Many of them seem to be almost universal. Some are regained at a certain point and then disappear again. Others are used until today. Most are finally lost, suppressed or become subterranean, largely through the developing doctrinal disapproval of the Christian church and, to a lesser extent, of Jewish law. It is all too easy to dismiss the largely homeopathic techniques as ineffective, folk remedies or old wives' tales. However, when the medical profession, from the eighteenth century onwards, starts to deal again with birth control, ancient knowledge resurfaces and is regained. Traces of that knowledge are certainly present in modern medical mechanical and chemical preparations.[68] Against this backdrop, it is hardly conceivable that only Israelite women lacked the resources or knowledge to exercise birth control if and when they wished and/or were able to do so. But before we proceed, some more detailed information concerning birth control on the time-place grid of the Southern Levant and Judaism-early Christianity seems to be in order.

Birth control in ancient Egypt and in Mesopotamia

Abortion (contraception after the fact) is recorded in texts of the end of the second millennium BCE from deir-el-Medina. Since deir-el-Medina was a village of workmen who constructed monuments at the close-by Valley of the Kings, this implies that abortion was known and practised throughout most social levels.[69] So is contraception: 'Prescription to make a woman cease to become pregnant for one, two or three years;[70] grind together finely a measure of acacia and dates with some honey. Moisten seed-wool with the mixture, and

---

[68] Riddle, *Contraception and Abortion from the Ancient World to the Renaissance*, esp. pp. 163–66.

[69] L. Manniche, *Sexual Life in Ancient Egypt* (London and New York: KPI, 1987), p. 17.

[70] Or 'periods'. See the different translation, discussion and elaboration in Riddle, *Contraception and Abortion*, pp. 69–72, and notes on p. 189.

insert it in the vagina' (from the Ebers Medical Papyrus, dated 1550–1500 BCE).[71] Tyldesley writes that,

> Several Contraceptives and even abortion-procuring prescriptions were available for those couples who wished to avoid pregnancy; these were generally concocted from a diverse range of curiously unpleasant ingredients and frequently included a measure of crocodile dung ... The efficacy of these methods is unknown ... Perhaps not surprisingly, no evidence of 'male' contraceptives such as condoms or recipes for potions to be applied to the male genitalia have been recovered; methods such as coitus interruptus ... or coitus obstructus ... would naturally leave no trace in the archaeological record.[72]

Tyldesley mentions contraceptives a few more times[73] but is never specific, apart from once when she attributes 'a certain contraceptive effect' to breast-feeding.[74] This lack of specificity, together with the general description quoted above, seems to point to her reluctance to discuss the practice of Egyptian birth control seriously.

In fact, Riddle supplies translations and/or discussions of the following medical documents about birth control, mostly for females but also for males: the Kahun Medical Papyrus (ca. 1850 BCE), the Ramesseum Papyrus IV (1784–1662 BCE), more of the Ebers Papyrus, and the Berlin Papyrus (1300 BCE). He also cites later Egyptian sources without specification.[75] Riddle even discusses the, apparently effective, abortive qualities of crocodile dung.[76] The female birth control preparations are to be taken orally or vaginally (by the insertion of a suppository). The substances cited (apart from the exotic animal faeces) are quite ordinary: honey, soda, dates, myrrh, acacia, onions, juniper and pine products, beans, beer and wine, celery, oil and more. These—in varied proportions, mixtures and manner of preparation—are used for various purposes: to induce menstruation, for causing spermicide, for contraception, for abortion. Riddle concludes that certain oral preparations were probably effective, if dangerous for the woman in improper amounts. He further writes,

> Vaginal suppositories appear in the oldest of Egyptian medical records and continue to appear in later papyri; all appear to draw on

---

[71] Tyldesley, *Daughters of Isis*, p. 62.
[72] Tyldesley, *Daughters of Isis*, pp. 62–3.
[73] Tyldesley, *Daughters of Isis*, pp. 32, 51, 78, 121.
[74] Tyldesley, *Daughters of Isis*, p. 78.
[75] Riddle, *Contraception and Abortion*, pp. 66–73, and notes pp. 188–90.
[76] Riddle, *Contraception and Abortion*, p. 67.

an archetype, or traditional formula, whose activity may have some basis for action. Given the uncertainties about texts, translations, and identifications, however, and given the lack of definitive pronouncements in modern science studies, one cannot draw conclusions. The importance of the Egyptian material is the presence of the concept that certain agents can prevent conception and cause an abortion. The idea of chemical means of birth control is thus as old as the surviving medical records. As for abortifacients, some were likely effective. Less confidence can be placed in the contraceptives, but here too there are grounds to postulate a rational use of drugs.[77]

It would therefore appear that female birth control is known from the beginning of the second millennium BCE; acknowledged in medical records; considered efficient, at least to a certain degree (why bother with repeatedly administering or recording it otherwise?); is mostly drug-based; and is preserved in an on-going tradition.

What about birth control in Mesopotamia? According to Karel van der Toorn, in ancient Mesopotamia (as well as in ancient Israel), failure to become pregnant fast branded a woman a sinner—in the eyes of others as well as in her own eyes. And he continues:

> Of course, there could also be technical handicaps at work. That people considered that a possibility appears, among other things, from a series of Akkadian incantations that tried to revive male potency. But Mesopotamians were not quick to ascribe impotency to divine retaliation. They thought rather of magic. Who knows how easily a jealous wife was able to pronounce a spell?[78]

For some reason, van der Toorn assumes that a Babylonian woman regularly and unconditionally wanted to become pregnant. In view of the acknowledged possibility of male impotence/sterility, be its attributed origin as it may; and in view of the danger inherent in pregnancy for everywoman, I question the validity of the generalization for all women. The absence of pregnancy may be attributed to 'technical handicaps', in his words! To be sure, van der Toorn's subject is women's religious life: religiously, women (and men) have to announce a wish to procreate, in Mesopotamia as in ancient Israel[s]. Was this always the case? Can it be assumed that women would want to become pregnant at all times, regardless of personal circumstances and other considerations, that a wish to regulate their own fertility never occurred to them? Should the pious sentiments

---

[77] Riddle, *Contraception and abortion*, p. 73.
[78] Van der Toorn, *From Her Cradle to Her Grave*, p. 77.

concerning childbirth that women express within a religious context, as is required of them, to be embraced uncritically? Van der Toorn's presentation seems a little too positivistic and one-sided. He mentions in passing texts which illustrate knowledge of miscarriage as well as protection against such an eventuality.[79] Such knowledge always entails its twin, knowledge of how to induce an abortion. Indeed, van der Toorn writes sketchily about women's culture, in a chapter entitled 'Repressed Emotions Take Their Toll: Women and Folk Religion'.[80] Women's knowledge of matters of fertility, birth control and contraception is hinted at in a subsection entitled 'Sorcery'. What could a woman do if her husband took another wife? Cast spells, try to reduce her husband's potency or harm her rival. How can she do this? We do not know, writes van der Toorn, how such witchcraft works: by burning a figurine, pronouncing incantations, obtaining physical traces of the victim, and also *the preparation of a magical potion of food, which then had to be administered by devious means*.[81] Indirectly, then, to be sure, van der Toorn could have constructed a picture of birth control in ancient Mesopotamia—even if he chose to relegate such practices from the sphere of the [established, male] religious to the sphere of [popular, female] folk religion. That he chose not to do it, in spite of the availability of M. Stol's book, is strange: while Stol maintains that very little is actually known about contraception in Mesopotamia, at least he discusses it and lists some references. That is, Stol does not confuse lack of information with the absence of evidence for praxis.[82] Furthermore, van der Toorn notes that, '. . . we can suspect the existence of so-called "Adonis gardens" (boxes of earth with quick growing kinds of grass, cared for by women as a form of fertility magic) but we have no firm proof'.[83] Van der Toorn does not even entertain the notion that such boxes could have contained anti-fertility as well as fertility herbs. As set out in Riddle's book *Contraception and Abortion*, such a 'garden' of useful herbs would have been a must for any practitioner of folk medicine, certainly for midwives and other female healers:[84] there can be no doubt that, in

---

[79] Van der Toorn, *From Her Cradle to Her Grave*, pp. 82–3.
[80] Van der Toorn, *From Her Cradle to Her Grave*, pp. 111–33.
[81] Van der Toorn, *From Her Cradle to Her Grave*, p. 114; my italics. See also S. Rollin, 'Women and Witchcraft in Ancient Assyria', in A. Cameron and A. Kuhrt (eds.), *Images of Women in Antiquity* (London: Croom Helm, 1983), pp. 34–45.
[82] Stol, *Zwangerschap en geboorte*, pp. 18–19.
[83] Van der Toorn, *From Her Cradle to Her Grave*, p. 144.
[84] On women as healers in general see C. Fontaine, 'The Social Role of Women

antiquity, women were involved in medical aspects of gynaecology as well as obstetrics.

It would seem that van der Toorn's presentation or, rather, non-presentation of women's probable knowledge about fertility and birth control in Babylonia (and ancient Israel) is instructive. He does not appear to be remotely interested in the topic: when he briefly discusses it, women's practices are demoted to 'witchcraft', perhaps also superstition. Recognition of infant mortality and pregnancy failure does *not* initiate a probe into possible implications beyond the necessity for further pregnancies. Women are presented as complying with the socio-religious, patriarchal system with urgency and eagerness. The relevant sources, as he writes, are scanty and originate in the dominant system. Let us read 'male' for dominant, for all the available documents—including the ones which express women's fervent prayers for children.[85] In short, on this count van der Toorn's book illustrates why and how we know very little about birth control and abortion practices in ancient Israel and in the culture of its neighbours. Van der Toorn complies with the biblical (and other ANE) texts and ideologies although he is fully aware of these texts' bias and limited value for any historical reconstruction, especially—but not only—for the reconstruction of ancient women's lives. As a result, the subject is virtually non-existent in his book. However, I am not at all sure that, in ancient Israel or ancient Mesopotamia, women did not have efficient, to a greater or lesser extent, means for regulating their own fertility. On the contrary, as suggested by evidence from surrounding cultures.

Birth control in the ancient Greek and Hellenistic worlds

Riddle presents an extensive review of medical texts relevant to gynaecology and fertility control from the Greek and Roman worlds. His review includes birth control and abortion terminology in the

---

in the World of Wisdom' in A. Brenner (ed.), *A Feminist Companion to Wisdom Literature* (Sheffield: Sheffield Academic Press, 1995), pp. 41–5; and 'Disabilities and Illness in the Bible: A Feminist Perspective', in A. Brenner (ed.), *A Feminist Companion to the Hebrew Bible in the New Testament* (Sheffield: Sheffield Academic Press, 1996), pp. 298–9.
[85] Van der Toorn, *From Her Cradle to Her Grave*, pp. 79–80.

Hippocratic corpus[86] and in Pliny the Elder (23–79 CE),[87] Scribonius Largus and Galen,[88] Dioscorides (first century CE) and Soranus (second century CE).[89] Riddle then goes on to discuss birth control and abortion along time/space lines in the late Roman empire and early medieval period,[90] the Middle Ages and the Christian Church,[91] Salerno and the twelfth century,[92] Arabic medicine and the late Middle Ages,[93] the Latin west and the Renaissance[94] and, finally, the post industrial revolution period in the west.[95]

One of Riddle's principal questions is, How and when did we lose the birth control/abortion information that the ancients seem to have had in abundance? That the ancients used mainly plant-derived drugs, and separated efficient plants from inefficient ones by processes of experimentation and observation of humans and animals, especially females, is no surprise. After all, this is how modern medicine rediscovered plants with anti-fertility or hormone properties, then started to synthesize them. For instance, in the 1930's willow, palm and pomegranate were found to contain sex hormones.[96]

In the ancient Greek and Roman cultures of the Mediterranean, anti-fertility and abortifacient plants (and some minerals) were known and used by women and medical men alike, although reluctantly by the latter on ethical and other grounds. The relevant literature is quite extensive, and points to widespread knowledge. This knowledge seems to have been transmitted along the axis of time as well as disseminated to various places. Furthermore, the same plants are mentioned again and again, from ancient Egypt of the beginning of the second millennium BCE to late antiquity and the early medieval period, and rediscovered recently. Most of these plants or plant

---

[86] Riddle, *Contraception and Abortion*, pp. 74–82.
[87] Riddle, *Contraception and Abortion*, pp. 82–4.
[88] Riddle, *Contraception and Abortion*, pp. 84–6.
[89] Riddle, *Contraception and Abortion*, pp. 25–65.
[90] Riddle, *Contraception and Abortion*, pp. 87–107.
[91] Riddle, *Contraception and Abortion*, pp. 108–17.
[92] Riddle, *Contraception and Abortion*, pp. 118–26.
[93] Riddle, *Contraception and Abortion*, pp. 127–34. For Arabic and Islamic ideologies and practices of contraception and abortion cf. Musallam, *Sex and Society in Islam*. Especially enlightening are the lists of materials used in various periods and types of literature, pp. 77–88 and 101–4.
[94] Riddle, *Contraception and Abortion*, pp. 135–57.
[95] Riddle, *Contraception and Abortion*, pp. 158–66. See also pp. 66–73 for Egyptian sources, discussed earlier.
[96] Riddle, *Contraception and Abortion*, pp. 87–8.

products—taken orally or vaginally; as prophylactics or after the event—were not exotic plants. They were common, easily found, easily prepared—as in ancient Egypt. The secret lay in using the correct part of the plant (root, leaves, bark, fruit etc.), at the correct stage for picking, with the correctly proportioned mixture of ingredients, and the proper application to a situation. Some of the products prescribed repeatedly for female birth control, inducement of menstruation and abortion are honey, dates, myrrh, acacia, onions, juniper and fir trees products, beans, beer and wine, celery, oil, birthwort, parsley, spikenard, coriander, cabbage, rue, dill, pepper, some ferns, cinnamon and some kinds of mint. Copper, rediscovered and used now in some IUD's, is known as a spermicide (taken orally or vaginally) from Egyptian texts through to the Hellenistic medical records and further, in Arabic and Islamic medical traditions.[97] Finally, surgical or pseudo-surgical procedures are known—be they performed by professional medical persons (usually males) on women, by women themselves on other women, and by women on their own bodies.

Birth control in early Judaic sources

Rabbinical texts show great preoccupation with menstruation and other female discharge phenomena connected to fertility, and with the implications of such discharges for women's participation in the cult. Similar if asymmetrical preoccupation is shown with regard to male sperm discharge. This preoccupation is in keeping with the biblical priestly (including H) preoccupation.[98] It would seem that both priestly/H and rabbinic attitudes to menstruation and female discharge are ambivalent. On the one hand, males are seriously warned against having sexual relations with a menstruant or otherwise discharging woman: the word for 'menses', נדה, is used to convey 'disgust, abomination' as well.[99] On the other hand, the link between menstruation and life was probably recognized: perhaps this is the

---

[97] Musallam, *Sex and Society in Islam*, pp. 60–88, including tables of contraceptive and abortifacient chemicals and methods in Arabic and Islamic literature (from p. 77).

[98] Lev. 12 and 15 are the chief prooftexts.

[99] For instance in Lev. 20.21; Num. 19 (5 times), 31.23; Ezek. 7.19–20, 18.6, 22.10, 36.17; Zec. 13.1, Lam. 1.17; 2 Chron. 29.5.

reason for a woman's longer transitional period after giving birth to a girl, which is double that prescribed for a male child (Lev. 12);[100] I would even suggest that the period prescribed in the HB for male cultic impurity after ejaculation or sexual intercourse (Lev. 15), which is shorter than a woman's and upheld as such in rabbinic literature, may have been motivated not by preferential treatment for males but, on the contrary, by the closer identification of the female with sexuality and procreation.[101]

In spite of the preoccupation with menstruation in particular and women in general, the question remains, How much knowledge of fertility/anti-fertility, and especially such knowledge as related specifically to gynaecology, was available in post-biblical communities of the last centuries BCE and the first centuries CE, as evidenced by rabbinic writings? The answer to this question is, in a nutshell, that the scope of gynaecological/fertility knowledge is quite extensive by comparison to biblical data. Rabbinic literature cannot be and is not here considered a direct derivative of biblical literature in any way. However, the amount of relevant knowledge in it, together with the inevitable links it demonstrates with the Graeco-Roman world and its knowledge, supports the fact that biblical literature could have been neither isolated from its neighbours' medical knowledge of anti-fertility and contraceptive agents, nor devoid of such knowledge altogether.

Miscarriage was certainly known and discussed.[102] So was abortion, 'which was not considered a transgression unless the fetus was viable'.[103] Furthermore, authorities for whom a woman's life supersedes that of a fetus, even prescribe surgical interference to induce an abortion in the case of fatal danger: 'when a woman has difficulty birthing, the fetus is cut in her stomach—even on the Sabbath—and is taken out limb by limb, because her life comes before his' (*Tos. Yeb.* 9.5). The passage certainly implies abortion by surgical means

---

[100] I. Be'er, 'Blood Discharge: On Female Im/Purity in the Priestly Code and in Biblical Narrative', in A. Brenner (ed.), *A Feminist Companion to Exodus to Deuteronomy* (Sheffield: Sheffield Academic Press, 1994), pp. 152–64.

[101] Whether the extensive rabbinic literature on menstruation was in fact put to practice by a majority in early communities, or just by rabinnic circles, is beside the point here, since our interest here is in rabbinic attitudes rather than actual early Jewish practice.

[102] For instance, *m. Nid.* 3.1–9, *Shab.* 10.2; *Tos. Nid.* 4.6, 9, 12; *b. Nid.* 18, 25, 26, 28; *Bab. Qam.* 83a; *Ḥul.* 77b; *j. Nid.* 50.3a; *Sif. Tazri'a* 1.3.

[103] 'Abortion', *Enc. Jud.*, vol. 2, pp. 98–101 (esp. 99), with rabbinic and secondary references.

although, to be sure, it is difficult to know to what stage of a potentially fatal pregnancy (and the foetus's viability) it refers.

Rabbinic Judaism gradually developed a doctrine of obligatory
procreation[104] that proscribed men from 'wasting seed'.[105] This doctrine in effect meant that while males had to refrain from inten-
tional birth control by *coitus interruptus*, masturbation and other means,
women remained unbound by the doctrine and much freer to pursue
birth control—although some rabbinic authorities were familiar
with Graeco-Roman theories of female seed.[106] While the Torah's
'Be fruitful and multiply' remained a basic tenet, circumstances as
well as the legitimate pleasure of male and female spouses were
taken into account. Should a man have sex with his wife, even
if it is dangerous for her to conceive or if she is post-menopausal?
Are anal and oral sex legitimate, even though they do not facilitate
procreation? The answer to those and similar questions is that, yes,
such sexual practices are allowed, since they strengthen mutual
affection and desire between [married] spouses. Inevitably, these two
directives—one pro-procreation, the other pro-desire—may come into
conflict. However, together and added to the recognition of the risks
women undertake in order to be fruitful, the two conflicting tendencies
leave a margin for the practice of female birth control that is tolerated
and even condoned in rabbinic discussions.[107]

Perhaps the simplest means for birth control practised by women
was a tampon, of cotton, wool or the like, referred to simply as מוך.
Rabbinic discussions as well Rashi's commentaries make it amply
clear that women knew how to use this mechanical device and used
it: it remained for the rabbis to try and regulate the praxis, allowing
it chiefly when a pregnancy would endanger a woman's well-being
or life, and bringing it into line with the procreation commandment.[108]
Let us remember that evidence of women's use of contraceptive
tampons is available already for ancient Egypt.

---

[104] As already in Philo. For a summary and references see A. Reinhartz, 'Parents
and Children: A Philonic Perspective', in Cohen (ed.), *The Jewish Family in Antiquity*,
pp. 61–88, esp. 69–70.

[105] Satlow, 'Wasted Seed', has a comprehensive discussion of this and related issues.

[106] Satlow; see also P.W. van der Horst, 'Sarah's Seminal Emission: Hebrews
11.11 in the Light of Ancient Embryology', in van der Horst, *Hellenism-Judaism-
Christianity: Essays on their Interaction* (Kampen: Kok-Pharos, 1994), pp. 203–23.

[107] Feldman, *Birth Control*; 'Birth Control', *Enc. Jud.*, vol. 4, pp. 1053–4.

[108] *Tos. Nid.* 2.6 (cf. Satlow, 'Wasted Seed', pp. 150–52, with references to addi-

Contraceptive drugs for women (of plant origin) are implied by the one mention of סמא דעיקרתא, 'drug of uprooting = abortive drug', mentioned as an efficient means in *b. Yeb.* 65b. This preparation is apparently taken orally, as implied by the 'cup of abortifacients' [drugs] of *Tos. Yeb.* 8.4; in *t. yer. Ab. Zar.* 2.40c there is a warning against letting a foreign midwife give such a 'cup' (כוס של עיקרין) to a Jewish woman: clearly, the art of female contraception is here associated with female medical personnel. Similarly, in the *b. Yeb.* passage a woman is associated with the self-administering of the drug[109] although, in another passage, males are the administering agents.[110] In *b. Shab.* 109b such contraceptive drugs, עיקרין, are mentioned for females and males alike, as explicitly stated by Rashi in his commentary for the passage. Rashi also knows of an orally administered abortive סם, 'drug of plant origin', used to induce abortion in a case of irregular pregnancy that endangers the woman (in his commentary to *b. Nid.* 40a).

The word סם designates 'drug' but also and more frequently and generally 'aromatic plant'. עיקרין, עקרתא are derived from the root sequence עקר, one of whose designations is to be or be made 'sterile'. While the identification of the plant products at issue is difficult to determine,[111] their presumably efficient nature can be assumed. In sum, it can be safely stated that, in early rabbinic culture, various forms of contraception and abortion are known and even legitimated in certain cases, especially when the life of prospective mothers is endangered. The apparent discord with prescriptions about procreation in general, and male seed in particular, creates tensions but does not obliterate the notion: contraception exists; women know about it, and so do men.

Back to ancient Israel and the biblical texts

Motherhood is one of the basic dogmas advocated by human society as we know it. An ideology of motherhood is indispensable for the

---

tional secondary literature on birth control in rabbinic literature); *b. Yeb.* 12b, 35a, 100b; *Ket.* 37a, 39a; *Nid.* 3a–b, 45a, *Ned.* 35b; *Esth. Rab.* 8.3; *Panim Aḥerim* 1.1.

[109] Cf. Riddle, *Contraception and Abortion*, pp. 61–2.

[110] See also *Mid. The.* for Ps. 106.5: Datan and Abiram sinned in that they made their wives drink an apparently contraceptive potion, hence the specific form of punishment they suffered.

[111] Riddle, *Contraception and Abortion*, p. 34, is tempted to identify this drug as

functionality and survival of any group, particularly for patriarchal organisations. Thus, buttressing the presumably biological-instinctive urge of females to parent children and care for them is a necessary part of female socialization. Women are subjected to pro-motherhood propaganda, be it implicit or explicit, from their early childhood: they are encouraged to become willing madonnas and they internalize the message, to their own and their society's detriment. This is the regular picture to be found in the ancient, so-called classical world.[112] The Bible offers no departures from this norm.

Centuries of Bible exegesis and interpretation have complied with biblical propaganda by idealizing the figure of the Mother. Many Bible feminist critics have acquiesced and even appropriated this idealized picture of biblical desire for motherhood as their own: after all, the ability to conceive and give birth is uniquely female/feminine. I have no quarrel with this tendency. I merely want to point out the facts, easily obscured by pro-motherhood propaganda, that so-called 'pro-life' policies might have meant early death for its ancient female adherents; and that female birth control, although almost completely eradicated [by males?] from the HB, perhaps in the interest of group survival, must have been practised in ancient Israel—like in several other ancient cultures of the southern Levant. It appears impossible that whereas contraception and other anti-fertility measures were known and practised all around ancient Israel and in early Judaism, and in earlier as well as later times, they were totally unknown in ancient Israel itself. The knowledge, part of which was certainly women's knowledge, was available but never explicitly disclosed by biblical literature.

An accidental omission of such data from the Bible is possible but not plausible, in the light of biblical procreation ideologies: it has been shown at the beginning of this Chapter that the so-called priestly writers were not the only ones to champion procreation as a supreme socio-religious value. The existence of Jewish sources, scanty as they are,

---

barrenwort, a plant of known anti-fertility properties, on the basis of the similarity of the name.

[112] See, for instance, N. Demand, *Birth, Death and Motherhood in Classical Greece* (Baltimore and London: Johns Hopkins University Press, 1994), especially on the 'Acculturation to Early Childbearing' and 'The Attitudes of the *Polis* to Childbirth' (pp. 102–40); S. Dixon, *The Roman Mother* (London and New York: Routledge, 1988), on 'The Official Encouragement of Maternity', pp. 71–103: 'In Rome, as in many societies, motherhood had always established or enhanced a woman's status. Fertility was associated with the general good' (p. 71).

is another pointer in this direction: contraception and anti-fertility are generally not discussed for their own sake but as incidental to other superordinate concerns. Finally, the association of anti-fertility as well as fertility-advancing knowledge with women might have contributed to its neglect (at best) or suppression (at worst).

It could have been expected that, if biblical writers/compilers—especially of the law codes—knew about [female] contraception but objected to it in principle, they would have prohibited it explicitly by formulating laws against it. In other words, are we here faced with authorly ignorance, disinterest, indifference or suppression? Ignorance can be ruled out, I think, as illustrated by the *sôṭâ* passage. So can disinterest and indifference, as evidenced by procreation ideologies. It is perhaps relevant to remember at this point that most of the biblical materials were authored, compiled, preserved, transmitted and later studied by males and for males, the true members of the community construct. F voices were largely edited out or muted out of it: only traces of those can be laboriously and uncertainly reconstructed.[113] If birth control was felt—as also in other cultures in general, including later Judaic sources—to fall primarily within the province of women's interest and praxis (and see below), then the silence about it fits in with other silences on women's lives. Women are the objects of/in most biblical texts, not the addressees of either requirements or prohibitions. Perhaps it was felt that, in their case, the procreation propaganda of the narratives (to distinguish from the law) was enough to preclude birth control and ensure co-operation. It can be freely granted that reading an omission is risky; it can also be granted that silence is as powerful a tool for negation as prohibition is. Furthermore, absence is not necessarily a signifier of disinterest. For instance, while the father-daughter incest category is completely absent from the incest lists in the Law,[114] this hardly means that such incest was *not* forbidden. It might simply mean that, in the light of virginity's value as a basic socio-economic commodity, father/daughter incest was understood as so destructive that it did not require any mention. Moreover, perhaps it was felt that contraception and abortion fell within the scope of human murder in general. At any rate, as in the case of F voices in biblical literature, only traces of birth control practices can be found. It remained for post-biblical

---

[113] See Brenner and van Dijk-Hemmes, *On Gendering Texts*.
[114] See Chapter 5, on incest.

Judaic sources, highly preoccupied with women's fertility while no less preoccupied with procreation than biblical literature and perhaps even more so, to acknowledge female (and male) contraceptive measures incidentally to other concerns.

And yet, the tracing of birth control and abortion information to biblical Israel might prove helpful not only for the reconstruction of a segment of ancient realia. It might also and simultaneously contribute to the interpretation of some biblical texts. Therefore, by way of closure, I would like to discuss two clusters of texts: texts on female involvement in magic, and SoS texts which contain multiple references to certain plants and aromatics.

A sorceress—do not let her live (Exod. 22.17)

Magic and witchcraft were an integral part of life in the ANE, including the so-called 'biblical' and 'post-biblical' worlds.[115] Women are imagined as closely linked with magic and sorcery, as succinctly expressed in *b. Sanhedrin* 67a: 'Most women know their way about magical practices'.[116] Practice of magic is specifically attributed to women also in Mesopotamian sources[117] and others. Most Jewish commentators, including sages as recorded in talmudic sources,[118] extend Exodus 22.17 to relate the absolute prohibition on magical practices, and the death penalty entailed, also to men—that is, they ungender this passage and harmonize it with other male-addressed prohibitions. Indeed, males (Exod. 7.11; Deut. 18.10; Jer. 27.9; Ezek. 13;

---

[115] A basic resource for background articles on witchcraft and magic in the ANE (in general) is J. Sasson (ed.), *Civilizations of the Ancient Near East* (New York: Charles Scribner's Sons, 1995), vol. 3. The relevant articles in this volume are, at least: J.F. Burgouts, 'Witchcraft, Magic and Divination in Ancient Egypt', pp. 1775–86; K. Weeks, 'Medicine, Surgery and Public Health in Ancient Egypt', pp. 1787–98; W. Farber, 'Witchcraft, Magic and Divination in Ancient Mesopotamia', pp. 1895–1910; R.B. Biggs, 'Medicine Surgery', pp. 1911–24; G. Frantz-Szabo, 'Hittite Witchcraft, Magic, and Divination', pp. 2007–20; J.-M. de Tarragon, 'Witchcraft, Magic and Divination in Canaan and Ancient Mesopotamia', pp. 2071–82. For these reference, as well as for many other references concerning witchcraft and magic in this Chapter, I am greatly indebted to Carole Fontaine.

[116] רוב הנשים מצויות בכשפים. Similarly also *yer. Sanh.* 7.25d.

[117] Z. Abusch, 'The Demonic Image of the Witch in Standard Babylonian Literature: The Reworking of Popular Conceptions by Learned Exorcists', in J. Neusner *et al.* (eds.), *Religion, Science, and Magic: In Concert and in Conflict* (New York: Oxford University Press), pp. 27–58.

[118] For example, *b. Ber.* 21b; *Sanh.* 60a, 67a and *yer. Sanh.* 7.25d; Rashi and Maimonides.

Dan. 2.2; 2 Chron. 33.6) as well as females (Exod. 22.17; 1 Sam. 28; 2 Kgs. 9.22; Isa. 47.9, 12; Ezec. 13; Mic. 5.11; Nah. 3.4, 5) are linked with varied and forbidden practices of sorcery and witchcraft. Nevertheless, not only the gendered F-object of Exod. 22.17 is odd. So is the death punishment decreed for the 'sorceress'. So is also the contextualization of the command within a passage dealing with sexual matters: in between the seduction of a virgin (vv. 15–16), and bestiality (v. 18). These problems or issues are already raised by the ancient and medieval Jewish commentators.

I would like to suggest that the passage be read as it is actually gendered, that is, a 'sorceress' should not be allowed to live. The question is, what is the specific witchcraft activity—referred to but not designated—that entails such a vehement judgement. It seems plausible that such an activity will be female-specific, connected to female wisdom, healing and medical practices. It seems plausible, because of the contextualization, that the female 'witch' has something to do with sexuality.[119] Women are midwives (explicitly in Gen. 35.16–17 and Exod. 1.15–22; implicitly in 1 Sam. 4.19–20, Ruth 4.13–17), they know about fertility drugs (Rachel and Leah and the דודאים fertility roots, Gen. 30.14–17). Women who knew about fertility and birth must have also known about their opposite, contraception and abortion. Devereux writes on abortionists,

> In most cases the woman herself performs the abortion, sometimes using singularly complicated or painful means to achieve her purpose. There are seemingly equally frequent references to assistance provided by unspecified old women. Expert or inexpert 'midwives' practice both in advanced societies... and in primitive societies... Physicians are sometimes more squeamish than medicine men and midwives about functioning as abortionists.[120]

---

[119] For instance, let us read some passages from E. Rose, *A Razor for a Goat: A Discussion of Certain Problems in the History of Witchcraft and Diabolism* (Toronto: University of Toronto Press, 1962). 'When a midwife was a witch (and probably most of them were; in a superstitious community they would need to be experts on charms), she was believed to be able to procure a painless delivery... Theologians were much occupied by the power of sorceresses to make a man impotent...' (p. 140). Rose rejects the attribution of malignant forces to 'witches' while admitting that their 'skill in poisons and abortifacients' must have been at least as strong as their powers to bless fertility (p. 141). In his view, women that were labelled 'witches' were herbalists, practising cults that were more religious than magical (pp. 143–44). See also pp. 146–51.

[120] G. Devereux, *A Study of Abortion in Primitive Societies* (New York: International Universities Press, 1955), p. 47.

In light of the predominant (and socially justified) procreation ideologies, such women do run the risk of being considered witches: they
undertake to deal with matters of life and death;[121] they seem to
have damaged the social fabric by helping women to regulate their
reproductive activities; their knowledge is dangerous to society and
its beliefs—as evidenced by persecutions to woman healers in much
later times. Indeed, the reading of the 'sorceress' as a medicine woman
or, more specifically, a female gynaecologist who deals with fertility
as well as anti-fertility measures, is helpful for understanding both
the content and context of this text. Such women's practices could
not have been restricted to verbal formulas and incantations: to
evaluate their practices as superstition only would be wide off the
mark. They must have had herbal and other knowledge, perhaps
also surgical knowledge, as is also true of their ANE 'sisters'[122] and
of women in all times, societies and cultures.[123] Recent literature on
the connections made between witchcraft, women and birth across
cultures and times, makes the links between female magicians and
fertility regulation in praxis and cultural theory abundantly clear.[124]
It is therefore plausible that HB texts, as well as extra-biblical Judaic
sources, implicitly share in the view of female sex and fertility experts
as 'witches'.

---

[121] Perhaps Ezek. 13.17–23, in which prophesying women are accused of magi-
cally 'trapping' individual souls' whereas prophesying men are accused of public
activity (vv. 2–16), is a case in point too.

[122] An instructive passage in Rashi's commentary to *b. Soṭ.* 21a relates a story
about a widow who was a sorceress and could either stop or 'open' a 'womb' by witchcraft, a praxis that was later disrupted through the intervention of a male labourer.

[123] Cf. T.R. Forbes, *The Midwife and the Witch* (New Haven and London: Yale
University Press, 1966)—esp. ch. 8, pp. 112–32, for midwives and witchcraft in the
fifteenth and seventeenth centuries in western Europe.

[124] Cf. articles in Neusner *et al.* (eds.), *Science and Magic*; A. Llewellyn Barstow,
Witchcraze: A New History of the European Witch Hunt (San Francisco: Harper/Pandora,
1994); S. Bovenschen, 'The Contemporary Witch, the Historical Witch and the
Witch Myth:', in B, P. Levack (ed.), *Articles on Witchcraft, Magic and Demonology* (New
York: Garland Publishing, 1992), vol. 10, pp. 83–119; A. Barstow, 'Women as Healers,
Women as Witches', *Old Westbury Review* 2 (1986), pp. 121–33; T.B. Benedek, 'The
Changing Relationship Between Midwives and Physicians During the Renaissance',
Bulletin of the History of Medicine 51 (1977), pp. 550–64; S.R. Burstein, 'Demonology
and Medicine in the 16th and 17th Centuries', *Folklore* (1955), pp. 16–33; J.B.
Donegan, *Women and Men Midwives: Medicine, Morality and Misogyny in Early America*
(Westport, CT: Greenwood Press, 1978; M. Green, 'Women's Medical Practice and
Health Care in Medieval Europe', *Signs* 14.2 (1989), pp. 434–73; L.B. Pinto, 'The Folk
Practice of Gynecology and Obstetrics in the Middle Ages', *Bulletin of the History of
Medicine* 47 (1973); R. Blumenfeld-Kosinski, *Not of Woman Born: Representation of Caesarean
Birth in Medieval and Renaissance Culture* (Ithaca, NY: Cornell University Press, 1989).

Plants, aromatics and perfumes: on reading the Song of Songs

Readers who interpret the SoS as a poem or poems of human love and sexual desire agree that the notions of 'garden' and 'orchard' in it have multiple, simultaneous and partly overlapping significations. The garden/orchard may be the physical surroundings the lovers inhabit. It may symbolize the world of love, for it is customary in many cultures to depict love against a pastoral background. Since garden/orchard is primarily and quantitatively associated with female lovers, it is also the female and 'her' desire for the male. Finally, since it appears to be specified as the locus of female sexuality in a scene of successful male seduction of a female lover (4.9–5.1), the 'garden' is also understood in this and similar passages as connoting female physical body parts.

The 'orchard' has shade trees (cedars, fir trees) but, principally, fruit trees—like vines, peaches or apricots (תפוח, 2.3, 5; 7.9; 8.5), figs, pomegranate (4.3, 13; 6.7, 11; 7.13; 8.2), date palm.[125] The 'garden' contains flowers, דודאים (fertility plants or aphrodisiacs?,[126] 7.14) and, mainly, spices and aromatic plants.

Smell appears to be an important constituent in the worlds of love and desire constructed within the texts of the SoS: so much so that many interpreters are tempted to overrate this constituent of human enjoyment for its own sake. Terms for aromatic plants and perfumes abound,[127] as well as their arrangement into whole 'gardens' (גן, גנה or ערוגה—6.2, 11; 7.13–14). Aromatic plants are associated with male lovers (1.3, 13–14) and their body parts (6.13); but, to a much larger extent, with female lovers (3.6). Female desire is metaphorized into perfumed substances (1.12; 5.5). Female genitalia are 'myrrh and frankincense' (4.6), a veritable perfume garden (4.12–5.1) which is the male

---

Specific materials concerning the ANE are to be found in S.D. Walters, 'The Sorceress and Her Apprentice: A Case Study of an Accusation', *JCS* 23 (1970), pp. 27–38; J. Black and A. Green, *Gods, Demons and Symbols of Ancient Mesopotamia: An Illustrated Dictionary* (Austin, TX: University of Texas, 1992), esp. pp. 67–8, 118, 124–28, 132–33.

[125] It is widely held that 'honey' in the Bible designates, unless otherwise specified (Judg. 14), date honey. Hence, the occurrences of 'honey' (נפת, דבש) in the SoS (4.11; 5.1) should be included here too.

[126] Although this plant is mentioned (Gen. 30.14–16) as an aphrodisiac or fertility agent (so also BDB), it might have—like other herbs—served for the opposite purpose as well.

[127] For identification and general discussion see A. Brenner, 'Aromatics and Perfumes in the Song of Songs', *JSOT* 25 (1983), pp. 75–81.

lover's domain (6.2; perhaps also v. 11, if attributed to a male-speaker-in-the-text). Among the aromatic substances mentioned are spikenard, myrrh, henna (the last two evoke males as well), frankincense, saffron, cane, cinnamon, aloes, 'and other spices' (4.13).

Quite a number of the plants repeatedly mentioned in the SoS have been used as female contraceptives and abortifacients throughout the Mediterranean world for, quite literally, ages. Pomegranates, honey, dates, fir trees products, [mixed] wine, oil, myrrh, spikenard and cinnamon feature in lists of such substances from the end of the second millennium BCE in Egypt and until the present. In the SoS sexual activity *never* culminates in pregnancy, neither does the book contain any mention of procreation ideology. I therefore suggest to add another stratum of interpretation to the text, namely, that the 'garden/orchard' is, coincidentally with its other significations, also a reassuring reference to and reminder of easily obtainable birth control facilities.

In spite of its overall unconventional character, the SoS is not devoid of knowledge of norms pertaining to female sexual behaviour, as illustrated by various references (1.6, 3.3, 5.7, 8.8–9). In such a social context it is imperative for a woman not to become illicitly pregnant (see the *sôṭâ* passage), not to seem to have lost her virginity. Therefore, for instance, a seductive male voice in 4.9–5.1 may be reassuring his lover through his recital of a list of aromatic plants which double as contraceptives that no consequences will have to be suffered. Or, an F invitation for a male lover to come to her mother's house, so that 'I will let you drink mingled wine, *pomegranate juice*' (8.2b) might be read as a reminder of contraception too—at least on a supplementary level. Most commentators concur that sexual consummation is finally allowed by the female lover. She seems to be convinced by the recital that the lover can come into 'his garden', which is her body (4.16). The male lover's jubilant last lines (5.1) leave no doubt as to his success. Similarly, the consistent association of women and pomegranates, a known source of female hormones that can be used in anti-fertility preparations, can be explained as an implicitly decorous and gentle reminder as to certain pomegranate's properties beyond its colour. And so can the insistent association of the female body or body parts with other certain plants, especially but not only aromatic plants.

Far be it from me to suggest that we confine the reading of the 'garden/orchard' notions of the SoS to contraception alone. I would merely like to suggest that if we add this level of interpretation to others—that is, read the 'garden/orchard' as signifying habitat, mutual love, female sexuality and desire, the female sexual body *and* potential fertility that is there but is rendered checked fertility—both our understanding of the SoS, and of contraception in ancient Israel, benefit thereby.

By way of conclusion

Knowledge of contraception and abortion belongs to the sphere of wisdom, in as much as knowledge of 'magic' and fertility and general medicine do. In ancient Israel practitioners of wisdom were women as well as men, although M wisdom was handed down to us on a much grander scale than F wisdom. Be the almost total absence of contraception knowledge (or F wisdom, for that matter) from biblical literature the outcome of deliberate design or otherwise, it seems reasonable to assume two things: that the actual knowledge existed; and that it was preserved and transmitted chiefly by women and for women.

CHAPTER FIVE

DEVIATION FROM SOCIO-SEXUAL BOUNDARIES, I: ON INCEST[1]

Introductory remarks and definitions

Incest taboos, like other sexual taboos,[2] define and express boundaries inside a society. Incest taboos are one of the means for organizing not only or simply [mostly heterosexual] sexual boundaries—who can have potentially reproductive sexual intercourse with whom; but also and primarily social boundaries—how should coupling and consequently parenting and lineage within a given society be structured. Interestingly, incest proscriptions and narratives in the HB encompass both kin incest and marriage incest, that is, the difference between the biological and the social is blurred by the lack of clearcut differentiation between the two categories. Therefore, the analysis of incest is highly significant for understanding HB attitudes to sex and gender.

In our western culture, 'incest' usually and immediately connotes a coercive/coerced sexual relationship between socially unequal blood kin, most usually initiated by an adult against an unwilling minor. In that sense, 'incest' constitutes a sub-category of sexual exploitation or harassment and is treated accordingly by legal systems. Not surprisingly, the usual, hierarchical age-and-gender stratification obtains in such cases, as in other social phenomena of patriarchal society. Statistically, the most common 'incest' event would involve an older male and a younger female. However, this modern notion of incest is not necessarily applicable, wholly or in detail, to notions of incest in cultures other than ours: Freud's Oedipal fantasy of primary son-mother incest does not conform to our empirical knowledge of our society. Therefore, when discussing biblical incest

---

[1] This Chapter is an extensive rewrite of my article, 'On Incest', in A. Brenner (ed.), *A Feminist Companion to Exodus to Deuteronomy* (Sheffield: Sheffield Academic Press, 1994), pp. 113–138.

[2] Such as adultery, 'homosexuality', prostitution, bestiality and cross-dressing, to be discussed in the next Chapter.

notions, a frame of reference drawn from the *biblical* material is in order. For the purpose of this study, then, I shall define 'incest' as,

(a) sexual [heterosexual] intercourse
(b) performed either by mutual consent, or else through unilateral coercion and/or trickery
(c) between sexually immature or sexually maturated persons,[3]
(d) who are related either as blood kin, or else
(e) as marriage kin.

In view of modern conceptions and colloquial usage, it appears that some elaboration of this working definition is necessary. Biblical notions of incest are extended from blood relations to include also in-laws of various categories (d, e). However, the prohibitions put forth are broader than the injunction not to marry: in fact, marital ties are seldom explicitly prohibited. The proscription is, first and foremost, against having sexual intercourse, hence without as well as with formal marriage. That both blood and marriage ties are included illuminates the dual nature of biblical incest prohibitions: this inclusion requires an interpretation that takes into account psycho-sociological factors rather than only biological (blood) factors.

The listing of both consent and, alternatively, coercion/trickery (b) draws attention to the fact that both are present in the HB, albeit distributed neatly between genres: whereas the prescriptive texts never relate to a combination of forceful or trick-motivated incest, the narrative texts may and do. For instance, as will be seen presently, coercion (rape) is primary in the Tamar-Amnon story; indeed, most commentators classify the story as a rape rather than incest story. In other stories—like those of Lot's daughters (Gen. 19.30–38) and Tamar and Judah (Gen. 38)—female trickery and male gullibility are thematically privileged over the incest theme. The almost total absence of the consent/non-consent consideration in the prescriptive texts (excluding Lev. 20.21), and the supremacy of other ideo-motifs (like paternal disrespect, sibling rivalry, female trickery) in the narrative texts, go to show (among other things) that the link between deliberate violence—physical and/or verbal—is presented as part of a certain sequence: social disorder, one of whose components is incest,

---

[3] I refer to 'sexually immature' and 'maturated' rather than to 'young persons' and 'adults' since the chronological age factor is not mentioned in the biblical passages to be discussed. Where a difference in age is implied, it is merely relative (like in the case of a forbidden son/mother relationship).

breeds social ills. The link between violence and incestuous behaviour patterns is in fact totally severed in the law codes, as if it did not merit any reference. In modern lore, however, incest is viewed as a potential cause rather than an outcome of social anarchy. Modern sociological research is greatly concerned with incest practised on children by their elder kin (usually male); biblical literature is apparently not concerned with this potential outcome of power relations.[4]

My aim is to consider the literary features and ideo-moralistic strategies relating to incest in narrative, law and prophetic texts; and to illuminate them by some modern theories of incest—sociological, anthropological, psychological, feminist and combinations thereof. I hope that the results of the transdisciplinary approach employed will constitute a small contribution toward the sociological knowledge of the construct we call 'ancient Israel'.

Incest in narrative and poetic texts

A juxtaposition of genres does not necessarily imply that different genres contain different approaches or ideologies. However, the preliminary results of reading different biblical genres which contain incest texts are surprising. It has already been noted that, in the narrative texts, the incest components differ considerably from their counterparts in the law and prophetic texts. The reasons for the seeming discrepancy probably pertain to the ambiguous emotive contents of incest, as evidenced by myth, fantasy and hero legends.

Brother-sister incest is implied in the wife-sister narratives (Gen. 12.10–13.2; 20; 26.1, 6–12). It is explicitly present in the stories about Amnon and Tamar (2 Sam. 13.1–22); and should be examined for the 'my sister, my bride' and 'my brother' addresses of lovers in the Song of Songs (SoS 4.9, 10, 12; 5.1, 2; 8.1–2; possibly also allusions in 6.9, 8.5b). Daughter-father incest is explicitly narrated about Lot's daughters (Gen. 19.30–38). It is an implicit underlying albeit sublimated and gradually fading motif in two other narratives, about Tamar and Judah (Gen. 38) and Ruth and Boaz (the Ruth scroll). A son-mother figure incest is present also in the shorter notes rather than the fully-fledged story about Absalom's uprising against his father

---

[4] On religious aspects of [modern] incest occurrences see A. Imbens and I. Jonker, *Christianity and Incest* (Turnbridge Wells: Burns & Oats, 1992).

David (2 Sam. 15.16, 16.21–23, 20.3). Son-father homosexual incest is perhaps present in the passage on the drunken Noah and his sons (Gen. 9.20–27).

In all the narratives cited, even when incest features as an explicit theme, it is not the most dominant theme. On the contrary: it is mostly subordinate to a stronger, superordinate theme. Another feature worth noting is the assignment of incestuous initiative to female figures (Lot's daughters, Tamar, Ruth), with the male figures assigned an object status. This stands in contrast to the positing of male addressees as the subjects of incest, and females as its objects, in the law and prophetic texts. Both female (Lot's daughters, Tamar, Ruth) and male (Abra[ha]m, Isaac) figures may be associated with trickery; violence in word and deed is attributed to male figures (Amnon, Absalom, perhaps also Noah's sons). Both elements of [gendered, male-specific] sexual violence and [bi-gendered, not gender-specific] sexual trickery are completely absent from the law/prophetic texts. Another conspicuous absence is the lack of specific, technical terms for incest in the narratives: neither the prescriptive terms nor others are present in the stories (excluding that of Noah and his sons). In short: context, gender roles, motifs, terminology and social concerns distinguish incest stories from incest proscriptions—again, possibly with the exception of the story about Noah and his sons. Similarly, no incest content seems to be attached to the male-voiced address 'my sister, my bride' of the Song of Songs (SoS 4.9, 10, 12; 5.1, 2). It is experienced as unproblematic by its repetition in the text itself and by most commentators. So is the female-voiced wistful 'I wish you were a [like] a brother to me . . .' (SoS 8.1–2), indulgently read as wishful thinking on the part of the female lover that a family relationship between her and the male lover would have made their union more viable.

Brother/sister incest

Implied brother-sister incest: the wife-sister stories

In the first wife-sister narrative (Gen. 12.10–13.2) it is gently implied that Sarai and the pharaoh have sexual intercourse[5] after Abram

---

[5] In biblical Hebrew the verb לקח, 'take' in such contexts, with a 'man' as the

asks Sarai to say that she is his sister, so that he does not suffer if any Egyptian desires her (12.13). The request is usually read as a ruse or blatant lie. But is it a complete lie? There is nothing in the text to suggest that Sarai is not Abram's sister *as well* as wife. Gen. 11.29 does not supply Sarai with a lineage. That absence can be read in two ways, although the mention of endogamy for Nahor makes its absence in Abra[ha]m's case look more like a lack than an absence.[6] Be that as it may, Abram's initiative of presenting Sarai as his sister is not overtly censored.[7] Abram makes a request, Sarai apparently obeys.[8] Neither the implied incest nor the half- or total

---

[grammatically implied] subject and a 'woman' as the [grammatical] object, may, approximately, signify 'marry', in the sense of formalize a union. That such a union consists, among other things or on its own, of sexual consummation is beyond doubt. The fact that here the passive form of לקח is used—'and the woman *was taken* (ותקח)'—may be read as a genteel side-stepping of the consummation issue, which has far-reaching ramifications for Abra[ha]m's paternity of Isaac who is still to be born. And see below for Lev. 20.17, 21.

[6] A strong tradition identifies Sarai with Yiskah, Abram's niece through his dead brother Haran. Some midrash instances (like *t. b. Meg.* 11.1, 14.1; *Seder Olam Rab.* 2; *Gen. Rab.* 46.1; *Yalkut Shimoni* 62, following *b. Sanh.* 69) make this identification, one of whose motives is undoubtedly to clear Abram's reputation somewhat. The same identification is made also by Josephus Flavius, who even foregoes the name Yiskah in favour of Sarah (*Ant.* 1.6.5; 1.12.2). For a survey of Gen. 12.10–13.2 in the Versions, midrash and ancient Jewish exegesis cf. Y. Zakovitch and A. Shinan, *Sarai and Abram in Egypt* (Research Project of the Institute of Jewish Studies Monograph Series, 1; Jerusalem: The Hebrew University, 1983 [Hebrew]). That kin endogamy is envisaged for Abra[ha]m's family is beyond dispute: the [non-incestuous] principle of marrying a niece/cousin is carried over to the third generation (Jacob and Esau). At any rate, Abra[ha]m's immediate lineage is somewhat muddled. The name Nahor appears in it twice, within successive generations, as his uncle (11.22–25; 1 Chron. 1.26) and also his brother (Gen. 11.26–27; cf. Josh 24.2) who married Haran's other daughter Milkah (Gen. 11.29). Whether this name repetition should be taken at face value or as an indication of lineage confusion (for Nahor's relationship with Abra[ha]m as well as for the latter's links with other members of this textual family) remains obscure.

[7] For another opinion, building on Sarai's silence-in-the-text, see F. van Dijk-Hemmes, 'Sarai's Exile', in A. Brenner (ed.), *A Feminist Companion to Genesis* (Sheffield: Sheffield Academic Press, 1993), pp. 222–34.

[8] Cf. also *Gen. Rab.* 41.2, 52.4; some Jewish sages apparently could not let Sarai/Sarah be potentially defiled without making a protest. On the other hand, they wanted her an obedient wife. Hence, Sarah is made to speak to God rather than to her husband. Seemingly, covert censorship of Abra[ha]m is thus implied. In the late *Sefer Ha-Yashar* Sarah is made to collaborate with Abraham, as quite clear from her interviews with the pharaoh (relating to Gen. 12) and Abimelek (relating to Gen. 20)—pp. 93 and 109 respectively in Dan's Hebrew edition (J. Dan [ed.], *Sefer Ha-Yashar* [Jerusalem: Bialik Institute, 1986]). In general, female figures in *Sefer Ha-Yashar* are given many more lines than in the source (biblical) text: cf., for instance, the retelling of Joseph and Potiphar's wife story (Gen. 39; pp. 199–205 in Dan's edition). This tendency to focus on women's roles may be explained by the possi-

lie seems scandalous. The chief themes are survival in a foreign presumably hostile land, by trickery if needs be, and the competition between the two males (Abram and the pharaoh), one of whom is backed by Yhwh. Readers face a dilemma. They/we do not even know what to prefer: a complete lie (Abram and Sarah are related, but not brother and sister); or a half lie (they are related hence, by definition, incestuously married as well as liars). Sarai is kept silent by the text, hence at the very most a passive accomplice. Attempts to clear Abram's name of the hideous crime of incest remain just that. The fact is that in this story incest, be it imagined or practised, is not problematized.

The moralistic edition of the same story in Gen. 20 (Abraham and Sarah in Gerar) 'corrects' quite a few moral and other difficulties present in 12.10–13.2.[9] The full responsibility for saying that Sarah is his sister is placed upon Abraham (20.2, 5). The previous ambiguities concerning a compromise of Sarah's virtue and her kin status, and Abraham's behaviour (half lie or a complete lie?), are resolved thus. Abimelek does not manage to touch Sarah before God intervenes. Abraham claims that Sarah is his half-sister, by his father although not by his mother (vv. 12–13): we know nothing of Sarah's lineage and, therefore, this claim might perhaps hold even if the information is new.[10] In this narrative, then, Abraham's lie is but half a lie, committed in self-defense against imaginary complications. Sarah neither denies nor affirms this: she remains silent. God too neither refutes nor confirms, but remains on Abraham's side against the hapless albeit righteous Abimelek. Abimelek himself, in an enigmatic utterance to Sarah (v. 16),[11] at least seems to accept Abraham's answer at face value. Whatever the 'facts' of the matter, numerous interpretive options can be entertained because of the textual ambiguities. It

---

bility that this late anthology (according to Dan, pp. 7–17, of the sixteenth rather than the eleventh or twelfth century, as previously dated) was compiled for women, somewhat like the Yiddish *Tsenah U-Re'enah*. However, more work should be done before this conjecture can be substantiated.

[9] I shall not discuss the relationship between the three stories here. Suffice be it to note that for the consecutive reader, be she or he an implied or a 'real' reader, Gen. 20 follows Gen. 12 and is followed by Gen. 26; hence, for those interested in a hermeneutic of suspicion, the former text is inevitably *read* as a comment on the latter.

[10] Cf. Again Abra[ha]m's lineage in ch. 11 and the absence of lineage for Sarah.

[11] Cf. *b. Sanh.* 56a (and Rashi's commentary to this passage); *Meg.* 15a, 28b; *Bab. Qam.* 93a. Abimelek's words to Sarah about the 'covering of the eyes' are interpreted as a covert curse. See also *Yalk. Shimeoni* 91.

seems that sexual relations and even marriage with a paternal half-sister are not considered incest here.[12] Or are they, but allowed in certain cases, insofar as certain [male] individuals are concerned?[13] This is perhaps corroborated by the Tamar and Amnon story, when Tamar tries to deter Amnon from raping her by insisting that David may agree to their marriage (2 Sam. 13.13; and see below). But, on the other hand, sexual union with paternal as well as maternal and half-sisters is prohibited by the law (Lev. 18.9, 20.17; Deut. 27.22); in Ezekiel 22.10–11, sexual relations with a paternal sister, apparently obtained by force,[14] are condemned together with two other incest categories (father and daughter, father-in-law and daughter-in-law). Also, the author/narrator of Gen. 26 certainly recognizes such a relationship as incestuous. Brother-sister sexual relations belong to the primary categories of kin incest not only in biblical law, but also in most cultures. In contemporary western society, brother-sister incest is one of the two most common blood incest categories, second only to the largest group of father-daughter incest.[15] On the whole, then, incest with a paternal sister (assuming that 'Abraham' is half-lying only) cannot be argued out of the text by interpretation or exegesis/midrash. It would therefore seem that in ch. 20 for Abraham, that is for the narrator, incest is less problematic than an admission

---

[12] For a summary of suggestions concerning the wife/sister situation, pointedly related to extra-Israelite ANE practices, and further bibliography cf. Rashkow, *The Phallacy of Genesis*, esp. pp. 31–2. Rashkow devotes a whole chapter to the first two wife/sister stories (pp. 26–48), and another to Abimelek's dream (Gen. 20; pp. 49–64).

[13] E.A. Speiser's commentary (*Genesis* [AB, 1; Garden City, NY: Doubleday, 1964)] can perhaps be read as an example of male complicity with the text: consciously or otherwise, and in the name of scholarship, Speiser supplies the textual Abraham with a perfectly adequate, comparative-cultural reasoning for what is, at most, a half lie. Cf. further Rashkow, *Phallacy*.

[14] The Heb. verb used in v. 11 is ענה pi., 'torture'. Previous consensus decrees that this verb, especially where it occurs with other lexemes of 'force', 'physical force' designates 'rape' (as in the narratives of Gen. 34, 2 Sam. 13; and the laws of Deut. 23). Cf. for other opinions and further literature L.M. Bechtel, 'What if Dinah Was not Raped?', *JSOT* 62 (1994), pp. 19–36; M. Weinfeld, *Deuteronomy and the Deuteronomic School* (Oxford: Clarendon, 1972), p. 286 n. 5; C. Pressler, *The View of Women Found in the Deuteronomic Family Laws* (BZAW, 216; Berlin/New York: de Gruyter, 1993), esp. pp. 37–8 n. 48.

[15] K.C. Meiselman, *Incest: A Psychological Study of Causes and Effects with Treatment Recommendations* (San Francisco: Jossey-Bass Publishers, 1978), esp. pp. 75–9, 293–98. Cf. also J. Irving's novel, *The Hotel New Hampshire* (New York: Pocket Books, 1981, 1982).

of dishonest, self-seeking deception. Ethical values assume precedence over sexual taboos. That this is not the only possible manner of resolving the conflict is clear.

An interesting development is the third story, about Isaac and Rebekah in the previously-mentioned Gerar, again with Abimelek (Gen. 26).[16] The woman is again the silent object of [implied] incest, the man the acting and speaking subject. But nothing happens: Isaac lies in preventive self-defense, the true nature of the relationship between man and wife is discovered by chance. And then Abimelek says to him, to paraphrase v. 10: What have you done? Somebody might have had intercourse with your wife and you would have made us guilty (of incest). Abimelek's words certainly contain a strong awareness of the adultery taboo, as supported by his protective command (v. 11). They also contain an awareness of sibling incest prohibitions. It appears that, on accidentally watching the pair make love,[17] Abimelek immediately infers that they are not siblings. This automatic inference can only mean that, for the narrator at least, the mere thought of incest is incomprehensible even where foreigners are concerned.

We find, then, that in the first two installments of the wife/sister series, on a sliding scale of gravity, adultery—be it deliberate or out of error—is a more serious offense than nuclear endogamy (brother-sister incest), be this narrative endogamy real or fictitious. It is initiated by the husband: the wife is silent but complies. This cooperation between spouses follows a strict patriarchal pattern—another pointer to the priority of matrimony over incest. The endangering of the woman's virtue[18] finally serves the issue of paternity as well. Significantly, though, the third instance (Gen. 26) regards brother-sister incest as a non-option: if Isaac makes love to Rebekah she *cannot* be his sister. This represents a shift of priorities. In short, the ambiguities are caused by the necessity to decide which social principle is the more important within a narrative framework of survival. Hence later

---

[16] The same Abimelek? This is of course problematic when read consecutively, after ch. 20, although the two other figures differ. One solution, of course, is to attribute each of the stories to a different source, although such an attribution misses the developmental thrust of the series somewhat. Another is to treat 'Abimelek' as a generic-local dynastic name, like 'Pharaoh'. The latter option was chosen, for instance, in Sefer *Ha-Yashar* (p. 125, Dan's edition).

[17] Heb. צחק pi., obviously with a play on the name Yitzhak = Isaac (and cf. also 21.9–10).

[18] Cf. R. Polzin, 'The Ancestress of Israel in Danger', *Semeia* 3 (1975), pp. 81–98.

commentators, including the author of Gen. 26, felt uncomfortable
with these stories and their thematized conflict and offered different
solutions.[19] The ambiguity of the triple claim which informs the
narratives—foreigners would commit adultery but not incest; nuclear
endogamy is permissible within the patriarchal household;[20] outright
or partial lying is somehow, to varying degrees, acceptable if survival
is at stake—compromises the patriarchal figures and necessitates
corrective interpretations and gap-filling.[21]

Explicit brother-sister incest: Amnon and Tamar (2 Sam. 13.1–22)

The possibility of excepting the paternal sister category from incest[22]
is further hinted at by Tamar's words to Amnon, her paternal brother.
Why rape me, she in effect asks, when we can marry if David
approves (v. 13)?[23] We have no way of knowing whether brother-
sister marriage, practised by some Egyptian dynasties,[24] is applicable

---

[19] For instance, Josephus plays down the story of Gen. 20 and completely ignores
the story in Gen. 26 (*Ant.* 1.12.1 and 1.17.2). Or the collection of sayings about
Isaac in *Yalk. Shimeoni* 111, which clearly castigates the patriarch about having sex
with Rebekah during daytime (as implied by Abimelek's ability to spy on them).

[20] As within the world at large. Adam and Eve are the closest blood kin; so are
their children. While the presentation of humanity as engendered by one primal
couple excludes a non-incestuous vision it is also, at one and the same time, testimony and witness to a deep-rooted human attraction to incest. The insistence on
endogamy in the patriarchal/matriarchal stories continues this [infantile, in psychoanalytic terms] trend while transforming and sublimating it. Sociologically, of course,
the function of patriarchal endogamy is different. Curiously, nuclear endogamy within
the founding patriarchal family reappears even in later midrash (many of whose
stories are, quite often, of earlier if difficult to locate origin). Thus in *Sefer Ha-Yashar*
Shimeon is unproblematically said to have married his [defiled by Shechem, Gen.
34] sister Dinah (p. 205 in Dan's edition).

[21] On the structural significance of the wife-sister 'myth' for understanding
Hebrew culture see S.D. Kunin, *The Logic of Incest*, pp. 262–63.

[22] Cf. the Athenian law: 'Hera ... the wife but also sister of Zeus, whose paradigmatic union would have been regarded as incest under Athenian law, which
authorized marriage between (half) brother and sister with a common father but
prohibited it with a common mother.'—N. Loraux, 'What Is a Goddess', in
P. Schmitt Pantel (ed.), *A History of Women in the West: I. From Ancient Times to Christian Saints* (Cambridge, MA/London: Harvard University Press, pp. 11–44 [22]; notes
on pp. 481–89.

[23] Again, *contra* Lev. 18.9, 20.17; Deut. 27.22. Josephus (*Ant.* 7.8.1) rejects the
possibility out of hand, calling it delay tactics on Tamar's part. Clearly, the rabbis
found the concept of paternal siblings' marriage problematic (in view of the Law),
hence the creative solutions in *b. Sanh.* 21 and elsewhere. See also Rashi and
Maimonides (*Mishneh Torah, Kings* 8.8).

[24] For summaries see, for instance, L. Manniche, *Sexual Life in Ancient Egypt*, p. 29:
'The royal family of the last three centuries BC, of Greek descent, provided numerous

to ancient Israel at any time. Her whole speech seems to imply that the נבלה she refers to, the 'abomination' of Amnon's behaviour, is his intention to *rape* her and her ensuing loss of virginity, not the incestuous relationship entailed (vv. 12–13).

The link between power politics and 'rape' hardly requires elaboration. The modern view of rape as a violent offense aimed at establishing the rapist's control over the raped person, be that person either a female or a male, and what it symbolizes is widely acknowledged nowadays. Indeed, power politics is the subject matter of the narrative in ch. 13 and beyond. Neither incest nor rape are the chief issues. The formulation of the exposition to the story—'. . . and Absalom, son of David, had a good-looking sister whose name was Tamar; and Amnon, son of David, loved her' (v. 1)—indicates that Tamar is just an object or pawn, standing between the paternal brothers in their bid for power and eventual inheritance. This is also borne out by the ensuing episodes, up to and including Absalom's revolt (to which we shall return later). Absalom guesses immediately upon seeing the tearful Tamar that Amnon is the culprit: this ready guess makes him an accomplice of sorts (prior knowledge, or even suspicion, could have perhaps been acted upon). He neither reacts immediately nor goes to David for justice: he advises Tamar to keep quiet for 'he is your brother' (v. 20): this enigmatic utterance can be interpreted in various ways[25] but certainly precludes David from a

---

examples of marriage between closely related persons, and for this reason Egypt has acquired a reputation of being the cradle of incest. This was supported by the very literal interpretation by the early Egyptologists of the words "sister" and "brother", used among lovers and married people. In Pharaonic Egypt incest was the exception, not the rule, but within the royal family special circumstances applied. For reasons of legitimacy a pharaoh might marry his half-sister, or perhaps one of his daughters. . . .' Or Joyce Tyldesley, *Daughters of Isis*, p. 48: 'With the exception of the royal family who intermarried to safeguard the dynastic succession and to emphasize their divine status, there is no real evidence for widespread brother-sister marriages until the Roman period, while parent-child incest is virtually unrecorded. The brother-sister marriages which are recorded are more likely to be between half-brothers and half-sisters than full siblings'; and cf. also pp. 197–203, 231 for the 18th dynasty. Tyldesley, like Manniche, attributes the opinion that Egyptians practised incest freely to the misunderstanding by modern scholars of ancient Egyptian usage of kinship terms as terms of endearment. But see below on the SoS usage of 'brother' and 'sister' for 'lover'.

[25] 'For he is your brother' is a gap that can be filled by the following conjecture: Absalom did not believe that Tamar will get justice against Amnon, the heir apparent, because of her inferior position as a woman and for reasons of family power politics. David knows and is angry, but does not do anything (v. 21), which might substantiate such a reading. Be that as it may, it is implied that Absalom (as

confrontation. Absalom kills Amnon (vv. 23–33) two years later. The reason given is that Absalom hated Amnon because he [Amnon] 'raped [ענה pi.] Tamar, his sister' (v. 22). This formulation indicates that the incest component is certainly present but secondary to the themes of rape, fraternal competition for the father's position and the dishonouring of a father.

Metaphorical sister-brother incest? The lovers in the Song of Songs[26]

In his monumental commentary Pope briefly discusses attempts to mask or unproblematize the sibling references in the SoS.[27] He further writes: 'The terms "brother" and "sister" are commonplace in many languages with reference to friendly relations without implication of consanguinity, incest, or "homosexuality", though by no means limited to purely Platonic relationships. The Semitic usage goes back at least to the Old Babylonian period . . .,'[28] and adds references to the wife-sister motif in Genesis[29] and the post-biblical Tobit (7.12, 15).

In his thoughtful and thought-provoking *Paradoxes of Paradise*, Francis Landy neither recoils from nor ignores the incestuous relationships implied by the sister/brother epithets used by the SoS lovers. Although he views them as 'metaphors', he writes that these references—and the many images of 'twins' in the SoS—constitute '. . . a regression to a time before relationships and prohibitions, to . . . a garden where everything is permissible'.[30] It seems reasonable to agree with Landy

---

well as Amnon) are guilty of dishonouring their father. It is worth noting that a link between dishonouring a father and incest is well-established as a non gender-specific component in relevant narratives (also Absalom and his father's concubines; the daughters and Lot, Tamar and Judah, Ruth and Boaz; the sons and Noah—and see below).

[26] SoS 4.9, 10, 12; 5.1, 2; 8.1–2; possibly also allusions in 6.9, 8.5b.

[27] So recently also, for instance, the one-sentence reference in R.E. Murphy, *The Song of Songs* (Hermeneia; Minneapolis: SCM Press, 1990), p. 160. For Murphy's references to a similar usage in Egyptian love poetry cf. also M.V. Fox, *The Song of Songs and Ancient Egyptian Love Songs* (Madison: University of Wisconsin, 1985). For another recent non-problematizing brief treatment of the brother/sister lovers theme cf. Y. Zakovitch, *The Song of Songs: Introduction and Commentary* (Hebrew; *Miqra le-Yisrael*; Tel Aviv: Am Oved and Magnes Press), p. 92. Here again, the fact that a comparative usage exists in other literatures seems to render it unproblematic in the SoS.

[28] Pope, *Song of Songs*, p. 480.

[29] Pope, *Song of Songs*, p. 481.

[30] F. Landy, *Paradoxes of Paradise*, p. 111; cf. also his Index of References and Index of Subjects (under 'Brother' and 'Sister').

that the desire to find a mirror image for the self in the loved one is at least partial motivation for the sister/brother epithets. Nevertheless, their [repressed? displaced?] incestuous fantasy contents cannot be denied, especially since the linguistic usage transcends language boundaries.[31] The fantasy of mutual, trans-gender sibling desire indicated is borne out by modern statistics: this is not to say that, in ancient Israel, it was tolerated in praxis. The poetic fantasy is of a maternal sibling relationship (8.1–2; and references to the 'mother's sons' who obviously wish to prevent their sister from consummating her desires—1.6; 8.8–10), thus complements the paternal sister fantasy of the wife-sister (Genesis) and Tamar-Amnon Narratives.

Child/parent incest

All the instances in biblical narrative of inter-generation incest between children and parents are attributed to the initiative of children, or child figures. In view of modern knowledge—parents or stepparents, especially stepfathers, tend to initiate incest with daughters and sons; their position of authority makes this viable—the biblical picture seems strange. There is no gender distinction here: such initiative is attributed to daughters as well as to sons. The motivation ascribed to the daughters, however, differs from that ascribed to the sons. The daughters initiate incest with fathers in order to produce sons. The sons initiate incest with the father's wife (or, perhaps, the father himself) as an index of their ascending power and the father's political demise, or for sexual gratification.

Explicit and implied daughter-father incest: Lot's daughters (Genesis 19.29–38), Tamar and Judah (Genesis 38), Ruth and Boaz

Curiously, the father-daughter incest category is totally absent from the prescriptive texts. More curiously still, it is by implication primary: is not the first woman, Eve, god's and the 'ādām's [un]natural daughter who steals the original phallus (the forbidden fruit) and then

---

[31] According to Manniche, *Sexual Life in ancient Egypt*, p. 29, and Tyldesley, *Daughters of Isis*, pp. 48–9, the linguistic usage of kinship terms for 'lovers' and 'spouses' in ancient Egypt should be discounted as evidence for widespread incestuous praxis. This approach seems reasonable. However, although such terms of endearment should not be overinterpreted, the sexual motivation behind them should not be ignored.

becomes, by displacement, the son-father sexual partner and a mother? In Freudian terms, seduction [theory] in the Bible antedates the Oedipal complex. As Ilona Rashkow states, something must be wrong with this picture.[32] Such a male fantasy of daughters seducing fathers would partially explain the series of narratives that begins with Lot and his daughters, continues with Tamar and Judah, and culminates in Ruth and Boaz.

In Genesis 19 Lot's daughters undoubtedly initiate incest with their unwitting father. Their motivation, although erroneous, is neither sexual gratification nor competition but the survival of the species. One gets the impression that their premeditated lack of respect for their father, expressed in their willingness to make him drink and to play the same trick twice on him, is as immoral as their incestuous behaviour, if not more so. Following Gunkel in his commentary on Genesis,[33] one suspects that the incestuous origins of Moab and Ben Ammi are derived from an extrabiblical myth, where divine incest is the prerogative of the gods. Therein lies one of the paradoxes biblical literature subscribes to. Incest is attributed to pagan goddesses and gods, and to humans of royal or similar descent and social status: myths and legends from Mesopotamia, Canaan, Ugarit and Egypt are replete with such incestuous stories that are far from pejorative in tone.[34] The biblical narratives, to distinguish from the legal materials, seem to recognize this attitude in a matter-of-fact manner.[35] Other issues, such as filial [dis]respect and female trickery, seem more central for the dominant ideology than the incest issue.

The narratives about Lot's daughters, Tamar and Ruth can be read as three installments in a series that supplies King David with a genealogy. The first story narrates the birth of the maternal forefather Moab. The second story narrates the birth of the paternal forefather Perez. The third story brings together Ruth the Moabite and Boaz of Perez's line. The first story blatantly depicts bloodkin incest of daughters (two of them!) and father, initiated by the daughters. In the second, a daughter-in-law initiates incestuous

---

[32] Rashkow, *The Phallacy of Genesis*, 'Daughters and Fathers in Genesis, Or, What Is Wrong with This Picture', pp. 65–84.

[33] H. Gunkel, *Genesis* (Göttingen: Vanderhoeck & Ruprecht, 1918), *ad loc.*

[34] Historically, though, even in ancient Egypt father-daughter [recorded] incestuous unions were rare: the list includes Seneferu, Ramesses II, Amenophis III, and perhaps Akhnaten.

[35] Cf. E. Leach, *Structural Interpretation of Biblical Myth* (Cambridge: Cambridge University Press, 1983), pp. 33–66, including plates; and esp. pp. 56–57 for the 'mytho-logic' that determines representations of incest.

intercourse with a marriage kin, her father-in-law, for the same reason: the survival of the male line. In the third, a daughter figure delivers a demand for marriage to a father figure[36] related to her by marriage. The motifs of daughterly initiative, wine and drinking, unwitting fatherly co-operation, daughterly trickery, family survival, and the daughter's desire for a son are present in various measures in all three stories. Viewed in the light of their results, all three are successful: the daughters who wish to become mothers acquire a son or sons. But the further away we get from the mythological origins (Lot's daughters), the closer we come to 'historical (in the biblical sense) facts', the more sublimated the incest contents becomes, until in Ruth it is hardly tenable, almost negligible. It is as if human desire for incest is acknowledged but relegated to far off, once-upon-a-time situations. This trend, like the similar trend in the three-part wife-sister series, reinforces the narrative ambiguity concerning father-daughter incest: the daughter is seductive, the father innocent; the story is repeated [and enjoyed?], then softened and sublimated.

Interestingly, in all three narratives the initiator of the incestuous act is a woman figure whereas, in the relevant prescriptive and prophetic material, only males are addressed as subjects-in-the-text. The implications of this fantasy for biblical notions of female morality are ambivalent, especially when the possibility of echoed goddess imagery is understood to inform these stories. If the latter possibility be entertained then the stories should be considered as originally complimentary to goddess/woman.[37] Once more, the incest content is not emphasized.

Son/father's wife incest: Reuben and Bilhah (Gen. 35.22, 49.3–4), Absalom and David's concubines (2 Sam. 15–16, 20)

Son/mother or son/father's wife incest heads the proscriptive-prescriptive lists (Lev. 18.7–8, 20.11; Deut. 27.20; cf. also Ezek. 22.10).[38] Clearly, this category of incest is the most reprehensible, be

---

[36] Boaz addresses Ruth as 'my daughter' (Ruth 2.8, 3.10). Even if this address implies recognition of her inferior social status or younger age (most readers tend to read Boaz as an older gentleman), the similarity of this story to the other two is striking.

[37] Cf. Gunkel, *Genesis*, for Gen. 19.30–38.

[38] Only in Lev. 18.7 does the biological 'mother' feature as a specific category of forbidden female kin. In the other lists the term 'father's wife' presumably designates both blood and marriage 'mothers'.

it with a consanguineous or relational 'mother'. It carries the gravest taboo.[39] Psychologically, it goes back to the pre-Oedipal male infantile attachment to the mother, hence threatens the father. Sociologically, the enactment of son/mother incest potentially undermines paternity patterns. It threatens the social hierarchy of the father's superiority by taking away his object of desire, thus symbolically his power.[40] In western societies, Meiselman writes, 'Incest between mother and son is regarded as being the least common and most intensely taboo form of heterosexual incest . . . the unique dependency relationship that usually exists between mother and child [*sic!*] seems to be antithetical to overt sexual behavior between them'; the phenomenon is rare but 'It may seem somewhat surprising, in view of the acknowledged rarity, to learn that there is a much more substantial literature relating to mother-son incest than is the case with sibling incest, which is widely regarded as the most common form',[41] although this bounty is relative.[42] Clinically, psychologists define most sons who initiate incest with their mother as having psycho-pathological personality disorders, including schizophrenia, since they have enacted their erotic feelings for the mother instead of suppressing them on the way to joining the father's world: in short, such sons have remained pre-Oedipal.[43] In cases of mother-initiated incest, the sons tend to become disturbed, ill or dysfunctional after the event[s].[44] All the case histories cited are between blood kin.

Somehow, it seems that in spite of its rarity, son-mother incest is treated more seriously in modern psycho-sociology than the more usual father-daughter or sibling incest. This parallels the strength of the taboo, and is borne out by male anxiety about the primal power of maternal sexuality and the need to cope with it. Against this background it comes as no surprise that, in the Bible, no blood son-

---

[39] Cf. Meiselman, Incest, pp. 22, 24, 74–5, 298–311.

[40] Rashkow, *Phallacy of Genesis*, pp. 88–92.

[41] Meiselman, *Incest*, p. 298.

[42] Meiselman, *Incest*, p. 309; she claims throughout her book that, although incest taboos and incestuous tendencies are acknowledged by psychoanalysis as fundamental to both human culture and psychological development, not much clinical literature is available on incest. While in recent years the taboo on discussing the taboo has been lifted somewhat—to the point that the issue is presented even in Television Soaps—the relative rarity of serious literature is still with us.

[43] Meiselman, *Incest*, pp. 299–302, with more literature and clinical interpretations.

[44] Meiselman, *Incest*, pp. 302–9.

mother incest is narrated. That such occurrences, rare in our own society, were as rare or rarer still in the ancient east Mediterranean world is possible. But the fantasy of the mother goddess and her son-spouse, as in the Innana/Ishtar and Dumuzi/Tammuz or Isis and Horus myths, testifies to its attraction and recognition. Occurrences, however, were either repressed as totally objectionable[45] or displaced onto the figure of the 'stepmother', the father's wife—a [biological] mother surrogate who is less threatening to both father and son than the primal mother figure.

An interesting case of apparently ceremonial son/father's wives incest obtains in 2 Samuel 15–16 and 20. When King David departs from Jerusalem to escape Absalom's revolt he leaves behind ten of his wives (פילנשים, secondary wives?) to 'guard the house' (15.16). Absalom follows his adviser Ahithophel's suggestion and publicly, symbolically, appears to take sexual possession of his father's wives (16.21–23). When David returns, the wives remain within his household in isolation: they are taken care of but remain in a condition of 'permanent widowhood' (20.3): David does not 'come to' them and they are forbidden to anyone else.[46]

It would seem that Absalom's intention was to consolidate his rule by forcibly inheriting his father's harem, thus drawing attention not only to his manly virility[47] but also to the political authority and power that virility symbolizes. This act constitutes a violation of the father: this is well understood and explicitly explained by Josephus, for instance, as a deliberate declaration of irreparable breach between son and father.[48] It reveals, unequivocally if in a twice-removed fashion, that the fight of the son *for* the mother love-object is rebellion *against* the father. No wonder, then, that Absalom must die; he dies because his hair, a well-recognized symbol of virility,

---

[45] Or should the short reference to Isaac's bringing Rebekah 'to his mother's tent' and finding consolation in his wife after his mother's demise (Gen. 24.67) be read as a veiled allusion?

[46] The Hebrew אלמנות חיות is difficult because of the pointing. Some of the translations render 'as living widows'; cf. commentaries.

[47] The power of the penis seems to symbolize power and authority in general. Thus symbolic demonstration of virility seems to have been, at least theoretically, a prerequisite for the legitimacy of a monarch's rule. So also in Ugaritic texts: the transformation of KRT into an efficient ruler is bound up with his siring a son; the god 'Il has to prove virility in order to retain at least a modicum of control.

[48] *Ant.* 7.9.5.

traps him in a tree (18.9–17; cf. 14.26).[49] And, measure for measure, according to one recorded tradition he dies sonless (18.18).[50]

Although the brief note about Reuben's 'lying with' Bilhah, his father's פילגש (Gen. 35.22) is cryptic, the plain meaning of the Hebrew שכב את ('[subject: male figure] lie with [object: female figure]') is clear. The motivation is not supplied: a displaced Oedipal attachment to a surrogate mother is one way of filling the gap. But so—in the light of Absalom's story—is also the attribution of Reuben's ascribed incest to his ambition to supplant his father. According to this interpretation the fictive Reuben—like Absalom—is implicitly accused of impatience and an ambition to consolidate his seniority of inheritance prematurely. Like Absalom, Reuben acts too hastily and before his father's demise, thus forfeiting his birthright as successor.[51] Jacob interprets this, and rightly, as a defilement of his own bed (Gen. 49.3–4). Even the Jewish sages who, according to their custom, creatively try to clear Reuben of incestuous behaviour, cannot ignore the anti-father thrust of his attitude: instead of incest, they settle for his making it impossible for Jacob to come to Bilhah's bed, in honour of his own mother (!).[52]

To summarize so far. Narratives which contain incest, the likes of which are known also from other sources in the ANE, thus furnish important clues as to the usage of incest motifs in biblical literature. In extrabiblical myth and epic incest is the prerogative of the gods and privileged individuals:[53] at least, it is acknowledged and even tolerated in narrative texts (Amnon and Tamar). On the other hand, incest is forbidden to the rest of humanity: so it is in the Law and prophetic passages. This double standard reflects the ambivalence incest phenomena inspire: attraction on the one hand, hence the license

---

[49] For a recognition of the upstart son/incest/hair associations see also *b. Soṭ.* 9 and *Yalkut Shimeoni* for 2 Samuel *18*.

[50] Although, according to 14.27 (before the son/father's wives incident), his virility is beyond doubt: he has three sons and a daughter called Tamar (14.27).

[51] Gen. 49.3–4. The anti-Reuben (and pro-Judah) polemics in the Joseph Cycle looks like another stage in the campaign to explain [away] the degradation and defamation of the eponym and the kin/social group 'Reuben' epitomizes. Sexual shaming, as Rashkow notes (*Phallacy of Genesis*, pp. 69–71), is a sure means for vilifying a rival.

[52] *M. Soṭ.* 1.8; *b. Soṭ.* 10a–b, *Shab.* 55a; *yer. Soṭ.* 1.16a, 17b; *Lev. Rab.* 9; *Tanḥ.* for Exod. 1. See also Rashi and RaMBaN for Gen. 35.22 and 49.3–4. For other attempts to whitewash Reuben see also *Gen. Rab.* 84, 85, 91.

[53] S. Freud, *Moses and Monotheism* (trans. K. Jones; New York: Random House, 1955).

projected onto the privileged; and aversion on the other hand, hence the prohibitions. In addition, the incestuous behaviour attributed to male and female figures highlights two other significant factors. One is the subordination of incest themes in the narratives to other superordinate themes, notably non gender-specific filial [dis]respect and male quest for power. The second is the possible origins of male-initiated incest patterns in the male quest for establishing sexual and social authority over the world, a quest symbolized by the sexual appropriation of their womenfolk and, perhaps in the case of Noah, also the father himself.

Son/father incest?: Noah and his son[s] (Gen. 9.18–27)

How is one to understand the story of Noah and his sons, immediately when the world is restored after the flood? Noah plants vines and gets drunk on the wine. He 'reveals' or 'exposes' himself inside his tent (v. 21): the verb formation used, ויתגל, is derived from the root גלה—'reveal' but also, euphemistically, 'expose [the genitals]', as in David's dancing immodestly in front of the Ark (2 Sam. 6.20). The same verb, or the verb 'see' (ראה) together with the word ערוה, 'nakedness' and a euphemism for 'genitals' (here in vv. 22 and 23), is the technical term for 'commit incest' in the prescriptive texts. So what happened? In what sense, 'literal' or 'metaphorical', did Noah 'expose' himself? Further difficulties are: Ham 'sees his father's nakedness' and tells his brothers (v. 22). He is not Noah's youngest son (the plain sense of בנו הקטן, v. 24) but the middle son (v. 18); why is Canaan, Ham's son, cursed by Noah rather than Ham (vv. 25–27)? The passage is clearly composite, which answers some of the difficulties. But the main difficulty is, what is described in such circumspect language and how could Noah, when he awoke from his drunken stupor, 'know what his youngest son has done'? In other words, what was the evidence available to Noah? A viewing of his nakedness by his offspring would have constituted an offense of disrespect but would have left no recognizable traces. Von Rad writes, delicately: 'Possibly the narrator suppressed something even more repulsive than mere looking (cf. v. 24, "what his youngest son had done to him")'.[54] Speiser recoils too; although 'nakedness' in his opinion

---

[54] G. von Rad, *Genesis* (OTL; rev. edn; Philadelphia: Westminster Press, 1972), p. 137.

connotes '*pudenda*; see the various injunctions in Lev. 18.6 ff.', he proceeds: 'The term itself relates to exposure . . . and does not necessarily imply sexual offenses'.[55] Simpson admits that 'In the primary, popular form of the story there probably occurred here . . . an account of an indecent attack by Canaan on his father [*sic!*]' but that it was 'omitted from motives of delicacy'.[56] A metaphorical-intertextual interpretation of this narrative seems preferable to a 'literal' interpretation, with the incest terms 'expose' and 'nakedness' read as euphemisms; the commentators draw back from this possibility with horror.

'Rav and Shemuel. One said, he [the son] castrated him [Noah]. One said, he [the son] had intercourse with him [Noah]' (*b. Sanh. 70a*; also quoted in *Yalk. Shimeoni* for Genesis, 61).[57] Disregarding the rabbis' possible motivation of shaming the eponymous Canaan as prototypic by attributing sexual sins to him, the fact remains that they read in the passage paternal disrespect (by the one son) and either paternal castration or, worse, homosexual incest.[58] Cassuto, who is well aware of the rabbis' interpretations, agrees with Ibn Ezra that the 'original', pre-Torah story might have contained a father-castration motif (like the story about Chronos and his father), 'perhaps even something more lewd', but that these motifs were disguised in the texts for reasons of modesty and tact.[59]

However, the Torah is quite outspoken about the Canaanites' sexual promiscuity in other places. The delicacy employed by modern commentators reflects their own sexual mores; the directness of the rabbis, whose motivation is transparent, in this case perhaps preserves traces of the passage's original (and primal) content. The

---

[55] E.A. Speiser, *Genesis*, p. 61. Speiser does his best to uphold his position by citing occurrences of נלה ערוה, 'expose nakedness' that do not connote incest (Gen. 42.9.12; Exod. 20.26). However, those occurrences are either metaphorical or of a different grammatical formation.

[56] C.A. Simpson, *The Book of Genesis* (IB, 1; Nashville and New York: Abingdon, 1952), p. 556.

[57] For more rabbinical responses to this story see also *Gen. Rab.* 36.

[58] Ironically, the incest, castration and 'homosexuality' that are attributed to Noah's son here are among the seven commandments binding upon all humanity, including the gentiles ('sons of Noah' is the specific rabbinical expressions). For the various lists of these commandments (all of which include incest) see the principal discussions: *b. Bab. Qam.* 38a; *Bab. Mets.* 90b; *Sanh.* 56a–b, 57b, 64a; *Ab. Zar.* 2b, 64b; and Maimonides, *Mishneh Torah*, Kings 9.

[59] M.D. Cassuto, *A Commentary on the Book of Genesis* (Hebrew; Jerusalem: Magnes, 1987), pp. 102–3.

density of themes encountered in other incest stories—wine and drunkenness, sibling rivalry, hostility towards the father, questions of succession[60]—points in the direction of incest. Son-initiated homosexual incest is undoubtedly more painful to contemplate than heterosexual incest; it has an kinky tinge.[61] The accusation, precisely because it is imprecise, is darkly shameful and shaming. Whether the allusion is to father castration or son-initiated father incest makes no difference to the deep structure. This story, like those of Absalom and Reuben, is another instance of the son's attempt to conquer the father and take over—an attempt which, given the patriarchal stamp of Scripture, is bound to fail.

An interesting reading of this passage is Kunin's. He calls it the 'sin of Ham', and writes: '. . . the incestuous relationship is inverted, being homosexual incest. By definition, homosexual incest is barren. This serves the opposite mythological function to heterosexual incest, which leads to fruitfulness. Inside plus inside (the incestuous relation) engenders divine fruitfulness'.[62] For Kunin, there are two 'basic sets of mythemes' in the HB: the 'distinctness of Israel', expressed in sacrifice and rebirth myths; and endogamy, which contains incest and danger (including the danger posed by woman) factors.[63] The episode of Noah blurs or, in Kunin's terminology, 'clouds' gender distinctions while excluding fruitfulness.

To conclude thus far. In narratives which feature explicit or implicit incest situations, the initiative may be assigned to either males or females. Male motivation in such texts may be personal survival, but always contains a strong component of competition against other males (fathers or brothers). Female motivation for incest initiative is presented as guardianship of social survival. Thus the incest theme is always narratively subordinated to another theme/concern, be it power or continuity. Both blood kin and marriage kin are involved in such narratives. Either sexual intercourse or marriage are invoked. Patriarchs

---

[60] Succession, acquiring the father's position and inheritance is one of the important issues in the passage; the curses and blessings deal precisely with the issue of fraternal hierarchy.

[61] As modern research shows, homosexual incest is rarer than heterosexual incest. In such cases, however, the older and more authoritative male partner (a father, father surrogate, uncle, and so on) initiate the incestuous act[s]. 'The most commonly reported kind of homosexual incest is the father-son combination . . . the sexual activity is nearly always initiated by the father' (Meiselman, *Incest*, pp. 312, 318).

[62] Kunin, *Logic of Incest*, p. 266.

[63] Kunin, *Logic of Incest*, p. 267.

and royals seem to enjoy mythic privileges which override incest considerations. One has to turn to biblical 'Law' to find explicit incest prohibitions addressed to [implied] ordinary persons.

Prescriptive/proscriptive texts (in law and prophetic books)

Specific terminology for incest per se is to be found in three law texts only: Leviticus 18 and 20,[64] where incest prohibitions are formulated in the strongest possible language; and also in Deuteronomy 27 (vv. 20, 22–23). A prophetic text which briefly alludes to incestuous practices (Ezek. 22.10–11) contains one specific incest term[65] and some rape terminology.[66] In all these texts incest appears among other categories of sexual transgressions, not as a separate list. It seems, therefore, that incest was not defined as a separate category but subsumed under the greater concern of sexual purity, as visualized by the societies that produced these texts (the same approach is exhibited by rabbinic legal texts). It is difficult to know whether lists of incestuous offenses (biblical לגלות ערוה, 'uncover nakedness', 'genitals' and by extension, 'sexual shame'; MH in the plural, [נילוי] עריות) ever existed as separate lists, then were incorporated into the wider framework of sexual offenses. I would argue nevertheless that the number of incest items in each source, always a formulaic number, points to the possibility of independent incest lists, later fragmented and incorporated into the wider framework.

The texts are exclusively addressed to males. Thus, the prescriptive formulations conceive of males as subjects of incest prohibitions and of females as their objects.[67] The question of consent, or its lack, does not arise. Yet, when a penalty is specified (as in Lev. 20), both the male subject of incest and the female object share it equally: there is no difference in fate for the presumed initiator and presumed [more] passive partner. Apparently, diminished subjecthood does not entail diminished responsibility. In the language of

---

[64] On the apparent contradiction between incest prohibitions and the law of Levirate marriage (Deut. 25.5–10) see below.

[65] ערות אב, 'nakedness of the father' = incest with father's wife. ערוה, 'nakedness' as technical term is repeatedly used in Lev. 18 and 20.

[66] ענה pi., 'torture', in numerous instances a euphemism for 'rape'.

[67] The rabbis and traditional Jewish commentators retain the biblical convention of addressing the male subject about the female object. Cf. *b. Sanh.* 58 and also 75a–b, 76a.

the Damascus Document, 'The law of incest is written in terms of males but it is the same for women' (CD V, ll. 9–10).[68] The age factor of the incest participants is not mentioned: it can be relativized in some cases (son-mother; father-granddaughter) but is hazy in others (son/father's wife). The prohibitions are absolute, unconditional—and so are the punishments, when mentioned. In all three, a mixture of blood-kindred and marriage-kindred females is cited as forbidden to the relevant males.[69] It remains to post-biblical halakhic literature to supplement, elaborate and organize the succinct biblical references and to supply the explanations, especially on the issues of age, consent, circumstances and penalization.[70]

The list of Leviticus 18 is the most unified. Following an introduction which attributes sexual ignominies to Egypt and Canaan (vv. 1–5) and a superscription (v. 6), a list of *twelve* categories of forbidden females is presented (vv. 7–18):

1. mother (v. 7);
2. father's wife (v. 8. Cf. Absalom and his father's wives, Reuben and Bilhah);
3. maternal and/or paternal sister, from the household or outside it (v. 9. Cf. the Tamar and Amnon story, the Genesis wife-sister motif);
4. son's or daughter's daughter (v. 10);
5. stepmother's daughter by the same father (v. 11);

---

[68] Translation from P.R. Davies, *The Damascus Covenant: An interpretation of the 'Damascus Document'* (JSOTSup, 25; Sheffield: *JSOT* Press, 1983), p. 245.

[69] The lack of distinction in classification into blood and marital kin proves difficult for interpreters. The terminology, and the punishments in the various cases, are not consistent enough to be of value. Neither is there a consistent movement from female next-of-kin to further next-of-kin to marital kin. For the terms and other difficulties of interpretation see, for instance: C.F. Keil and F. Delitzsch, *Commentary on the Old Testament: The Pentateuch* (Grand Rapids: Eerdmans, rep. 1980), pp. 411–18, 426–8; J.R. Porter, *Leviticus* (Cambridge: Cambridge University Press, 1976), pp. 143–65; N.H. Snaith, *Leviticus and Numbers* (New Century Bible; London: Nelson, 1967), pp. 123–5, 136–41. I shall here confine myself to general principles, not to comments on the terms themselves. A consideration on the critical positions adopted by interpreters will be presented below.

[70] For a summary of the halakhic positions on incest (including a concise explanation of how and why the rabbinical list of forbidden females was amplified and expanded considerably, and the status of the added categories), see Joseph Caro's synopsis in the *Shulhan Arukh*, the *Even Ha-Ezer* section, 15 (from the sixteenth century and, since the seventeenth century, authoritative for orthodox world Jewry); also 'Incest', *Enc. Jud.* (Jerusalem: Keter, 1971), vol. 8, pp. 1316–18.

6. paternal blood aunt (v. 12);[71]
7. maternal blood aunt (v. 13);[72]
8. paternal blood uncle's wife (v. 14);
9. daughter-in-law (v. 15. Cf. the Tamar and Judah story);
10. brother's wife (v. 16; in contrast to the Levirate law, Deut. 25.5–10; Ruth 1);[73]
11. woman and her daughter, and their female descendants (v. 17);
12. woman and her sister (v. 18. But cf. the Jacob narratives).[74]

Other sexual prohibitions follow (vv. 19–23: of intercourse with menstruating women; adultery; sacrifice of 'seed' to Moloch; male 'homosexuality'; bestiality committed by male and female humans[75]).[76] Finally, an exhortation in the style of vv. 1–5 concludes the pericope (vv. 24–30). No penalties are prescribed. When an argument is given for forbidding the liaisons proscribed, they are linked with either the kin structure (for instance vv. 12, 13) or apparently shameful (ערוה, 'nakedness', metaphorically 'shame'; like in v. 8, 10). As Rashkow points out, the absence of an explicit prohibition about father-daughter

---

[71] In Exod. 6.20 Amram takes his 'aunt' or, according to the commentators, paternal aunt for wife. The LXX has 'niece' instead of 'aunt'. This may be a tendentious emendation in the spirit of this proscription: so B.S. Childs, *The Book of Exodus: A critical Theological Commentary* (OTL; Philadelphia: Westminster Press, 1974), pp. 110–11.

[72] The maternal blood aunt is singled out for mention in the CD (V, l. 9), perhaps polemically against prevalent praxis.
Keil-Delitzsch, *The Pentateuch* (1980, p. 412) count both maternal and paternal aunt as one category. In view of the terminology and the formulaic numerical arrangement of the other lists, I have retained the number of categories indicated by this biblical text. The distinction often found by anthropologists between the social taboos concerning paternal as against maternal kin (so also in the biblical narratives cited above; and upheld by the biblical practice of referring explicitly to both lineages) justifies this distinction too. On the other hand, the separation of the category 'aunt' into two, in contrast for instance to the unification of the 'sister' category (v. 9), might have resulted from the wish to schematize the list into twelve items.

[73] This necessitates a discussion in the Mishna and Talmud (for instance, *b. Yeb.* 7–8).

[74] See Kunin, *Logic of Incest*, pp. 263–64.

[75] This additional list is again of a formulaic number, seven this time. A wish to achieve this numerical framework might have informed the presentation of woman as separate subject of the bestiality prohibition, in a style absent from the rest of the chapter.

[76] Whether the additional list is originally independent (see its formulaic number of items), or part of an expanded original list of sexual prohibitions (see ch. 20 and Deut. 27), here it is contextualized inside the exhortation frame, and the significance of the arrangement should be dealt with as such.

or daughter-father incest (exactly the type of incest present in the narratives of David's genealogy) is conspicuous.[77] This absence is so glaring that rabbis and traditional commentators had to deduce its covert existence in the text by various means.[78] Another 'absence' is the prohibition to have sexual intercourse with one's niece, a mirror reflection on the prohibition on sexual relations with an aunt of any sort.[79] It would seem that the addressing of males only may lead to certain inconsistencies.

The list of Leviticus 20 is of a somewhat different nature. Again, a short introduction (vv. 7–8) precedes the list and an exhortation concludes it (vv. 22–24).[80] Again, there obtains no consistency in the listing of female blood kin and marital kin. Again, the premise of addressing males in the matter of forbidden females is retained. Nevertheless, there are differences. The female partner is described as less passive: she is depicted as 'active' (the subject of a verb in the active mode) in two cases (vv. 12, a man with his daughter-in-law; v. 17, a man with paternal and maternal brother/sister). The terminology differs slightly from that of Leviticus 18. Punishments are prescribed for both parties in the various categories of incestuous liaisons. The *seven* categories of forbidden females here do not form a unified list but are positioned within other categories of sexual transgressions.[81] Nevertheless, the ground covered by this list basically

---

[77] Rashkow, *Phallacy of Genesis*, pp. 65–84.

[78] Cf. *b. Sanh.* 75a–b and 76a: the category of 'woman and her daughter . . . and her son's daughter and her daughter's daughter' (Lev. 18.17) is read as including a man's daughter, since he is the son of his forbidden mother (v. 7) whose female descendants are forbidden to him to the third generation (at least). Rashi simply states (for v. 10) that if a granddaughter is forbidden, this is surely applicable to a daughter (בת בנך קל וחמר לבתך). Maimonides (*Mishneh Torah, Sexual Prohibitions*, Introduction) lists the daughter as his sixth category, after the mother, father's wife, sister, the daughter of a father's wife and son's daughter.

[79] Interestingly, the CD singles out the paternal blood niece for a specific mention, seemingly as an example of female responsibility for incestuous behaviours: so it is when the brother's daughter 'exposes the nakedness' of her father's brother, for she (Davies, *The Damascus Covenant*, p. 245, translates 'for he', that is, the uncle) is kin' (CD, V, ll. 10–11.

[80] A short paragraph on dietary laws, or rather the distinction between 'clean' and 'unclean' meat follows (v. 25), once more with its own concluding formula (v. 26). Thus the conclusion of the incest passage (vv. 22–24) also serves as an introduction for the next section. We shall have to come back to the associative principle that underlies the editorial arrangement at this point.

[81] The number of items, however, perhaps points to the existence of an original incest list which was disbanded and expanded to allow for a larger socio-sexual context. Once more, if we exclude the reference to parental disrespect (v. 9) on

corresponds to that of chapter 18. The close correspondence raises the problem of understanding the editorial policy—why the inclusion of both lists within such a short contextual span?[82]

The seven categories of forbidden females in Leviticus 20 are:

1. father's wife (v. 11 = Lev. 18, nos. 1, 2. See also Deut. 23.1);
2. daughter-in-law (v. 12 = Lev. 18, no. 9);
3. woman and daughter (v. 14 = Lev. 18, no. 11);
4. maternal and/or paternal sister (v. 17, Lev. 18, no. 3);[83]
5. maternal or paternal blood aunt (v. 19 = Lev. 18, nos. 6, 7);
6. uncle's wife (v. 20 = Lev. 18, no. 8);
7. brother's wife (v. 21 = Lev. 18, no. 10).

Unlisted here—by comparison to Leviticus 18—are a man's grand-daughter (18.10, no. 4); his stepmother's daughter by the same father (18.11, no. 5); a woman and her sister (18.18, no. 12). Once more, the daughter figure is absent from the list.

Deuteronomy 27.14–26 contains a set of *twelve* 'commandments', ostensibly to be recited by Levites and answered by the community at the entrance to Canaan. The prescribed ceremony defines the passage as a declaration of faith, a covenant undertaken by the whole (male) community, partly parallel in situation and content to the Sinai tradition. Each item is introduced by the term אָרוּר, 'cursed be [the man who]' . . . The commandments range from a prohibition on visual representations of the divine (v. 15) to a binding obligation to fulfill the oath undertaken (v. 26), with a spectrum of religious, social and economic issues in between. Interestingly, this most solemn credo includes *three* items of forbidden incestuous relationships, with the following categories of females:

---

grounds of theme, a twelve-item list emerges in this passage too (although, as a whole, it includes additional material).

[82] See commentaries. However, no convincing answer—literary, source-critical, etc.—for this textual state of affairs is supplied.

[83] The formulation here is, 'And if a man *takes* his sister . . .,' before the usual terms of 'see/expose nakedness' is introduced. In the other cases, apart from the 'taking' of the brother's wife, the initial term employed is 'lie'. Whether the verb 'take', also used to refer to the act of 'take in marriage' (with a male subject) has that designation here is difficult to determine. Perhaps this is also the case for the seventh category (forbidden brother's wife). One possibility is to attribute the differences to the literary process and the composite character of the list. Another is to consider, once more, a polemical thrust against actual practices.

1. father's wife (v. 20 = Lev. 18 nos. 1 and 2, Lev. 20 no. 1);
2. paternal or maternal sister (v. 22 = Lev. 18 no. 3, Lev. 20 no. 4);[84]
3. mother-in-law (v. 23; presumably a part equivalent to the Leviticus category of 'mother and daughter', ch. 18 no. 11 and ch. 20 no. 3).

Curiously, the short list of Ezekiel 22 (a so-called 'prophetic' text) also cites *three* categories of forbidden females within an accusation addressed, as usual, to males:

1. father's wife (22.10);
2. daughter-in-law (v. 11);
3. sister (v. 11).

Thus, the two three-item lists share two categories (father's wife and sister); the third, although a female (mother or daughter) in-law features in both, differs.

It is worth noting at this point that the law or custom of יבום, Levirate marriage (prescribed in Deut. 25.5–10; probably reflected in Ruth 1.11–13 and Gen. 38), contradicts the incest prohibition on sexual intercourse with a sister-in-law (Lev. 18.16 and 20.21). This contradiction can be explained away by citing the different source provenance of the Leviticus and Deuteronomy passages. Might it also be narrowly accommodated by interpreting the incest prohibition as referring to a brother's wife while he is still alive, whereas the Levirate prescription refers to the situation after the brother's childless demise? This second solution seems improbable because of the terms used in Leviticus 20.21: 'And a man who takes (יקח) his brother's wife . . . they shall be childless'. לקח, 'take' a woman, often signifies 'in marriage'; furthermore, whereas the purpose of Levirate marriage is to produce an heir for the deceased man's 'name', that is, line, the penalty for both here is that they remain childless. Also, the brother/sister-in-law relationship is called נדה, a strong term used as a euphemism for the pollution generated by a menstruant. Hence, this verse can be read as a polemic against the Levirate law. Nonetheless,

---

[84] This is the only occasion when gender mutuality of action is envisaged. The reason might be historical (if the list is composite, this accounts for the different styles). However, in view of the relative tolerance of sibling incest in numerous cultures, this might also be read as a special case of mutual consent. The implication might be that such cases were known—and condemned out of hand.

within the broader biblical context Levirate arrangements override
the relevant incest prohibition, probably because they provide for
the preservation of paternal lineage, demarcation of family property,
continuation of the deceased male's memory, and social survival
in general. The overriding concerns that the prescription for יבום
represents constitute additional pointers towards the partly fluid
nature of incest prohibitions, which is to be expected when religious
morality facilitates social order.

The proscriptive/prescriptive sources undoubtedly exhibit a marked
horror of incestuous relations, which is not the case in the narrative
passages cited: let us remember that in the narratives socio-moral
issues other than incest were dominant. The horror of incest, well
expressed in the prescriptive and (prophetic) terminology chosen
and the punishments prescribed for the relevant offenses, makes no
distinction between blood kin and marital kin forbidden females, as
attested by their co-mingled listing. The greatest taboos seem to attach
to a biological mother and/or a father's wife, a barely differentiated
category which obtains in all three lists. The next place goes to the
blood sister, be she paternal or maternal (again in all three). These
two broad categories could be explained as reaction formation to
pagan myths and practices of royal inbreeding. The mother-son union
is characteristic of goddess myths, as well as of Oedipus-type ones;
the sister-brother union is quite common in myth too (and, as we
have seen, it is the second most common incestuous liaison, after a
father-daughter relationship). The emphasis on these categories can
be understood as covert religious polemics.[85] However, the insistence
on other categories too, such as various in-law females, should be
taken into account as a determinative signifier for the biblical system
of incest prohibitions. But before the discussion can continue, a brief
survey of some modern theories about incest seems to be in order.

---

[85] Examples of incorporating pagan myths linked with incest while ostensibly
rejecting them is to be found in Ezekiel 16 and 23. The hyperbole presenting god as
a loving husband and Samaria-Israel/Jerusalem-Judah as an adulterous wife contains
strong incestuous elements. In ch. 16, Yhwh adopts a metaphorical 'foundling' then
weds her—the text, especially v. 6 onwards, is strongly reminiscent of a birth as
well as a defloration scene; a father figure/daughter incest is implied. In ch. 23,
God's two 'wives', Samaria and Judah, are presented as maternal sisters (v. 2); Lev.
18.18 forbids a male union with two sisters. It is discomfiting that a text such as
Ezek. 16 or 23, whose choice of the metaphorical sinner is 'woman' and whose
language is so sexist and violent, also contains fantasies of incest.

Theories about incest

The origin of incest taboos is much debated. Although commonly believed to be universal, even a cursory anthropological survey shows graded variations in the horror, prescription, and classification of the incest attitudes adopted by various societies.

The biological and socio-biological explanations which cite incest taboos as 'uniquely human',[86] instinctive safeguards against the consequences of inbreeding, can hardly be taken seriously.[87] Genetic knowledge was not available to ancient or so-called 'primitive' societies; the suggestion that deductive observation rather than proper knowledge might have motivated the taboos is offset by statistical considerations[88] as well as two other factors: the lack of universality in attitudes towards incest—for instance, classifications in numerous societies concerning a paternal vs. maternal sister differ;[89] and the extension of the taboo from blood (consanguineous) to marital kin. It is therefore preferable to regard incest as a cultural phenomenon— indeed, the cultural phenomenon par excellence, a link between nature and culture, thus within the realm of psychology, anthropology, and sociology rather than exclusively in the realm of biology or sociobiology.[90]

Most psychological explanations which go beyond the notion that a deep-rooted, common human revulsion is supposedly caused by incest, broadly fall into two categories. The psychoanalytic (Freudian) approach and its offshoots cite a primary incest scene (the Oedipal situation) whose successful resolution is mandatory for emotional and mental development. This approach, and the reading of incest myths and ancient literature according to it, shares the phallologocentric

---

[86] For recent refutations of the 'uniquely human' character of human incest prohibitions see, however, studies of animal behaviour and social organization in the wild—especially primates—cited in W. Arens, *The Original Sin: Incest and Its Meaning* (New York and Oxford: Oxford University Press, 1986), pp. 85–95. Such refutations have obvious implications for the alleged nature/culture ambiguity of incest prohibitions. And see below.

[87] Contra Meiselman, *Incest*, pp. 1–26; and see below.

[88] 'The economic systems of some primitive or archaic societies severely limit population size, and it is precisely for a population of such a size that the regulation of consanguineous marriages can have only negligible genetic consequences.' (C. Lévi-Strauss, *The Elementary Structure of Kinship* [Boston: Beacon Press, 1965 = 1969], p. 16).

[89] Cf. the biblical wife-sister motif, and the Tamar and Amnon story.

[90] See also Arens, *The Original Sin*, pp. 102–21.

bias of the biblical law tradition. An incest situation which necessitates resolution and breeds taboo as its safeguard is interpreted by
positing male development at its centre and relegating females to the
status of object or, at the very least, an other.[91]

Another psychological view cites familiarity, social and/or sexual,
as a serious obstacle for maintaining positive sexual tension and
therefore reproduction; hence, according to it, the tendency—in the
animal as well as human world—to outbreed. This would explain
the inclusion of both blood and marital kin females within the taboo.
But this theory, for example, does not explain why the biblical sister
taboo extends in Lev. 18.9 to sisters born and bred outside the
household. In general it seems that the biblical (prescriptive) relational categories are undifferentiated by blood, marital, or familiar
oppositions: a female kin is classified by her relatedness to a male,
be that relatedness of whatever nature, biological or social. For other
insubstantialities of this second psychological theory the reader is
referred to Lévi-Strauss[92] and Arens.[93]

A middle-of-the road position between psychology and sociology
is suggested, for instance, by Meiselman. She insists that,

> It now seems that the harmful effects of inbreeding are sufficient to have
> mediated the natural selection of incest avoidance behaviors in both
> animals and humans . . . In no way, however, should the reemergence
> of the biological explanation be taken to imply that humans have an
> innate, instinctive aversion to incest; there is no evidence that the in-
> cest taboo is not learned by each individual through his or her early
> interactions with family members and other societal agents . . . The fact
> that the incest taboo is extended beyond the nuclear family in very
> different ways in different societies still strongly suggests that it serves
> other social and psychological purposes . . . once established within the

[91] Some feminists believe that the bulk of Freudian and Lacanian teachings can
be redeemed for feminism, in spite of the teachings' inherently androcentric bias. My
own view is that the banishment of woman from the symbolic order, her imaged
position as a parallel or outsider/other, excludes such a possibility. Hence, I would
prefer theories of development and subject-object relations that are equally if differently
applicable to the emotional and mental development of either or both genders: for
instance, M. Klein, *The Selected Melanie Klein* (ed. by J. Mitchell; New York: Free
Press, 1987), whose perspectives appeal to me much more. Cf. also Nancy Chodorow,
Feminism and Psychoanalytic Theory (Cambridge, MA: Polity Press, 1989); Karen Horney,
Feminine Psychology (ed. by K. Helman; New York: Norton, 1967); and Carol Gilligan,
In a Different Voice (Cambridge, MA: Harvard University Press, 1982). See also Rashkow,
Phallacy of Genesis, 'Father and Daughter'.
[92] Lévi-Strauss, *The Elementary Structure of Kinship*, pp. 16–19.
[93] Arens, *The Original Sin*, pp. 80–4.

nuclear family, the taboo would tend to generalize to other relatives in a pattern dependent on the kinship system of each society'.[94]

Some of the influences that cause variations in the intensity and contents of nuclear family incest in various societies, as cited by Meiselman, are: relative tolerance to incest relationships that conform to the regular dominance hierarchy in a certain society; condemnation of sexual relations with pre-puberty individuals; an almost universal societal preference for same-generation sexual unions; and the destructiveness of overt incest for a male or female dependent on the parent for nurturance. The interaction of these factors positions a mother/son incest as the most reprehensible; does not affect heterosexual sibling relationships, unless the sister is older; and the father-daughter incest occupies an intermediate position between the two.[95]

Sociological theories usually take into account the inclusion of non-consanguineous kin within taboo prohibitions. Some derive their arguments from observations of exogamy/endogamy rules (Durkheim and others, as cited in Lévi-Strauss).[96] These explanations are illuminating albeit ultimately unsatisfactory in their quest to establish a universal/historicized account for a disparate but widely distributed phenomenon. The problem is complex: given the inherent ambiguity of incest institutions (see the psychological theories), it is not easy, to quote Lévi-Strauss, 'to discover what profound and omnipresent causes could account for the regulation of the relationships between the sexes in every society and age'.[97]

Lévi-Strauss himself commences to discuss the socio-economic regulatory force of incest prohibitions which enables the economic survival of societies by balancing them as units of exchange, whereby male wife-donors and wife-takers can pursue their activities without socio-sexual interference.[98]

The biblical texts, however, do not confine incest prohibitions to marriage between kin but extend them to *sexual intercourse* between those same kin; the socio-economic theory does not apply as successfully to those extra-marital situations. Nonetheless, this approach certainly explains, among other things, why biblical texts focus on

---

[94] Meiselman, *Incest*, pp. 22–3.
[95] Meiselman, *Incest*, pp. 23–6.
[96] *The Elementary Structure of Kinship*, pp. 19–23.
[97] *The Elementary Structure of Kinship*, p. 23.
[98] In *The Elementary Structures of Kinship*. Also C. Lévi-Strauss, *The View from Afar* (New York: Basic Books, 1985), pp. 88–97.

male-initiated incest, since this textual phenomenon can now be related to an [extra-linguistic] act of establishing male authority instead of being evaluated as merely deviant, sexually motivated male behaviour.

An interim understanding which, at this juncture, seems to fit the assumptions underlying biblical prohibitions makes socio-psychological sense concerning male-initiated vs. female-initiated incest. When biblical female figures commit incest, they allegedly do it for the survival of their social unit—in order to breed a son. The situation is different in the case of males, as addressed by the prescriptive formulations. Incest taboos addressed to males may thus be understood as a collective male sanction against other aggressive, power-seeking males who might attempt to seize power over society's basic commodity/currency (women), beginning with their own female relatives. Such an understanding might also explain further the bias of mythology and royal legends in favour of incest, as gleaned from ancient and modern sources (including the biblical narratives cited). in Arens' view, which seems attractive because it establishes a correlation between sex and power,[99] one has to look for the 'relationship between the forbidden sexual act and the exercise of power'.[100] Similarly Gerda Lerner, who asks why women, and not men or young children, became the basic social commodity to be exchanged,[101] concludes:

> Sometime during the agricultural revolution relatively egalitarian societies with a sexual division of labour based on biological necessity gave way to more highly structured societies in which both private property and the exchange of women based on incest taboos and exogamy were common. The earlier societies were often matrilineal and matrilocal, while the latter surviving societies were predominantly patrilineal and patrilocal . . . The more complex societies featured a division of labor no longer based only on biological distinctions, but also on hierarchy and the power of some men over other men and women. A number of scholars have concluded that the shift here described coincides with the formation of archaic states . . .[102]

However, Lerner does not go beyond this general linkage of women's oppression and incest taboos.

---

[99] See the discussion concerning Amnon's raping of Tamar above.
[100] *The Original Sin*, pp. 140–9; the quotation is from p. 148.
[101] G. Lerner, *The Creation of Patriarchy* (Oxford: Oxford University Press, 1986), pp. 24–5.
[102] Lerner, *Patriarchy*, pp. 24–53; the citation is from p. 53.

Evelyn Reed's approach[103] contests the view that incest taboos are the primary foundations of human culture and social organization. She commences from the hypothesis that matriarchy preceded patriarchy, and that in the matriarchal clan all females were forbidden to a male as mothers; therefore, any male member of a clan had to outbreed. The development of incest taboos is thus assigned to the institution of the family, whose development is linked with patriarchy. In Reed's view, 'The oldest and most important taboo prohibitions are the two basic laws of totemism: namely not to kill the totem animal, and to avoid sexual intercourse with totem companions of the other sex'.[104]

Reed's approach is helpful in linking sexual taboo, exogamy and dietary taboos, a linkage which we shall come to later. It is also conducive to understanding the biblical address of males in the prescriptive texts. However, the trend of social evolution she delineates—from matriarchy to patriarchy, from clan to family—remains unsubstantiated. In addition, the argument for an implied primal incest prohibition involving mother-figures and son-figures weakens her case considerably, in view of the fact that it is a rarely documented occurrence (although more widely present in myth and [male-produced?] fantasy).

Sociological theories of incest clearly contribute to our understanding of biblical incest prohibitions, but they do not adequately explain the sense of moral aversion attached to incest in the Law. The functional role of the aversion, together with the repetitious proximity of incest lists in Lev. 18 and 20, are not accounted for by sociobiology either. Freudian-inspired psychoanalytic theories, centered as they are on male development, imply a basic ambiguity in human attitudes; this is helpful for the understanding of the human and mythic/royal contrast but unhelpful in its marginalization of woman, presented in proscriptive biblical sources as the object of incest. Cultural, especially structural-cultural, approaches contribute some principles of organization (the inclusion of both blood and non-blood kin, exogamy, mytho-logic) but do not explain specifics of the biblical Law system.[105] Reed's theory of a secondary male-invented

---

[103] E. Reed, *Woman's Evolution: From Matriarchal Clan to Patriarchal Family* (New York: Pathfinder Press, 1975), pp. 3–26.

[104] Reed, *Woman's Evolution*, p. 23.

[105] Although, to be sure, Lévi-Strauss' remark that laxity in incest prohibitions on

incest taboo is attractive, but rests on the unverifiable premise of primal matriarchy. Lerner's hypothesis of tying the inauguration of incest taboos with the shift from matrilineality/matrilocality to patrilineality/patrilocality and to changes in economy, demography and organizational patterns is more balanced than Reed's and is useful for the discussion. Nonetheless, it too does not account for specific features of the biblical prohibitions. By and large, the socio-anthropological hypotheses reported are valuable for positing biblical attitudes towards incest within a broader framework. However, a more specific principle of organization for those proscriptive biblical attitudes still remains to be supplied. The question raised by Lévi-Strauss—Since the universal nature of incest specifics is questionable, what is its function in any given society?—breeds a question specific to the biblical law passages. What, within their verbal and literary contexts, are the functions and significance of those incest 'laws' for the social system they reflect?[106]

Back to the prescriptive texts

Mary Douglas writes, in connection with the Leviticus dietary laws:

> We can conclude that holiness is exemplified by completeness. Holiness requires that individuals shall conform to the class to which they belong. And holiness requires that different classes of things shall not be confused.[107]

Her remark seems equally applicable to the Leviticus and Deuteronomy incest prohibitions. Some of her positions in *Purity and Danger* (1966) and *Implicit Meanings* (1975)[108] will be adopted here and used, together with the theories listed above, for rereading the biblical incest prohibitions.

The moral aspects of social regulation of sex and related issues is but one facet, admittedly a most significant one, of the manner in which society organizes itself into coherent, practicable sets. Ambiguities mostly lead to compartmentalization and confinement of what is

---

the paternal side is characteristic of male-dominated societies (*The View from Afar* [1985], pp. 88–97) illuminates, for instance, Gen. 20 and 2 Sam. 13. See above.

[106] 'Reflect', of course, in a complex rather than a simple, one-to-one correspondence of texts to extratextual reality.

[107] M. Douglas, *Purity and Danger* (London: Routledge & Kegan Paul, 1966), p. 53.

[108] M. Douglas, *Implicit Meanings* (London and Boston: Routledge & Kegan Paul, 1975).

perceived as their source. A split between the psychological and social aspects of 'reality' often occurs. The question rephrased is, then: Against the backdrop of other data concerning biblical Israel,[109] what is the structural social function of the incest prohibitions cited?

Biblical writings set great store by emphasizing the differences between the community in which they originate and other communities. This insistence is perhaps the product of insecurity; the similarities rather than dissimilarities to contiguous communities is considered a serious threat to social (inclusive of religious, ethnic, cultural, and other aspects) identity. Attempts to define the community's ideological and practicable boundaries, both outwards and inwards, are therefore extremely pronounced. External boundaries are delineated by exhortations to be unlike the foreign Others. Internal boundaries divide—first and foremost—the two human genders and, concurrently, classes of entities and things. Ironically, there is no clear differentiation in the texts between the concern for external boundaries and the concern for internal boundaries: both appear together within the same contexts, perhaps because they are experienced as the two sides of the same coin.

The society described in the Bible is by and large patriarchal, with the בית אב, the 'father's house' as its basic family unit.[110] This nuclear kin unit typically encompasses two to three generations of blood kin, marital kin and dependents; eventually it splits off into new 'father's houses'.[111] In accordance with the principle of boundary-setting described, there is great concern for paternal linearity (genealogies!) and preservation of paternal inheritance. That concern is amply expressed in all biblical genres but, especially, in the prescriptive texts. And among the prescriptive texts, the preservation of paternity and resultant issues is particularly evident in the priestly writings (of which Leviticus, of course, is a prominent part).

In that society, whose extant literature habitually defines it as male dominated, woman is indeed the basic social currency without whom

---

[109] Which is not synonymous with 'ancient Israel', that is, the actual historical Israel outside the biblical sources, of which our knowledge is scant indeed. Cf. Davies, *In Search of 'Ancient Israel'*.

[110] But see C. Meyers ('To her Mother's House', in Brenner [ed.], *A Feminist Companion to Ruth*, pp. 85–114) for the alternative though rare בית אם, 'mother's house'.

[111] Cf. S. Bendor, *The Bet 'Ab in Israel from the Settlement to the End of the Monarchy: The Social Structure of Ancient Israel* (in Hebrew; Tel Aviv: Afik and Sifriat Po'alim, 1986).

economy and hierarchy can be neither established nor regulated (as in Lévi-Strauss's analyses of other societies). Simultaneously, woman and female 'sexuality' are often perceived as stereotypically ambiguous, hence threats to the desirable social order. Male sexual appropriation of dependent and other females can therefore be interpreted as a socially-conditioned response, a reaction formation designed to exercise control over those female ambiguities; hence the designation of incest prohibitions as addressed to males (whereas, in the narratives, female figures commit incest in the service of patriarchal lineality).

The concern with paternity can be viewed as a component of attitudes towards women in biblical literature, especially in genres which attempt to regulate social behaviour. Synchronously, it can also be viewed as a component of a set which indeed includes gender issues but, at the same time, has a much broader scope and further ramifications. Seen thus, incest belongs to a set of rules and prescriptions whose concern is to delimit and fix the internal boundaries of descent.

There are numerous examples within biblical Law and outside it for this underlying concern with social boundaries and their regulation outside the incest sphere and, moreover, outside the sexual sphere. Such concern is evident in varied arenas of life. The relevant 'laws', irrespective of the problem of their enactment or its absence, can mostly be understood by referral to the issue of establishing formal distinctions, an issue which was apparently perceived as more urgent the closer the entities to be delineated were deemed to be (as in incest prohibitions). For instance, the recurrent admonitions against intermarriages with the land's inhabitants can now be reinterpreted in the light of the fluid ethnic-cultural identity of the so-called 'Israelites' and 'Judahites' during the late Bronze age and the Iron age. Attempts to define the fluid borderlines between the sacred and the profane abound; ambiguities and fluidity apparently accentuate the need for specific regulations concerning the enforced separation of similar entities. The recommended boundaries, it seems, are mandatory safeguards for the desired cultural identity of the community which sought to publish them.[112]

---

[112] For an analysis of this argument and the following details, as applied specifically to 'homosexuality' and conceived independently of my own, see Boyarin, 'Are There any Jews', pp. 340–345. Also: T.M. Thurston, 'Leviticus 18:22 and the Prohi-

Biblical prohibitions of admixtures (שעטנז, כלאים)

The life loci of biblical regulations concerning admixtures of similar entities vary. However, in the case of explicit prescriptions[113] the textual loci are similar and/or identical with those of incest. This is particularly apparent wherever other sexual matters, apart from incest prohibitions, are referred to.

Within the agriculture field, *domestic animals* should not be inbred: as we learn from Leviticus 19.19, a horse and an ass should not be mated. How this regulation accounts for the widely spread (extra-textual) use of פרדה, פרד, 'mule' is perplexing. Domestic animals of similar function should be separated into distinctive classes: Deuteronomy 22.10 forbids the working of an ox and ass together. Various 'commonsense' explanations can be forwarded at this point. Nevertheless, ox and ass can be used together and must have been so used, otherwise why attempt to reject the phenomenon? It seems reasonable to assume that the domestic beasts' similarity, offset by their obviously different identities, is the key to the separation. The same principle is applied to *cloth* in general (Lev. 19.19) and to wool and linen in particular (Deut. 22.11). *Agricultural produce* (Lev. 19.19, Deut. 22.9) should be cultivated separately.

Within roughly the same contexts of agricultural mixture distinctions of some sexual offenses are listed: *adultery* (Lev. 18.20, 20.10), *the wearing of transsexual clothing* (Deut. 22.5), '*homosexuality*' (male; Lev. 20.13), *bestiality* (committed by male and female; Lev. 18.23,[114] 20.15–16; Deut. 27.21). The textual contiguity of such general sexual offenses and incest seems obviously motivated by the extra-textual referent (sex). I would like to suggest an additional criterion for the contiguity—as is the case in Leviticus 20—as a framing context for incest prohibitions.

---

bition of Homosexual Acts' in M.L. Stemmeler and J.M. Clark, *Homophobia and the Judaeo-Christian* Tradition (Dallas, 1990); S. Bigger, 'The Family Laws of Leviticus 18 in Their Settings', *JBL* 98 (1979), pp. 187–203. For a critique of Thurston and Bigger's positions on this issue see also Olyan, '"And with a Male"', esp. pp. 199–202.

[113] To distinguish from implicit deductions gleaned from other biblical genres, like narrative prose and poetry.

[114] Where the prohibition is defined as תבל, like for having sex with a daughter-in-law (Lev. 20.12). If תבל signifies 'improper mixing', then the case for viewing incest as such is made stronger. See T. Frymer-Kensky, 'Law and Philosophy: The Case of Sex in the Bible', *Semeia* 49 (1989), pp. 95–7; and for this term as well as the term תועבה see Olyan, '"And with a Male"', p. 180 n. 3 and p. 205; and Boyarin, 'Are There Any Jews', pp. 343–45.

From the perspective of hierarchy and social control, both incest prohibitions and other sexual prohibitions require the establishment of strict social boundaries; incest is one component among others—and not always the most important. I would also suggest that the loud protests against 'homosexuality', trans-sexuality and bestiality serve the same ideological purpose of avoiding mixtures in the interest of social order and stability. Thus incest and non-heterosexual practices are both constituents of a larger set of prohibitions; and so is adultery, the threat to known family structures.[115]

We now come to the sphere of food/eating. The principles behind the dietary laws concerning eatable ('clean') and uneatable ('unclean') animals (Lev. 11, 20.25; Deut. 22) have been and still are much debated. No attempted interpretation should, of course, account for all of them; governing principles are nonetheless necessary so that some sense can be made of the seemingly arbitrary list. I here adopt Mary Douglas's interpretation, namely, that an animal (be it fowl, fish or mammal) is eatable when it is not a borderline case. In her phrases, '. . . the underlying principle of cleanness in animals is that they shall conform fully to their class. Those species are unclean which are imperfect members of their class, or whose class membership confounds the general scheme of the world'.[116] Once more, the governing principle seems to be that of boundaries or lack of them, a principle that is especially significant in the case of ambiguous, related but hardly differentiated entities.[117]

Coming back to matters of gender and socialization, the separation and confinement of women in general and especially those prescriptions concerning menstruation, female genital discharge and postnatal conditions,[118] again betray the same informing principle: precisely when women are at their most ambiguous (after a birth, during a period), when their life force seems to clash irreconcilably with their socially inferior status, they are confined and any transaction with them suspended until the ambiguity is temporarily contained by time and ritual. Like in other instances, a confusion of similar elements perceived to be related but simultaneously contradictory calls

---

[115] *Contra* Olyan, '"And with a Male"'.

[116] Douglas, *Purity and Danger*, p. 55.

[117] I suggest that, in addition to its presumed religious polemic value, the injunction against eating 'a kid in its mother's milk' (Exod. 23.19, 34.6; Deut. 14.21) belongs to the same set of boundary-drawing.

[118] Cf. Ilana Be'er's article, 'Blood Discharge', in Brenner (ed.), *A Feminist Companion to Exodus—Deuteronomy*, pp. 155–68.

for the stringent measures.[119] Such measures are especially required whenever the fluid borderlines between the sacred and the profane are experienced as potentially threatened.[120] Whether we are convinced by Frymer-Kensky's definition of the Hebrew god's desexualization[121] or not, her remarks about the danger sexuality embodies for social boundaries[122] are certainly convincing, as are her definition of biblical cultic activities as sexuality-free and characterization of public interest in controlling sexual behaviour.[123]

In conclusion

I subscribe to Mary Douglas's rule: in the investigation of social phenomena psychological motivation should be separated from sociological motivation. The two might certainly coincide or partly overlap. While the one may be conceived of as subtext for the other, their affiliations are complex, which does not allow for direct correspondences between potentiality and actuality.

From the psychoanalytical perspective, incest is a deep-rooted human fantasy, especially a male fantasy. In that fantasy, desire for sex and control are intermingled. But in the enactment of this fantasy, to distinguish from the fantasy's primal nature, there seems to occur a shift in balance between the two components. Like in other forms of sexual practices, incest behaviour may constitute a bid for acquiring social domination through sexual stamping. Women may make sexual bids for social power too; however, male use of sexual subordination is encouraged by social mores and praxis. Psychology, including individual psychology, is culture-bound. And individual sexual bids for power, be their gender constituency as it may, are prohibited by society when judged disruptive. In that respect, incest

---

[119] See Douglas, *Implicit Meanings*, pp. 47–82.

[120] Cf. M. Eliade, *The Sacred and the Profane: The Nature of Religion* (New York: Harper, 1961). A case in point are the marriage rules prescribed for the priests, much tougher than ordinary exogamous and endogamous practices. Another example is that of the 'good looking [female] prisoner' of war (Deut. 21.10–14). Her period of waiting, like any period of mourning, is designed to make the difference between her former and present state of existence total. Other instances concern rituals of transition at the appropriate life junctions, and so on. The point of these examples is that, like in the cases of incest and (especially priestly) marriage, the concern with paternity is an important factor.

[121] Frymer-Kensky, 'Law and Philosophy', pp. 89–102, esp. 89–91.

[122] Frymer-Kensky, 'Law and Philosophy', pp. 95–7.

[123] Frymer-Kensky, 'Law and Philosophy', pp. 97–8.

is no different from other forms of social behaviour which are considered dangerous for the accepted social order and therefore morally and ideologically deviant. Furthermore, incest may thus be considered a form of sexual violence: although both partners might consent, the social gain for the socially dominant partner (in our culture, usually the male) far exceeds the inferior partner's profit (even when that partner is the initiator of incestuous behaviour, see the biblical incest narratives initiated by female figures). Given the fact that woman in the HB represents socio-cultural danger, her inside/ outside position in incestuous situations emphasizes women's outsider status in the fabric of their society and the threat they pose for that society.[124] 'The opposition between the inside and the outside is the structural centre of the texts dealing with women in the biblical and rabbinic texts'.[125]

Admixtures of similar yet different entities are prohibited; these prohibitions are structurally and motivationally similar to incest prohibitions. In Frymer-Kensky's view too incest presents the danger of blurring social boundaries, for the structure of the family as well as the larger social unit.[126] A social concern for establishing boundaries and well-defined identities[127] links the series of admixture prohibitions to the extent that both appear to be constituents of a broader set. Kunin, who analyzes biblical incest laws and stories in terms of social structure and myth, points out how instructive incest is for understanding the basically endogamous nature of the biblical (and later rabbinic) cultures.[128] Lerner's placing of the emergence of incest taboo at a transition from nomadism to settlement, from one kind of economy to another, and from one social organization to a new one, comes to mind. Such needs for recurrent social organization can perhaps be applied to the situation of the ancient Israelites/Judahites. Lerner also connects women's oppression with (prehistoric) socio/economic transition. The same principle can be

---

[124] Kunin, *Logic of Incest*, pp. 261–62.

[125] Kunin, *Logic of Incest*, p. 262.

[126] Frymer-Kensky, 'Law and Philosophy', pp. 95–7. 'The desire to maintain categories is also a cosmic issue', as shown by the need 'to divide humanity from the divine realm' (in the story of Gen. 6.1–4, 'the sons of god/the god' and the human 'daughters')—p. 96.

[127] The same priestly concern is projected unto the world in the priestly material contained in Gen. 1–11. God's first step is to separate before he creates the world. In the Flood, the differences between heaven and earth are obliterated, never to recur by divine will. The J account contributes its consent to the definition of boundaries through the tower/city story, ch. 11.

[128] Kunin, *Logic of Incest*, pp. 267–69.

related to historical transition. Thus, the concern for biblical boundaries is particularly noticeable in the ever-elusive endeavor to safeguard paternity. This concern is also energetically applied to the regulating of various sexual phenomena. Incest is obviously included within those phenomena—as are adultery (Lev. 18.20, 18.10; Ezek. 22.11), 'homosexuality', trans-sexuality and bestiality,[129] all of them socio-sexual phenomena deemed worthy of preemptive proscription.[130] The anxiety concerning the paternity problem further explains why biblical incest language has the male as addressee and subject-in-the-text in most law cases. The care invested in the prescriptive formulations first and foremost betrays a male worry over the continuation of the male line, that is, over social organization as constructed by males. It also reflects male worry over the control of insurgent, ambitious other males.

Ultimately, incest should not be debated in isolation from other social measures and institutions but within the structural paradigm of a given society—in the present case ancient Israel and its mores, as present within the biblical texts (law and narrative) and behind them. Paradigmatic shifts rather than universal generalizations seem to underlie trans-cultural differentials of incest, as of other socio-moral institutions. Intertexts from comparative ancient cultures provide helpful illumination for such *cultural differences*. The two examples I would like to cite are, respectively, the relevant sections in the Hammurabi Code and the Hittite Laws.

In the Hammurabi Code, four categories of 'forbidden females' are listed; the addressee, like in the biblical prescriptive material, is the male, presumably the initiator of the incestuous act.

1. Daughter. A father/daughter incest does feature here (section 154), while this category is missing from the biblical law (although not the narrative) material. The punishment the prohibition entails is far lighter than any biblical punishment for incest: the father has to leave the city.[131]

---

[129] To return to the inclusion of cursing a father and mother injunction within the incest contexts (Lev. 20.9, Deut. 27.16). This can be explained by the perception of the cursing as a symbolic act of overturning authority. As such, this too is an instance of overstepping basic boundaries, mandatory for the preservation of social order.

[130] A truism but seems in order here: the preemptive preoccupation with incest should be regarded as solid evidence for its widespread practice within ancient Israelite societies.

[131] The Hammurabi Code, section 154; cf. T.J. Meek's translation in J.B. Pritchard (ed.), *Ancient Near Eastern Texts Relating to the Old Testament* (Princeton, NJ: Princeton University Press, 1950), p. 172.

2. Daughter-in-law, before (section 156) or after (section 155) her union with the son is consummated. In the first instance, she is dismissed from the family with a small payment, so that she can marry another; in the second, the male offender undergoes the water ordeal.
3. Mother, after the father's death (section 157); both offenders will be burnt to death.
4. Stepmother who has borne the father children, after the father's death (section 158); the man will be cut off from the parental home.[132]

The Hammurabi Code deals with two types, a male's daughters and mothers, be they blood kin or marriage kin. (Other categories mentioned in the biblical texts are missing.) A clear distinction is drawn between the two types of relatedness, a distinction well-expressed in the penalties prescribed. Considerations of ownership override those of paternity or boundaries, although the latter are present too. This is evidenced by the relatively moderate punishment for incest with daughter, or with daughter-in-law. The single red boundary, perhaps the only one morally horrifying,[133] is intercourse with a blood mother, which entails a death sentence. Obviously, incest in early second-millennium Mesopotamia, as indicated by the Hammurabi Code, exhibits social concerns that are far removed from the biblical ones.

The Hittite laws are similarly addressed. The categories of forbidden females following two sections on bestiality are:

1. Blood mother (section 189).
2. Blood daughter (189).
3. A man's intercourse with a blood son.[133a]

All three are capital offenses.

4. A stepmother is forbidden only during the father's lifetime (section 190).

---

[132] Meek in Prichard, *Ancient Near Eastern Texts*, pp. 172–3. Cf. also Lerner, *The Creation of Patriarchy*, p. 116.

[133] Since it is formulated in such a way ('after the father's death') as to pretend that its occurrence during the father's lifetime is inconceivable.

[133a] The inclusion of a son, presumably a minor, as an object of ['homosexual'] incest supports the understanding of both incest and 'homosexual' prohibitions as male-power regulations rather than 'just' sexual regulations, in as much as they testify once more to known cases of sexual abuse of minors (not only females) by the powerful *pater familias*. See further on slaves, section 194.

5. Blood-related females (sisters, or mothers and daughters) can be taken as co-wives as long as they live in separate localities (section 191); but otherwise intercourse with kindred blood females—mothers and daughters—is forbidden until one of them dies (section 195).

6. A wife's sister is allowed in marriage after the wife's death (section 192).

7. A sister-in-law is permitted to her dead husband's brothers (section 193), but while the husband is alive that is a capital offense (section 195).

8. No blood kin limitations obtain in sexual relations with slave girls, be the subjects (males) or the objects (females) involved related among themselves (section 194).[134]

It would seem that in Hittite incest laws blood relatedness is the most significant principle (unless the blood kin are non-persons, that is, slaves; and even that principle fades after the blood relative's death. One can speculate as to the reasons for this emphasis on biological kinship. A concern for boundaries of biological kinship implies interest in the *ownership* of females and in the paternal transmission of property. Unlike the biblical material, the extension of the incest concern to marital kinship is minimal. The differences in categories and emphasis between the Hittite society, as it wishes to present itself through its laws, and the biblical (Israelite?) society and its incest laws, are considerable.

It seems, then, that the *phenomenon* of incest probably occurs in all or most human societies; but the formulations, regulations and taboos associated with it are not universal. Thus, reading our modern definitions of incest into the relevant biblical texts—or any other culturally different text—may not always be helpful.

---

[134] Cf. A. Goetze's translation in Pritchard, *Ancient Near Eastern Texts*, p. 196.

CHAPTER SIX

DEVIATION FROM SOCIO-SEXUAL BOUNDARIES, II: ON ADULTERY, SEXUAL COERCION, GENDER-BENDER BEHAVIOUR, BESTIALITY AND PROSTITUTION

Both texts that report/narrate the beginning of humanity[1] (the so-called P account, Gen. 1–2.4a; and the so-called J narrative about the garden, 2.4b–4.2a)[2] state that the world is hierarchic and differentiated. Difference, to a greater or lesser degree, is a primary condition in the world as divinely created. Humans come in sexually differentiated monogamous pairs. Males are superordinate. The human sex drive is or should be motivated by procreation. Polygamy is interjected immediately (Gen. 4.19) and is socially acceptable. The basic social order is introduced, then, in these two texts as a power structure which is hierarchic, heterosexual, patriarchal and procreation-oriented.[3] In other words, the nuclear social order is introduced as a 'natural', in the sense of primeval and primary, order in as well as out of the human social sphere. Other texts too—especially the juridical texts but also narratives—make it amply clear that the gendering of human sexual behaviours, be the behaviours socially acceptable or otherwise, is governed by this naturally/divinely ordained male authority for the purpose of regulating societal survival, which is equated with continuity.

---

[1] For the purpose of the following description, as for the rest of the discussion in this book, it makes no difference which of the texts is relatively or absolutely earlier and which is later. Nor does it matter what the authors' provenance is. It is highly significant that, in spite of the differences and variations in the visions underlying each and both texts, the basic views they contain concerning social structure and continuity are highly similar. Clearly, I hardly agree with feminist critics (like P. Trible, *God and the Rhetoric of Sexuality* and elsewhere; Bal, *Lethal Love*, pp. 104–130) who detect a difference with regard to female social status between Gen. 1 and Gen. 2–3. See also P. Milne, 'The Patriarchal Stamp of Scripture', in A. Brenner (ed.), *A Feminist Companion to Genesis* (Sheffield: Sheffield Academic Press, 1993), pp. 146–72.

[2] For the inclusion of Gen. 4.1–2a (Eve gives birth to Cain and names him, then gives birth to Abel) in the Garden story, rather than reading 3.24 traditionally as its ending, see I. Pardes, *Countertraditions*, pp. 39–59.

[3] For details see Chapter 4, 'Sex, Procreation and Contraception'.

Against this utilitarian ideological background, it is hardly surprising that breaches of the created order are treated as serious aberrations of not only accepted social principles, but also the 'natural' (in the sense of 'created' for the universe, including human society) principles that govern the world. Incest blurs patrilineal distinctions, hence is a threat to the social order. Adultery and fornication endanger male confidence and dominance by jeopardizing the indisputable knowledge of paternity, as does the restoration of marriage after a divorce and after the woman has been married to another husband meanwhile.[4] Sexual coercion of females or males (there is no specific term for our 'rape') threatens the males the females are related to. Whatever the textually significant status of the female involved—daughter or sister or betrothed or wife, virgin or otherwise—sexually abusing her violates at least the honour of the males she is subordinate to, not to mention other social and economic properties that are conceived of as male rights and obligations.[5] Prostitution is acknowledged, even tolerated, but its [female] practitioners are depicted as societally liminal. Homosexuality, in any form, is neither reproductive nor observant of sexual difference; it transforms males into females and, in at least some forms, renders them the objects of shame instead of subjects of honour.[6] Gender-bender dressing, once more, blots out some visual, easy to recognize sex and hence gender difference. Bestiality blurs the difference between the human and the more inferior if similar animalistic. In short, potential deviation from norms is viewed as damaging to the social texture; the moral and religious is highly pragmatic. Deviations from sexual norms are presented as crimes against the community, as [re]constructed in the biblical texts.

In recent years, phenomena defined in and by the HB as sexual illicitness—especially but not only as linked to gendered social status—have been analysed in many publications, particularly in feminist works. In this Chapter I do not set out to give a comprehensive account of the phenomena under discussion. Rather than

---

[4] Pressler, The View of *Women Found in the Deuteronomic Family Laws*, pp. 45–62. As Pressler summarizes, the law of Deut. 24.4 'quite precisely denies the first husband's authority over the woman for the sake of the purity of the community and in order to support the patrilineal family structure' (p. 62).

[5] Pressler, *Women in the Deuteronomic Family Laws*, pp. 35–43.

[6] K. Stone, 'Gender and Homosexuality in Judges 19: Subject—Honor, Object—Shame?', *JSOT* 67 (1995), pp. 87–107.

repeat extensively the views advanced in these [post] modern publications and in older ones, the following remarks are intended as a short dialogue with several of the views advanced in various such publications. My main concern is with the definitions of the terms for socio-sexual 'aberrations', proceeding from the premise—aptly discussed in these publications—that the terms' significations are not necessarily equivalent or analogous to contemporary concepts.

Adultery

When the subject/agent of adultery is male, it is immaterial whether he is married or single. The same applies when the male is the object of adultery and a female is its subject/agent. When a female is the object, the very nature of the offense, its very definition, hinges on the female's marital status. If she is single, then the illicitness of the relationship is linked to a potential loss of virginity and the attendant loss of honour[7] and potential income for her father's house (Exod. 22.15–16; Deut. 22.28–29), including her mother and other members of the household. This is considered a less severe offense than adultery, as evidenced by the lesser punishments prescribed by the law. If the female partner is betrothed or married, then the punishment is severe and, when consent between agent and object is to be plausibly assumed, meted out to both partners. It follows, then, that 'adultery' is specifically and exactly the sexual penetration of a betrothed or married female by a male (whose marital status is immaterial for the definition).[8] 'Adultery' is therefore a specific case of 'fornication'—a blanket term covering all occurrences of illicit (non-sanctioned, unmarried) heterosexual intercourse.

As in the case of incest, prescriptive (juridical and prophetic) texts are almost always much more severe with regard to adultery than narrative texts.[9] Indeed, Judah judges that Tamar should be executed,

---

[7] On the issue of honour and shame in biblical literature and in the Southern Levant in general see S. Olyan, 'Honor, Shame, and Covenant Relations in Ancient Israel and Its Environment', *JBL* 115.2 (1996), pp. 201–18 (with comprehensive bibliography); L.M. Bechtel, 'Shame as a Sanction of Social Control in Biblical Israel: Juridical, Political and Social Shaming', *JSOT* 49 (1991), pp. 47–76; L.R. Klein, 'Honor and Shame in Esther', in A. Brenner (ed.), *A Feminist Companion to Esther, Judith and Susanna* (Sheffield: Sheffield Academic Press, 1995), pp. 149–75.

[8] Pressler, *Women in the Deuteronomic Family Laws*, pp. 19–43. Cf. there for an assessment of the Deut. laws against the background of relevant ANE cognate materials.

[9] For the historical development of the Deuteronomy prescriptive texts, and their

since her pregnancy occurs while she is still linked to his household by marriage; hence, she is presumably an adulterer (Gen. 38). But the pharaoh is punished but not killed for his hinted-at sexual intercourse with Sarai (12.10–20); she, however, is returned to her husband, her consent or lack thereof not commented upon. Reuben is apparently reprimanded (49.3–4) for having sex with Bilhah (35.22), whose consent to the act or its lack is a matter of silence. Joseph refuses the sexual advances of his master's wife: however, his refusal is general and does not cite fear of punishment as a motive (39.8–9). At any rate, even when the master apparently believes his wife's allegations of Joseph's behaviour, he sends Joseph to prison (that is, to wait for a decision concerning his fate) rather than punish him by death (vv. 17–20). David is reprimanded and punished for his sexual liaison with the married Bath Sheba (2 Sam. 11–12) but neither of the two, Bath Sheba's consent or its lack notwithstanding, is executed or struck dead. Even when the male agent of adultery dies or is punished not long after he commits the offense, it seems that other factors apart from the reported adultery—such as violence committed against other males, dishonouring a father and rebelling against him (Absalom and David's concubines, 2 Sam. 16.21–23, 20.3), or power/ownership considerations (the woman of Gibeah, Judg. 19)—are as weighty. Apparently, outside the law and the prophets, adultery can be overlooked by both the affected human males concerned and the divine, much like the situation prescribed in section 129 of the Hammurabi Law.[10] In the Law, however, adultery is a lethal and fatal offense. In prophetic literature, female-motivated adultery becomes the trope of 'Israel's apostasy'. In both genres, adultery is considered a type of 'prostitution' (and see below). In sum, texts which are generically and explicitly concerned with the preservation of social order construct adultery as a greater danger to social boundaries than the narrative texts, to the extent that in Ezekiel adultery is equated with the shedding of blood (16.38; 23.37, 45). Not surprisingly, perhaps, in these latter texts female configurations are presented as

---

postbiblical application as anchored in the assessment of their severity, see A. Rofé, *Introduction to the Book of Deuteronomy* (Heb.; Jerusalem: Academon, 1988), pp. 141–58 (with bibliography and references to ANE materials as well as to rabbinic literature, medieval Jewish commentators).

[10] In the case of proven adultery, the husband of the implicated woman as well as the 'king' may decide to spare either or both guilty parties.

the agents and initiators of adultery much more often than they are
so in the prescriptive texts.[11]

לא תנאף, 'You shall not commit adultery', is introduced in the
decalogue (Exod. 20.14 = Deut. 5.18) within a cluster of maxims for
regulating basic societal behaviour. The maxims progress from the
assurance of inter-generational continuity (treatment of [elderly]
parents) and peer safety (proscription of human killing), to securing
personal possessions (against adultery and stealing), just legal practice
(against perjury) and back to stability of ownership (against desiring
others males' property). The addressee is a male. Another male's
wife is one of the objects listed in the injunction against 'desiring'
(Exod. 20.17, in second place after 'house'; in Deut. 5.21 the object
'wife' heads the list of desirable possessions). The linguistic data
apparently reflects social norms; the 'prophetic' twist, in which woman
figures serve as symbols of wilful adultery, appears like a highly creative
innovation when compared with both the law and narrative texts,
where male-initiated adultery appears like much more of a threat to
social stability and patriarchal order than female-initiated adultery.

'Rape'

The [modern] concept of 'rape', as defined in western legal systems, is
non-existent in biblical language as we have it. Modern legal systems,
such as the system in the state of Israel (my home base), define 'rape'
as a criminal offense. Rape is, in other words, a matter to be resolved
by the legal system of the social organization (the state). It consists of
bodily sexual violation (including penetration but not limited to it)
performed by an active agent on a non-consenting recipient. The
key issue is corporeal, inclusive of sexual, autonomy and the right to
choose, the human right denied to the attacked by the attacker.
Degrees of violence and coercion are recognized; shades of sexual
harassment are differentiated; verbal threats and the activation of

---

[11] The sequence נאף (Qal and Pi.) and its nominal derivatives occurs in the HB
31 times. Of these occurrences, ten times is the grammatical subject a female figure
or figures in prophetic literature (Jer. 3.8; Ezek. 16.32, 38; 23.37 [twice], 45 [twice];
Hos. 3.1, 4.13, 14), to compare with twice in Lev. 20.10 and once in Prov. 30.20.
The nominal נאפוף, 'adultery' is also attributed to a female figure in Hos. 2.4, as is
the abstract plural [?] נאפים in Jer. 13.27 and Ezek. 23.43.

power relations are taken into the assessment of the violation event.

Biblical literature, be it narrative or prescriptive, lacks not only a specific term for 'rape' but also a conceptual reference to it. Some of the terms employed are gender-specific and others are not. At any rate, none of them corresponds fully to the western category of 'rape'. For instance, the general euphemism for 'have sexual intercourse with', ידע (with an accusative), is used for homosexual 'rape' (Gen. 19.5; Judg. 19.22). Verbs denoting violence, such as חזק (Qal and Hif.) and ענה (Pi.) denote the activation of physical force for obtaining sexual intercourse (שכב, with the preposition 'with' or followed by an accusative) on the part of their subject-attacker when he is a male and the recipient is a female (Gen. 34.2; Exod. 22.15–16; Deut. 22.23–29; Judg. 19.24, cf. v. 25; 2 Sam. 13.11–12, 14). In other words, neither males nor females are ever 'raped' in the HB. In that sense, discussions whether Dinah is 'raped',[12] or whether 'rape' is meant in the prescriptions of Exodus. 22 or Deut. 22,[13] are largely beside the point.

This holds for female as well as male recipients of 'rape', according to the western system. And yet, the partial overlap *and* the differences in the terminology employed for female and male 'rape' point to a gendered view of sexual violation. As Carolyn Pressler convincingly argues, in the HB free men are presented as sexually autonomous whereas women lack sexual autonomy: their 'sexuality' is governed by the dominant males to whom they are related. Pressler's analysis of the sexual violation laws in Deuteronomy 22 shows that 'sexual violation of women is an invasion of male legal and social claims', and that 'a raped woman or girl is damaged goods'.[14] Her conclusions are applicable to 'rape' narratives as well as to the law of Exod. 22.15–16. In other words, the 'rapist' of a female injures not the female object of the sexual violation but, first and foremost and almost exclusively, the relational male legally responsible for her. In Ken

---

[12] Bechtel, What if Dinah is not Raped?

[13] For a full treatment of this issue see Pressler, *Women in the Deuteronomic Family Laws*, pp. 35–41, esp. for Pressler's refutation of M. Weinfeld in his *Deuteronomy and the Deuteronomic School* (Oxford: Clarendon Press, 1972), p. 286.

[14] C. Pressler, 'Sexual Violence and Deuteronomic Law', in A. Brenner (ed.), *A Feminist Companion to Exodus to Deuteronomy* (Sheffield: Sheffield Academic Press, 1994), pp. 102–12 (citation from p. 112), and *Women in the Deuteronomic Family Laws*, pp. 35–41.

Stone's words, 'There seem to be quite a number of narrative texts in which a woman is represented as the means with which one male challenges the honor and power of another male. Moreover, the nature of this challenge is quite frequently a sexual one. . . .'[15]

It follows that the desire 'that is expressed more directly here [in Judg. 19] by homosexual rape [is] that of power over, and dishonor of, another man'.[16] The threat of sexual violations of males (Gen. 19; Judg. 19) is couched in terms of 'knowledge'. The 'knowing' agent aspires to establish power and control over other male newcomers, experienced as potential usurpers of male knowledge and power. Physical penetration of a male by another male would establish that goal by de-masculinizing the penetrated alien males, by making them into women[17] not indirectly, through a female intermediary, but directly. Physical force serves to symbolically humiliate, to shame and to render the penetrated male into a social inferior—a subordinate like a woman, slaves and minors of both genders.

To conclude so far. 'Rape' of females and males in the HB, each in its own way, signifies an attempt to enforce or regulate social hierarchy among males by means of sexual activity. The object of 'rape', be it a male or a female, is a token of the agent's status or hoped-for status within the male community. Therefore, the category 'rape' is not an independent category. In the case of 'raped' females, 'rape' falls under the category 'family laws' (Pressler's formulation)— that is, the laws governing the functionality of the idealized norm, the 'house of the father' (בית אב);[18] and emblematizes power relations in or outside the 'family' (in the case of homosexual rape). The lust for power is presented as the prime motive for the sexual violation of females, not only of males. Although love and desire are not excluded from the description and play a role in the unfolding of, for instance, the stories about Dinah (Gen. 34) or Tamar (2 Sam. 13),

---

[15] Stone, 'Gender and Homosexuality', p. 102.

[16] Stone, 'Gender and Homosexuality', p. 103.

[17] M.L. Satlow, '"They Abused Him Like a Woman": Homoeroticism, Gender Blurring, and the Rabbis in Late Antiquity', *Journal for the History of Sexuality* 5.1 (1994), pp. 1–25.

[18] Although, to be sure, it is impossible to speak about one type only of 'biblical' family, as it is equally improper to speak of only one 'type' of Jewish family in postbiblical literature and times. See the essays in S.J.D. Cohen (ed.), *The Jewish Family in Antiquity* (Atlanta: Scholars Press, 1993), esp. M. Peskowitz, 'Family/ies in Antiquity: Evidence from Tannaitic Literature and Roman Galilean Architecture', pp. 9–36.

these are political stories about the struggle of males, in both instances the female object's brothers, for power.

[Male] homosexuality

Like 'adultery' and 'rape', our 'homosexuality' has no equivalent concept in either biblical literature or in any other culture in Mediterranean antiquity, rabbinic literature included. Sexual orientation was seen as typical, but not exclusive.[19] A sexual agent in such cultures is, by definition, a male. He is defined by his potential to actively penetrate a sexual body, not necessarily by the receptive, passive object of his desire and penetration. Boyarin's remark on talmudic culture is equally applicable to the culture reflected in the Bible: '. . . this culture, insofar as we can know it, does not know of a general category of the homosexual (as a typology of human beings) or even of homosexuality (as a bounded set of same-sex practices)'.[20] The taxonomy is different: there is no clear-cut binary opposition between heterosexuality and [male] homosexuality.[21]

There are two prescriptive texts against male 'homosexuality': Lev. 18.22 and 20.13. Two narrative texts, Genesis 19 and Judges 19, contain a threat of male 'rape' by males, in which women are substituted (by intention and actuality respectively) as the sexual object. In two other narratives, the narrative about Ehud son of Gera and Eglon king of Moab (Judg. 3)[22] and the narrative about Noah and his sons (Gen. 9),[23] there possibly are hints of 'homosexual' behaviour. Several preliminary, general, interconnected questions are relevant to all these sources. Who is implicated? What sexual activities are attributed to either of the partners in the male-male act? What is the status of each of these male partners, especially in the Law? Ultimately, Who is condemned for the same-sex sexual behaviour, and why? How is

---

[19] D.N. Fewell and D.M. Gunn, *Gender, Power & Promise: The Subject of the Bible's First Story* (Nashville: Abingdon Press, 1993), p. 192 n. 10.

[20] Boyarin, 'Are There Any Jews', p. 337.

[21] Boyarin, 'Are There Any Jews', pp. 334–35; cf. also pp. 338–39.

[22] A. Brenner, 'Who's Afraid of Feminist Criticism? Who's Afraid of Biblical Humour? The Case of the Obtuse Foreign Ruler in the Hebrew Bible', *JSOT* 63 (1994), pp. 38–55; and references there to Alter, *The Art of Biblical Narrative, esp.* pp. 37–41.

[23] See Chapter 5, pp. 107–110.

the paucity of the occurrences to be explained—as evidence of biblical
abhorrence of 'homosexuality', or its relative lack in ancient Israelite
societies as reflected in their extant literatures?

Boyarin,[24] Olyan[25] and Satlow[26] agree that the proscription in the
Leviticus (H) corpus is not against homoerotic activities in general
but, specifically, against male anal intercourse—as amply illustrated
by the less obscure discussions in later Jewish literature and other
cultures of late antiquity. The term משכבי אשה ('the lying down of a
woman'), which refers to the forbidden activity, defines it as [active]
penetration/[passive] receptivity of penetration for the respective
[male] partners. Olyan shows how the partly analogous idiom משכב
זכר ('the lying down of a man'; Num. 31.17, 18, 35 and Judg.
21.11, 12) refers to [male] vaginal penetration [of a woman], thus
strengthening the understanding of משכב as 'penetration'.[27] The
question is, which partner of this sexual act—the insertive or the
receptive—is implicated by the law. Olyan believes that the insertive
partner is the one addressed in Lev. 18.22, whereas the change to
the plural formulation in 20.13 implicates both partners through a
development of the law.[28] In Boyarin's formulation, '. . . when one
man "uses" another man as a "female" he causes a transgression of
the borders between male and female'.[29]

What about the receptive partner? Boyarin, Olyan, Satlow and
Fewell and Gunn agree that his gender position as male is compromised:
by being inserted, he becomes a 'woman'. Boyarin links the position
of the receptive partner with cross-dressing and gender differentiation
in general: 'men penetrate, women are penetrated; so for a man to
be penetrated constitutes a "mixing" of kinds analogous to cross-
dressing'.[30] Olyan refers to ANE materials to suggest that 'the receptive
partner in a male-male coupling was viewed in this legal setting as
the equivalent of a woman'.[31] Satlow discusses the position of the
'pathic'—the penetrated partner—in classical and rabbinic sources,
showing that 'Palestinian rabbinic discourse on homoeroticism is

---

[24] 'Are There Any Jews', esp. pp. 336–37.
[25] '"And with a Male You Shall Not Lie"', esp. pp. 184–97.
[26] Satlow, 'They Abused Him Like a Woman', p. 5.
[27] '"And with a Male You Shall Not Lie"', pp. 183–86; similarly Satlow,
pp. 5–6. Cf. pp. 24–6 above.
[28] '"And with a Male You Shall Not Lie"', pp. 186–88.
[29] 'Are There Any Jews', p. 343.
[30] 'Are There Any Jews', pp. 345–47.
[31] '"And with a Male You Shall Not Lie"', p. 193.

characterized by two traits: concern over gender boundaries and the divinely ordained limits on sexuality'.[32]

Fewell and Gunn agree in principle and introduce the issue of waste of seed:

> The ultimate confusion is for a man, equipped with phallus and the divine seed, to equate himself with a woman, phallus-less and (from the male point of view) seed-less. For patriarchy, that confusion is intolerable, unacceptable, an abomination.[33]

The issue of misuse or 'waste' of seed is also discussed by Olyan,[34] with references to Bigger,[35] Eilberg-Schwartz[36] and Biale,[37] among others.

The brief sketch above illustrates how 'homosexuality', as a category, does not obtain in biblical as well as talmudic culture. Issues like cross-dressing, female 'homosexuality' (see below), 'waste of seed', gender identity, social hierarchy, social boundaries and extrabiblical cultural cognates are crucial for the understanding of the Leviticus laws and their continuation in Jewish culture. This explains why the laws appear together with similar proscriptions designed to maintain social boundaries. It follows that a total condemnation of [male] homosexuality per se does not obtain in early Jewish literature. The negative evaluation of either 'active' or 'passive' partner of the [anal] male-male intercourse is condemned for the socially *symbolic*, to distinguish from the *actual/sexual*, practice. To quote Ken Stone,

> Male homosexual contact is forbidden because it confuses the boundaries between gendered subject-object categories. This confusion is considered abominable to the authors of the Levitical codes, who went to great lengths to map out the distinctions and categories in terms of which the world ought to be ordered and to condemn any activity that was thought to disrupt this system of ordered purity . . .[38]

Thus, the chief issue in the mirror stories about the males of Sodom (Gen. 19) and Gibeah (Judg. 19) is not [homo]sexuality but their wish to establish social control on other males, to the extent that

---

32 '"They Abused Him Like a Woman"', p. 23.
33 Fewell and Gunn, *Gender, Power, & Promise*, p. 108.
34 '"And with a Male You Shall Not Lie"', pp. 197–204.
35 S. Bigger, 'The Family Laws of Leviticus 18 in Their Setting'.
36 H. Eilberg-Schwartz, *The Savage in Judaism*, p. 183.
37 D. Biale, *Eros and the Jews*, p. 29.
38 Stone, 'Gender and Homosexuality', p. 98.

they disregard social valves like hospitality—and, in the latter case more than in the former, also the appalling treatment of women.[39] If the narrative about the drunken Noah and his sons (Gen. 9) is read as a story containing traces of 'homosexuality', then the 'homosexual' or any other, similar 'sexual' trace (like incest, father's castration) is subordinate to the dominant social requirement for the son/s to accept a father's authority.[40] In the story of Ehud and Eglon (Judg. 3), Ehud is the symbolic and actual penetrating male and Eglon the penetrated male. The penetrated is the butt of the joke—a foreign, feminized male ruler treated with contempt and subjected to *anal* humour; Ehud, although the story's hero, does not escape at least implied criticism for his method.[41]

The views I have presented above differ in details but, on the whole, share important traits such as differentiation between partners, re-examination of terminology and taxonomy, recognition of sexuality as reflection of cultural mores and the significance of the way gender relations are conceptualized in a culture for its vision of individual sexuality. Thus, central to the discussion of [male] 'homosexuality' is the comprehension of females as receptive/passive and of males as penetrating/active agents. The implications of this world view are clear-cut and not specific to biblical, or 'Israelite', or Jewish culture in antiquity. Strictly speaking, only free (non-slave) adult males, those who have a penis/phallus, possess a sexuality. This sexuality can be properly used, that is, for procreation. It can be misused, that is, according to some sources for [anal] intercourse, or with another male or for animal penetration (see below). The divinely-ordained function of the phallus/penis, when not exercised, cancels out not only the 'natural' male identity of its physical bearer but also his class and social identity. Another important implication, easily cross-referenced with the results of other analyses, is that the system is anchored in the view that females are not 'women', in the sense that they do not possess an independent sexuality of their own. Thus,

---

[39] Boyarin, 'Are There Any Jews', pp. 354–55; cf. Y. Amit, *The Book of Judges: The Art of Editing* (Heb.; Jerusalem: Bialik, 1992), pp. 311–24; S. Niditch, 'The "Sodomite" Theme in Judges 19–20: Family, Community, and Social Disintegration', *CBQ* 44 (1982), pp. 365–78; P. Trible, *Texts of Terror* (Philadelphia: Fortress, 1984), from p. 65.
[40] For possible 'incest' traces in the narrative cf. Ch. 5.
[41] Brenner, 'Who's afraid of Feminist Criticism', pp. 45–7; Alter, *The Art of Biblical Narrative*, pp. 37–41.

females have sex and sexual desire; but, as they are gendered in the HB, they do not have sexuality.[42]

[Female] homosexuality

Why is female-female sexual behaviour not mentioned in the HB? The omission is intriguing since, paradoxically, a principle of female sexual responsibility—especially in the cases of suspected sexual offenses—is in evidence. This is the case for loss of virginity, adultery and female participation in bestiality (Lev. 18.23, 20.16). Baruch Levine speculates that, perhaps, female-female intercourse was 'less common' than male-male intercourse; or that the usual address of the law (in Lev. 18 and 20) is to male subjects, hence the omission.[43] The assumption that female-female sexual behaviour was 'less common' than male-male sexual practice is indefensible as it is irrefutable; the address of males as agents excludes no female responsibility for sexual transgressions of any kind, as already noted.

Some potential answers can perhaps be gleaned from the references in rabbinic sources.[44] According to Boyarin, rabbinic acknowledgement of the possibility of female-female sexual relationship, and the reason for its negative evaluation (so that women do not become promiscuous with men), support the notion that 'homosexuality' per se is not a known category in rabbinic literature although the Torah itself is interested in regulating female sexual behaviour.[45] According to Satlow's analysis of a passage in the Jerusalem Talmud (*Giṭṭ.* 8.10.49c), the attitude of the sages to female homoeroticism in this passage is ambivalent; in another passage it is not condemned per se—unlike male-male sex, it is not considered a criminal offense; the condemnation is reserved for female-female marriage, that is, the gender-blurring of a female behaving as a male.[46] Satlow continues to establish 'the rabbinic anxiety over gender blurring' by discussing rabbinic attitudes to having sexual relations with hermaphrodites.[47] Judith

---

[42] Cf. Boyarin, 'Are There Any Jews', pp. 353–55.

[43] B. Levine for Lev. 18.22 in M. Weinfeld (ed.), *Leviticus* (Heb.; World of the Bible Encyclopedia; Ramat Gan: Revivim, 1987), p. 127.

[44] For instance *Tos. Soṭ.* 5.7, *b. Sanh.* 69b, *Yeb.* 76a, *Shab.* 65; *yer. Giṭṭ.* 8.10, 49c.

[45] 'Are There Any Jews', pp. 339–40.

[46] Satlow, '"They Abused Him Like a Woman"', pp. 15–17.

[47] '"They Abused Him Like a Woman"', pp. 17–18.

Romney Wagner thinks that, because female-female sexual activities
threaten neither women's ability to conceive children nor the establishment of paternity when they do conceive, the rabbis were largely
uninterested in women's sexual liaisons with partners other than
mature males. 'Psychologically', Wagner wrote, 'they did not perceive
lesbian activity as "real" sex—as is proven by their analogizing it to
the case of the mother and her minor son'.[48] All these answers and
a combination thereof, together with a lack of interest (on the part
of the biblical male authors) and accidental omission, are equally
applicable. None is either verifiable or unverifiable. All are governed
by the twin notions of women's 'inferior' sexuality, if they have
'sexuality' at all, and by the different gendering of same-sex sexual
practices in the world of the HB and rabbinic culture (and, to a
large extent, their traditional or male/mainstream interpreters).

Cross-dressing

The proscription of cross-dressing (Deut. 22.5) includes both males
and females, in that order. Like in matters of sexual penetration,
here too the issue is that of gender:[49] 'The Torah's language is very
explicit; it is the "use" of a male as a female that is *tō ʿēbâ*, the
crossing of a body from the God-given category to another, analogous
to the wearing of clothes that belong to the other sex, by nature as
it were'.[50] Boyarin, therefore, views the objection to cross-dressing
as another particular example of the general biblical prohibitions
concerning hybrids and mixtures.

However, the extention of the cross-dressing taboo in rabbinic texts
to feminized behaviour of males in general, again betrays an anxiety
about male sexual identity. This anxiety, which Satlow presents as
concern over gender blurring, requires further specification.[51] It seems
to exceed the straight-forward wish to supply visual parameters for
the sexual identity of males and females. Similarly, in the biblical
texts, although both men and women are forbidden to cross-dress,
the formulation is such that the male garment, or the male wearing

---

[48] In an e-mail message on the Iudaious list, September 21st, 1995.
[49] *Contra* J. Milgrom, '*tō ʿēbâ*', *Enc. Biblica* (Heb.; Jerusalem: Bialik, 1965–88), vol. 8,
p. 467, who attributes this and other prohibitions to theological differentiation between
'Israelites' and the religious practices of other nations.
[50] Boyarin, 'Are There Any Jews', p. 343.
[51] Satlow, '"They Abused Him Like a Woman"', pp. 12–14.

a woman's garment, are the [grammatical and actual] subjects of the prohibition.[52] In other words, the anxiety is about *male* sexual and social identity. In spite of the mention of women's cross-dressing, the anxiety is not truly paralleled for both genders. As in previous instances, the safeguarding of male sexual autonomy is of uppermost importance, for it signifies male social supremacy.

Bestiality

The link made in the HB between male-male sexual behaviour and human (of both male and female, in that order)-[domestic] animal sexual behaviour in unmistakable. In two occurrences of the prohibition, a locational link is immediately apparent. Lev. 18.22 (against male-male [anal] intercourse) is directly followed by the taboo on bestiality (vv. 23–24). Lev. 20.13 is followed almost directly by the taboo on bestiality for both men and women (vv. 15–16). As Satlow points out, a similar connection between the two behaviours is made also in rabbinic literature by spatial and linguistic associations.[53] In Deut. 27.21 no such link is made, and the addressed agent is a male only: the taboo is 'sandwiched' between prohibition on incest with a father's wife (v. 20) and with a sister and mother-in-law (vv. 21, 22). Curiously, the biological sex of the 'domestic animal' (בהמה) implicated is not mentioned in either the case of the male agent or of the female agent. Theoretically, at least, a same-sex sexual behaviour between a human and an animal is thus not excluded. The formulation of the prohibition in Exod. 22.18, like in Deut. 27.21, is addressed to a male (in the singular). In the Exodus and Leviticus 20 occurences, bestiality entails death sentence: in the former for the human practitioner, in the latter for both humans and domestic animals involved.

---

[52] Boyarin's translation, 'The woman shall not wear that which pertains unto a man, neither shall a man put on a woman's garment . . .' (p. 342), like other translations, is less than accurate in making the 'woman' the grammatical subject of the first clause. The Hebrew text reads, לא יהיה כלי גבר על אשה ולא ילבש גבר שמלת אשה. This should translate approximately as, 'There will be no man's clothing on a woman, nor will a man wear a woman's garment'. For the Heb. כלי as 'clothing, piece of clothing', an equivalent of the biblical בגד, see many examples in MH. For the understanding of כלי as 'utensil' rather than 'clothing' see Milgrom, 'tō 'ēbâ', p. 467.

[53] Satlow, '"They Abused Him Like a Woman"', pp. 22–3.

The motivation which underlies the taboo, as well as the punishment, appears at first to be identical for both genders. On reflection, though, a gendered nuancing is at least possible if not necessarily certain. The subject/agent position of the woman here is hardly surprising: women are associated with *animal* lust elsewhere in the HB too (Ezekiel 16 and 23; Jeremiah 2). The insistence of Leviticus 20 that the responsibility and punishment for sexual transgression to be shared by female and male culprits is extreme, to the extent of including the poor animal in the punishment for bestiality; however, this inclusivity does *not* imply a recognition of either female or animal independent sexuality.

The taboo for both females and males is probably grounded in two factors. According to Genesis 1, and the picture does not vary much in the rest of the HB, the 'natural' order of things is hierarchic. The descending order in which living things are organized is inverted to the sequence of their creation. The creating god stands at the head of the 'natural' structure and is accompanied there by other godly figures. Man, woman, mammals, fowl, fish and vegetation follow. For human males or females to have sexual intercourse with anything but their own opposite sex constitutes a violation of this divinely ordained scheme of the world. It would also constitute a mixing of separated categories, as against the biblical abhorrence of 'unnatural' mixtures. Humans are a separate species, hence should not 'mix seed' with other species that are divinely ordained to be separate. Perhaps this is also one of the notions behind Yhwh's anger in the elusive story about the fruitful sexual liaisons that 'the sons of god' or 'the sons of the gods' initiate with 'the daughters of man' (Gen. 6.1–4). The ensuing offspring, the famous giants, are the result of a mixture of human and divine 'seed'; they are an aberration of categorized order.

For men, a [wasted] ejaculation is explicitly mentioned in Lev. 20.15. The waste or the mixing of seed is implied (by male-animal as well as by male-male intercourse). Perhaps, as Olyan suggests, for H texts such mixture of human-animal seed defiles the land.[54] For females, the chief transgression is probably different. From the hierarchic and stereotypic point of view, there is a role reversal inherent in the woman-animal situation. It is inconceivable that the animal— and a domesticated animal, a בהמה (whose status, despite its usefulness,

---

[54] Olyan, "'And with a Male You Shall Not lie'", pp. 199–204.

is lower in the scheme of things than that of wild, often romanticized animals)—would be the initiator. In such a situation the
'woman' is an agent, she 'would stand' (תעמד, 18.24) in front of the
animal or 'would come near' (תקרב, 20.16) it, thus departing from
the properly passive receptive position which is conceived of as innately
female. At any event, for both genders bestiality implies a violation
of natural, divinely established hierarchy and order (procreation before
sexual activities for their own sake) that cannot be socially tolerated.

Prostitution

Not surprisingly, there is no HB term which corresponds to our
'prostitute'. The verbal sequence זנה and its nominal derivatives
may denote 'prostitute', 'prostitution', 'harlot/ry' or the like in some
contexts. In others its denotations are either 'have illicit sexual
intercourse' or 'fornicate, be promiscuous', in parallelism and with a
similar sense to נאף. It is therefore preferable to distinguish between
the phenomenon of 'prostitution' (selling sexual intercourse for payment)
and the root זנה.[55] Related to the question of the social phenomena
is the issue of alleged 'sacred' prostitution, both female and male, in
ancient Israel and the ANE in general. Within the discussion of זנה,
the abundant utilization of the root in the divine/human marriage
metaphor merits some attention.

Phyllis Bird, who in an important essay analyzes in some detail
the significations of the root זנה and the nominal זונה ('harlot, prostitute'), writes: 'The semantic relationship between the verbal and
nominal uses of the root is, in fact, complex, affected in part at least
by the figurative usage[56] that dominates in the Hebrew Bible and
invites interchange'.[57] Indeed, her statement can be corroborated by
quantitative survey of the data. The verb—in the Qal, Pu. and Hif.—
occurs sixty times, followed by various prepositions. In twenty-one
instances the verb's subject is a female and the activity denoted appears
to be fornication or adultery. In the other instances, a figurative usage

---

[55] P. Bird, '"To Play the Harlot": An Inquiry into an Old Testament Metaphor',
in P.L. Day (ed.), *Gender and Difference in Ancient Israel* (Minneapolis: Fortress, 1989),
pp. 75–76. See also T.D. Setel, 'Prophets and Pornography'.

[56] 'Figurative', that is, for turning away from Yhwh and esp. in the divine/
human marriage metaphor.

[57] Bird, '"To Play the Harlot"', p. 78.

of 'turn away from Yhwh' and/or 'towards other gods' has also males
or 'the land' as the verb's subject. The distribution of the verb is
wide, from the Torah to Chronicles, with about a third of the
occurrences in pornoprophetic passages. The nominal (Qal participle)
זונה is gender-specific and feminine only: 'harlot', 'female prostitute'.
It occurs thirty-four times, eleven of which in the pornoprophetic
passages. The nominal זנות, 'fornication, promiscuity' occurs nine times,
all but once (Num. 14.33) in the pornoprophetic passages. זנונים, with
a meaning similar to זנות, occurs twelve times, only twice (Gen. 38.24,
2 Kgs. 9.22) outside the pornoprophetic passages. תזנות, another
synonym, looks like an Ezekiel invention (twenty times).[58] Three
conclusions are immediately apparent in this quantitative-statistical
mini-survey. One, that most of the occurrences of the verb and the
nominal forms are in the pornoprophetic passages. Two, that Bird is
correct in asserting that the base meaning of the sequence זנה ('have
illegitimate religious tendencies') in the HB is not transparently
connected to the nominal זונה, 'prostitute'.[59] And three, that the use
of the same verbal sequence for designating female prostitution and
promiscuity on the one hand, and for designating male illegitimate
religious beliefs and practices on the other hand, establishes an
unmistakable association that is hardly complementary to women and
their sexual behaviour. However, Bird assumes cautiously that the
connection could not have been the integration of 'sacred' or 'cultic'
prostitution into the cult of ancient Israel, in spite of the parallelism
found in some texts between זונה and קדשה, 'a consecrated female'.[60]
Gruber goes even further than Bird in rejecting the 'cultic prostitution'
option for זונה.[61]

The word קדשה is paired off with זונה, 'prostitute' in the Tamar
and Judah story (Gen. 38.21, 22) and in Hosea (4.14), and with the
masculine form קדש once in Deuteronomy (23.18). קדש also appears
four more times in Kings.[62] Both forms have been translated and
interpreted as 'cultic prostitutes' of both genders in many modern
works, although not in ancient translations.[63] Gruber shows that קדש

---

[58] The word זמה, with the meaning 'fornication, promiscuity, adultery' (figurative
or otherwise), often appears in Ezekiel as a synonym for זנה-derived nouns.

[59] Bird, '"To Play the Harlot"', p. 79.

[60] Bird, '"To Play the Harlot"', pp. 87–89.

[61] M.I. Gruber, The Hebrew qĕdēšāh and Her Canaanite and Akkadian Cognates',
in Gruber, The Motherhood of God and Other Studies, pp. 17–47.

[62] 1 Kgs. 14.24, 15.12, 22.47; 2 Kgs. 23.7.

[63] Gruber, 'The Hebrew qĕdēšāh', pp. 22–4 n. 9.

and קְדֵשָׁה, a true pair grammatically, are not symmetrical in their designation of social function, or vocation. The קָדֵשׁ was a cultic official, but there is no evidence that he was a male prostitute or a male cult prostitute.[64] He also argues convincingly that neither the Hebrew term קְדֵשָׁה nor its Akkadian semantically cognate term qadištu (and the Ugaritic and Phoenician cognates) designate a woman whose function is that of a temple prostitute[65] but, simply, 'she who is set apart' (be she a temple functionary or not).[66]

The phrase 'she who is set apart' depicts well the situation of the prostitutes/harlots in the BH. They are marginal and liminal,[67] tolerated; but attitudes towards them are ambivalent. They are despised and socially isolated. In her analysis of three 'harlot' stories—Tamar's (Gen. 38), Rahab's (Josh. 2) and the two women who come to Solomon for judgement—Bird illustrates how such attitudes supply the presuppositions that inform the stories.[68] Even in stories where the prostitute/harlot has a central role, in Bird's words, 'The harlot heroine, or protagonist, remains a harlot. She is lifted for a moment, as an individual, into the spotlight by the storyteller, but her place remains in the shadows of Israelite society'.[69]

This evaluation of the prostitute's social station is certainly correct—for biblical literature, at any rate. However, there are traces of information that may point to paradoxical possibilities. The prescriptive demand that priests do not marry 'harlots' (Lev. 21.7, 14) implies that, in spite of their vocation and non-virginity, prostitutes could and did marry (outside the scope of priestly ideology). Whether Hosea's wife or wives were a harlot or harlots is a moot point (Hos. 1–3); but the command delivered to him, although shocking, supports the possibility of prostitutes marrying, if against the prevalent moral ideology.

Rahab (Josh. 2) has a house. So do the two women who come before Solomon for judgement.[70] In other words, be their marginal position as it may, they own real estate. Such ownership is not the

---

[64] M.I. Gruber, 'The qādēš in the Book of Kings and in Other Sources', *Tarbiz* 52 (1983), pp. 167–76 (Heb.).

[65] Gruber, 'The Hebrew qĕdēšāh', pp. 25–47.

[66] Gruber, 'The Hebrew qĕdēšāh', esp. p. 46.

[67] S. Niditch, 'The Wronged Woman Righted: An Analysis of Genesis 38', *HThR* 72 (1979), p. 147.

[68] P. Bird, 'The Harlot as Heroine: Narrative Art and Social Presupposition in Three Old Testament Texts', *Semeia* 46 (1989), pp. 119–39.

[69] Bird, 'The Harlot as Heroine', p. 133.

[70] Bird, 'The Harlot as Heroine', p. 132, argues that the women's house is a

usual lot of relational women in the HB. Relational, proper women
who are protected by a male (father, brother, son, another male
relative, husband) do not own property. Even a widow, like Naomi
(Ruth 4), has to sell her land. But a prostitute, or so it seems, has
economic autonomy if not social status.

But perhaps the interpretation should be turned the other way
around? Perhaps, in at least some cases, a woman figure that does
not conform to her dictated normative role is called a 'harlot/
prostitute' precisely for this, and for no other reason? If she is not
faithful to her husband, like the זרה woman of Proverbs 7 or any
other woman, she is a 'harlot' or 'plays the harlot'. If she leaves her
husband and runs back to her father, like the Levite's wife later raped
and tortured in Gibeah, she 'acts like a harlot' (Judg. 19.2). If she
seduces a man actively, like Tamar does to Judah (Gen. 38),[71] she is
a 'harlot' (cf. Jer. 3.3). If she is an enterprising woman of leadership
qualities, like Jezebel, she is a whore and a witch (2 Kgs. 9.22). If
she loses her virginity while she is still in her father's house, she
brings 'harlotry' to her father's house (Deut. 22.21; cf. Gen. 34.31).
If she is a single unmarried mother she is a whore, unless a higher
principle is at stake (1 Kgs. 3; cf. Gen. 38.24–26). If she is domi-
neering, she is a 'harlot' (Ezek. 16.30). The 'harlotry' of Jephthah's
mother is questionable, in view of his unquestionable paternity and
life in his father's household until his half-brothers expel him so that
he does not share the paternal inheritance (Judg. 11.1–3); the nameless
mother's epithet is a literary device, it defines Jephthah's origins as
humble, no more than that. It is not at all clear what Rahab's sexual
activities are, beyond and apart from the appellation given to her:
another literary device? In short, a woman figure that does not
conform to the conventional role of daughter, wife or married mother
as required, and even more so if she initiates sexual activity (like in
the pornoprophetic metaphor), a woman figure that disregards the
social proprieties runs the risk of being called 'whore'. Interestingly,
the only narrated woman who unmistakably practises her vocation is
the whore/prostitute Samson 'comes to' in Gaza (Judg. 16.1). Women
are not allowed 'sexuality' apart from in the Song of Songs although,

brothel. This is also argued by many commentators for Rahab's house. Be that as
it may, the fact remains that Rahab and the women have a house.
[71] F. van Dijk-Hemmes, 'Tamar and the Limits of Patriarchy: Between Rape and
Seduction', in M. Bal (ed.), *Anti-Covenant: Counter-Reading Women's Lives in the Hebrew
Bible* (Bible and Literature, 22; Sheffield: Almond Press, 1989), pp. 135–56.

even there, punishment is due for unconventional female behaviour (SoS 5.7). If they are initiators of sexual activity, they risk being labeled 'harlots' or 'whores'.

I am not trying to claim that there were no prostitutes in ancient Israel. There most probably were vocational prostitutes, males (although there is no HB term for male prostitutes) as well as females, although almost certainly *not* so-called cultic or sacred prostitutes. Occasional prostitution, as suggested by van der Toorn, is a distinct possibility.[72] That female prostitutes were marginal and liminal seems very likely, since they are a threat to 'decent' women as well as to men. What I am trying to point out is that, in a corpus of literature that depicts female sexual behaviour as suspect at best, dangerous and destructive to the fabric of society if not tightly controlled at worst, signs of female independent behaviour—be such behaviour of a sexual nature or otherwise—would be branded as 'harlotry' in order to transpose such defiant phenomena decisively to the realm of the undesired and socially marginalized.

Conclusions

Phenomena that are conceived by a society as aberrations of social conduct permit the etic observer a glimpse into the contours and boundaries, external and internal, of that society. Sexual mores are an important criterion for boundaries and social organizations, perhaps one of the most primary criteria. Biblical writers, whoever they were, expressed in their texts their own ideas about how their societies worked or how they wished them to work. In that sense, the HB is a sociological document even if it does not necessarily reflect historical 'realities'.

In this document, the presentations of adultery, sexual coercion, gender-bender behaviour, bestiality and prostitution exhibit several common traits.

- All the terms used neither overlap nor fully correspond to contemporary terms signifying similar sexual behaviours. In other words, the conceptualizations of sexual behaviour found

---

[72] K. van der Toorn, 'Female Prostitution in Payment of Vows in Ancient Israel', *JBL* 108 (1989), pp. 193–205.

in the HB are different from modern, western, middle-class conceptualizations of sexual morality.

• The attitudes towards aberrations are more severe in the so-called priestly (including the H texts) and prophetic texts than in narrative texts.

• The terms are gendered: what they signify in reference to male behaviour does not match what is signified for female behaviour.

• The definitions of aberrations are characterized by a deep concern for patriarchal values: paternity, 'seed', male honour and shame, male control over females, and hierarchic order. A concern for avoiding mixtures, well attested in other areas of human experience, is much in evidence.

• Males are, at least to a certain extent, sexually autonomous. 'Decent' Females are not. Nevertheless, [textual] females do not enjoy a diminished sense of responsibility to match their diminished sexuality. This conclusion corresponds to the conclusions gleaned from the analysis of incest in biblical prescriptive texts (Chapter 5).

CHAPTER SEVEN

PORNOPROPHETICS REVISITED: SOME ADDITIONAL REFLECTIONS[1]

Some seductive passages in the books attributed to the 'prophets' contain specifically allocated images of gender relations and gendered sexuality. These images are inflexible in that they invariably reflect female sexuality as negative and male sexuality as neutral or positive. Therefore such passages—like Hosea 1–3, Jeremiah 2–5, Ezekiel 16 and 23 and Deutero-Isaiah 47—have been branded 'pornography' by some readers, notably feminist readers. These passages contain variations on the twin-image of the faithful husband and his promiscuous wife. The husband is god; the wife variously represents Samaria, Jerusalem, Judah, the Israelites, the Judahites— in short, the addressed territories and, by contiguity, the religio-political communities.[2] The textual speaker sides with the divine 'husband' to the point of identification. For example, 'Hosea' is reportedly involved with an אשת זנונים, 'wife of harlotry' (chs. 1 and 2), and the same or possibly another woman is depicted as promiscuous (ch. 3). Grammatically, the textual voice is a first person singular masculine voice. Interpreters are divided on the question, Did Hosea's mission shape his marital life or did his unfortunate marital life shape his prophetic destiny? Be the answer to that interesting question what it may, and theological considerations do of course determine the interpretive position taken, the affinities of male mainstream commentators with 'Hosea' are noticeable.[3] This 'prophetic' textual voice, then, can be constructed as a male voice, is in fact gendered by the reader as such. At any rate, the text is neither perceived of

---

[1] A much shorter and earlier version of this chapter was delivered at the AAR/SBL conference in Chicago, November 1994.

[2] Related passages which contain images of 'harlots' as other cities conquered by Yhwh and similarly punished are Nah. 3.4–7 (on Nineveh) and Isa. 47.1–12 (on Babylon).

[3] Cf. for instance C.R. Fontaine, 'Hosea' and 'A Response to Hosea', and Y. Sherwood, 'Boxing Gomer: Controlling the deviant Woman in Hosea 1–3', in A. Brenner (ed.), *A Feminist Companion to the Latter Prophets* (Sheffield: Sheffield academic Press, 1995), pp. 40–69 and 101–125 respectively, for comments on commentaries to Hosea, and for alternative analyses.

as, nor—perhaps—intended to be, gender-neutral. Consequently, the
dual image of husband/wife and, implicitly, male/female sexuality is
unbalanced. The 'husband' is divine, proper, faithful, positive, voiced.
The 'wife' is human, morally corrupt, faithless, negative, silent or
silenced: her voice, if heard at all, is embedded within the male
discourse of the text. The message, though indirect, is clear. 'Wifely'
loyalty is to be learnt through re-education and punishment, including
exposure and public shaming. A metaphor for a wayward people
who deserve their fate, a 'true-life' situation utilized for religious
instruction: that was the critical consensus before feminist Bible critics
started to problematize the husband/wife image.

    D. Setel has written about such passages in Hosea and other texts.[4]
F. van Dijk-Hemmes has discussed Hosea 1–3[5] and Ezekiel 23.[6] I wrote
a comparison of chs. 2–5 in Jeremiah with a modern pornographic
novel, the *Story of O*.[7] However, many other readers have viewed and
continue to view these same passages as merely 'erotic imagery',
utilized for a theological purpose. Indeed, the latter approach has been
standard in Bible interpretation from antiquity until quite recently.
Objections to viewing the husband/wife image as pornography have
been and still are numerous; and even when the pornographic contents
is not denied, its anti-woman bias is disputed. In addition, ostensibly
politically-correct attitudes towards pornography are invoked for the
sake of personal freedom and personal choice[8] and, thus, the social
thrust of the image for contemporary readers is ostensibly minimized.
For instance, in a recent response to van Dijk-Hemmes's and my
own work, R. Carroll severely chastises us for our partisan attitudes

---

    [4] D.T. Setel, 'Prophets and Pornography: Female Sexual Imagery in Hosea', in
Russell (ed.), *Feminist Interpretations of the Bible*, pp. 86–95.
    [5] F. van Dijk-Hemmes, 'The Imagination of Power and the Power of Imagina-
tion: An Intertextual Analysis of Two Biblical Love Songs—The Song of Songs and
Hosea 2', *JSOT* 44 (1989), pp. 75–88. Reprinted in Brenner (ed.), *A Feminist Companion to the Song of Songs*, pp. 156–70.
    [6] F. van Dijk-Hemmes, 'The Metaphorization of Woman in Prophetic Speech:
An Analysis of Ezekiel 23', in Brenner and van Dijk-Hemmes, *On Gendering Texts*,
pp. 167–176.
    [7] A. Brenner, 'On "Jeremiah" and the Poetics of (Prophetic?) Pornography', in
On Gendering Texts, pp. 177–193.
    [8] For a refutation of such and similar arguments, in the American legal setting,
see the short essays under the heading 'Pornography and the First Amendment' by
various contributors in L. Lederer (ed.), *Take Back the Night: Women on Pornography*
(New York: Morrow, 1980), pp. 239–58. Although published in 1978, the refutations
still rings fresh and true—and valid.

in indiscriminately rejecting pornography as a consumer object in general, hence also for making too much of the biblical passages discussed.[9]

There is hardly disagreement about the function of such passages: they are widely recognized to be religio-political propaganda. So much of the authorial intent is considered obvious, whoever the author[s]. I feel, however, that the allegedly propagandistic constituents should be articulated in the light of modern definitions of propaganda. The debate about these loaded texts centres on the dual problem of the texts' definition as either eroticism or pornography, either realistic (objective?) metaphor or image rooted in anti-female disposition on the one hand; and the issue of modern readings of 'historical', that is, culturally different texts of the past on the other hand. Somehow, interpreters who are seduced by the image tend to 'understand' its function and validity as 'erotic'. Resistant and more suspicious readers, those who refuse to be co-opted by the texts into adopting their inherent focalization, tend to disapprove of their pornographic thrust and anti-female bias—even if, to consider the minimalist position of Phyllis Bird with regard to the Hosean texts, the metaphor's 'female orientation does not *single out* women for condemnation' (my italics).[10] Both factions are motivated by their own worldviews and specific ideologies.

My personal position is a feminist variant, one of a few existing feminist approaches. I would like to add some reflections to the ongoing debate from that standpoint. The following remarks are based on previous work I have done on this issue and are much indebted to recent work by others.[11] The strategy I adopt is to move between the present and the past and vice versa, since I find that a rigid linearity in treating this loaded subject is impossible for me to attain. A consideration of propaganda in general will precede a change of direction, to the definition/examination of pornography vis-à-vis

---

[9] R.P. Carroll, 'Desire under the Terebinths: On Pornographic Representations in the Prophets—A Response', in Brenner (ed.), *A Feminist Companion to the Latter Prophets*, pp. 275–307. Recently see also R. Carroll, 'Whorusalamin A Tale of Three Cities as Three Sisters', in B. Becking and M. Dijkstra (eds.), *On Reading Prophetic Texts: Gender-Related and Other Studies in Memory of Fokkelien van Dijk-Hemmes* (Leiden: Brill, 1996), pp. 67–82.

[10] Bird, '"To Play the Harlot"', p. 89.

[11] My own work has been published in *On Gendering Texts*, pp. 177–93, and a revised version in *A Feminist Companion to the Latter Prophets*, pp. 256–74. Other works have been cited above and will be cited presently.

eroticism. That will be followed by some brief notes on the propagandistic nature of 'prophetic' literature, and a discussion of the similarities between propaganda and pornographic representations, within
modern contexts and also within the biblical materials. Then, some
more aspects of biblical literature in general and the 'prophetic'
husband/wife metaphor in particular will be referred to, again in
order to answer the questions: Are these texts propaganda, are they
porno-religious propaganda? And what are the hallmarks of HB social
order and pornography, of which the husband/wife metaphor is the
most blatant example? In essence, then, the strategy I adopt here is
akin to that of my previous work on what I and others view as biblical
pornoprophetic literature. And, once again, I find it helpful to draw
a comparison between modern representations and biblical ones.

What is propaganda?

I proceed from a minimalist postulate: propaganda is a transaction
of verbal [rhetorical] communication [information] designed by its
initiator[s] to persuade the recipients of communication to accept its
message[s], then formulate new opinions, then act on the newly
acquired position. The techniques employed for accomplishing
persuasion may include the following devices.[12]

  A. Use of stereotyping. Stereotypes, generalizations and catch
     phrases are a great aid to persuasion: details are perceived
     as hindrance to the process of establishing influence. Hence,
     the use of a progressively more limited stock of stereotypes
     becomes more and more noticeable as a piece of propaganda
     becomes more virulent. Suffice it at this point to mention
     just a few stereotypes that have featured largely in western
     history: 'black', 'foreigner', 'mad', 'Jew', 'feminist'.
  B. Naming and Name substitution follow the principle of uncom-
     plicated economy in much the same way stereotyping does.
  C. Selection. In order to convince, only certain facts pertaining
     to a case are presented, instead of as full a picture as possible.

---

[12] The following list of devices and their use in pornography (see below) is largely
derived from B. LaBelle, 'The Propaganda of Misogyny', in Lederer (ed.), *Take Back
the Night*, pp. 174–78, 324; which is, in turn, based on J.A. Brown, *Techniques of
Persuasion* (New York: Penguin, 1963).

Consequently, the addressee's vision is limited by the absence of data as well as by its presence.

D. Exaggeration and Lying. Even the partial presentation of a situation or information constitutes a lie by omission; the manipulation of opinion by direct lying may be used as well, with the reasoning that the end justifies the means. Paradoxically, of course, propaganda always claims *a* truth, if not *the* truth.

E. Repetition is part and parcel of propaganda, be it political or ideological or commercial: a cursory glance at any contemporary large advertising campaign for consumer goods will verify this beyond any doubt. Repetition may be monotonous or else varied. At any rate, sheer repetition makes the verbally repeated entity acquire a non-verbal existence of its own: remembrance is essential to persuasion. Repetition also desensitizes the target audience as to the nature/origin of the claims made.

F. The selected idea[s] is [are] promoted as positive, beneficial and possessing a liberating potential.

G. By way of supporting the promotion of a propagated idea, promises and threats are closely linked to its acceptance or non-acceptance. An equation is made between acceptance and liberation of sorts on the one hand, non-acceptance and oppression or lack on the other hand. Shaming of opponents falls under this heading as well as under others (like, for instance lying, and the targeting of a scapegoat—see below).

H. Particular examples are utilized to make general points, as a complementary technique to stereotyping. Heroes and anti-heroes feature largely in such examples.

I. Anti-heroes fill the important role of enemy. The pinpointing of an enemy or a scapegoat diverts attention, creates solidarity between propagandist and addressees, and effectively bonds the creators and consumers of propaganda through hatred and/or aversion. Thus the boundaries of the hoped-for community of opinion and action are doubly defined by positive ('for') as well as negative ('against') markers.

J. So as to substantiate its claim for truth, propaganda always appeals to authority in order to legitimate itself and acquire respectability and authority of its own. Appeals may be made to history and the wisdom of the past; to contemporaneous history and currently accepted wisdom; to 'common sense';

to the law, institutions, celebrities, culture, expertise, science;
to religion and its institutions; and, ultimately, to a god.

These techniques and devices are hardly unique to propaganda: some
or most are routinely used as rhetorical devices in other genres of
communication. However, in propaganda—which is about the domination of the target's mind prior to its activation—they are present
as a cluster. If propaganda's end justifies the means, all available
means can be and are enlisted.

Before we can ask the question, Are the same or similar techniques
deployed for both [modern and ancient] propaganda and [modern
and ancient] pornography, some reflections on pornography per se
are in order, together with an evaluation of the differences between
pornography and eroticism.

What is pornography? What is eroticism?

By general consensus, and as reflected in and by dictionary entries,
pornography is the representation of sexual acts which arouses sexual
excitement. Some definitions add that the pornographic representation
is *designed* to arouse sexual desire: thus, authorial intent and motivation
are implied. Even without going further, it can be noted at the outset
that the 'prophetic' husband/wife and related images fall well within
the dictionary definitions of pornography on this count. Assuming
for the moment that the husband/wife images do constitute propaganda, which virtually all commentators confirm (but which, nevertheless, we shall come back to examine later), they must have had
an appeal for their target audience.[13] The use of sex as an appeal for
selling everything and anything is not an invention of the modern
advertising world. In that sense, although religious ideas rather than
sex or male control (see below) *per se* are being sold by the 'prophets',
sexual arousal is used as a tool for securing attention, influence and
potential persuasion.

One of pornography's basic constituents is its appeal to, and/or
attempt to [re]create, sexual fantasy. The appeal to the seemingly
imaginary and extraordinary may express one of the differences
between erotic representations (of what is within personal experience)

---

[13] Brenner, *On Gendering Texts*, pp. 178–79.

and pornographic representations (of what is conjured up as 'potential' or 'possible'). It so happens that usually, in mainstream definitions of sexual fantasy, no distinction is made between genders. It is widely assumed that female and male sexual fantasies are identical or similar; alternatively, when a need to admit gendered variables in fantasy is recognized, gendered fantasy is viewed as at least complementary, like in the sado-masochistic twin image. The fact that, culturally, male sexual fantasies have been and still are presented as universally and transgenderwise valid is usually ignored or not commented upon. The assumed male dominance and female compliance in this representation of bi-gender sexual fantasy is seldom contested. It is accepted unquestioningly. This is highly unsurprising: why should representations of sexuality, be their definition what it may, differ by a presumably non-gendered content from other gendered socio-cultural phenomena? And how does this fixed-role convention contribute to the definition of a visual or literary representation as pornographic? In other words, once more, wherein lies the difference between 'erotics' or even so-called 'soft porn' on the one hand, and 'pornography' or 'hard porn' on the other hand? I shall by-pass the joke about pornography and geography, but not without a moment's pause: conventions, variations in taste and norms, spatial and temporal and individual determinants, do indeed motivate the making of distinctions between eroticism and pornography. Readerly location and self-location are certainly crucial here.

From my gendered perspective, the lack of gender differentiation in attributing or creating a sexual fantasy may mutate that fantasy into a pornographic fantasy through lack of curiousity, or knowledge, about the Other's desire. Other determinants may be the objectification of female sexuality and the representation of fixed sexual roles, with the female serving the male. The same goes for the repeated humiliation of woman or a woman's image through sexual violence, and 'her' bodily exposure (in language or vision) to public view within a shaming framework (and more on that later). The same applies to the all too frequent depictions of females as lesser than human males: as slaves, as servants, as minors, as animals. Admittedly, then, multiple criteria are necessary for distinguishing between pornographic and erotic representations, over and apart from the recognition of cultural and individual variations.

Some common ground can nevertheless be demarcated even though exact definitions are elusive, or inadequate. To illustrate from the

HB. The Song of Songs is explicitly sexual and lets us gaze at naked
or partially naked women at our leisure; and yet, most readers—
and I include myself among those—experience it as erotic rather
than pornographic. Although the SoS contains elements of female
nakedness[14] and explicit references to sexuality, thus may activate
sexual fantasy if the reader of either gender is that way inclined,
there are neither gender debasement nor fixed gender roles in it. We
do view female and male figurations in the SoS, but the fantasies
described are differentiated as well as mutually inclusive. It goes
without saying, then, that pornography, according to the guidelines
I adopt, does not concern just *what* is being seen and said, neither
simply the bluntness nor the explicitness of the sexual object conjured
up and gazed at, be it male or female, but also the *how* used in the
representation. Wherever I detect an underlining world view of gender
asymmetry and female otherness, there I tend to respond by screaming,
Pornography. And so far, the multiple criteria of exposure, shaming,
asymmetry and objectification certainly feature in the 'prophetic'
passages that we shall come back to later.

Furthermore and logically, pornography is not simply the representation of sexual fantasy but that of *violent* sexual fantasy. Even if
we reject essentialism, the obvious facts that women (as a group) are
physically weaker than men and that their bodies are physically
penetrated in male-female sex should be given due consideration:
potentially and actually, women's bodies are more deeply affected by
sexual acts than [heterosexual] men's. Women are also, again as a
group, inferior social agents. Hence, sexual violence can and is
exercised upon them in order to control their bodies and minds. How
should sexual violence practised by the strong [male? older person?
social superior of either gender?] on the weak [females? children[15] of

---

[14] And, if to a lesser extent, male nakedness.
[15] In Ezekiel 16 a first-person voice speaking for Yhwh narrates the story of a
male who finds a female baby, raises and then weds her; the metaphorical female
baby is Jerusalem (vv. 1–14). This fantasy of turning a 'daughter' into a 'bride' goes
sour, according to the indignant speaker. Since the daughter figure is silent throughout the process, we may assume that she consents. We may also view the story,
however, as reflexive of incest practices about which daughters had no say. The
speaker certainly expects us to side with him against the disobedient daughter. On
father-daughter incest see above, Chapter 5. Suffice be it here to note that child
molestation is well represented in modern pornography; cf. pp. 119–184 in Lederer
(ed.), *Take Back the Night*, esp. on *Playboy* and other [soft porn?] magazines. The link
between the pornographization of women and of children is well explained there.

both genders? socially inferior persons?] be assessed, then: as erotic or pornographic?

In my view violence does not have much to do with Eros. Violence is a distortion of Eros, a corruption or sublimation. Although violence may express Eros, its ultimate motivation is physical and social control. It can and should be admitted that when violence occurs in sexual relations women are much more vulnerable than men. Is sexual violence motivated by desire? Perhaps by frustrated desire. In our culture, the license to gratify desire, immediately and even violently, is the privilege of the socially dominant. In our culture, this is the prerogative of males (as a group). And when violence enters the sexual fantasy, it mutates that fantasy into pornography.[16] I shall not refer here to the platitude of the Eros/Thanatos duality: suffice be it to note that to merely equate violence with Thanatos is to miss the mark widely. I am also less essentialistic-deterministic about gendered sexual mechanisms than other feminist critics. Here I obviously part company from feminist writers like Andrea Dworkin,[17] or Camille Paglia.[18] I do not define heterosexual sexual activity a-priori as violence against women, nor necessarily view sex as a war game. However, certain sex and gender differentials, although banal, cannot be ruled out of the discussion.

In assessing the differences between erotics and pornography I take my cue from Susan Griffin,[19] whose views in *Pornography and Silence* I shall summarize briefly and comment upon. According to Griffin pornography is a cultural phenomenon which, paradoxically, is accepted as a positive antidote to [negative, threatening] nature. Culture triumphs over nature through the agency of human knowledge.

The depiction of the female object as doubly inferior—by gender and by age—obtains also in Ezekiel 23.3.

[16] For recent views about violence and pornography see, for instance: C. Itzin (ed.), *Pornography: Women, Violence, and Civil Liberties* (Oxford: Oxford University Press, 1993); S. Gubar and J. Hoff (eds.), *For Adult Eyes Only: The Dilemma of Violent Pornography* (Bloomington: Indiana University Press, 1989); N.M. Malamuth and E. Donnerstein, *Pornography and Sexual Aggression* (Orlando: Academic Press, 1984).

[17] A. Dworkin's work is well known and much objected to, sometimes with violent criticism (cf. for instance Carroll, 'Desire', p. 281). For the sake of convenience I'll refer here to two items: her *Pornography: Men Possessing Women* (New York: Putnam, 1981); and two short pieces in Lederer (ed.), *Take back the Night*: 'Why so-called Radical Men Love and Need Pornography' (pp. 148–54), and 'For Men, Freedom of Speech; for Women, Silence Please' (pp. 256–58).

[18] For instance in C. Paglia, *Sexual Personae: Art and Decadence from Nefertiti to Emily Dickinson* (New York: Vintage Books, 1991).

[19] S. Griffin, *Pornography and Silence*.

Knowledge is control; to control is to know. The pornographic mind seeks to achieve control over its own carnal (natural) self and the other's corporeal and carnal self by enslaving the other's body. The ensuing violence evidences the futility of the project. No lasting epistemology of the self or the other can be gained or sustained by upholding the dual equation self=culture/other=nature, and by organizing the binary opposition of self/other relationship into a relationship of control and submission. The fatal split between self and other, culture and nature, soul and body suffered by the pornographic mind cannot be healed, and Eros is destroyed by the pornographic fantasy instead of being nourished by it. Since males (as a group) are more likely to participate in or practise pornography voluntarily, women—and social inferiors, and minors of both genders— are its more common objects. The inferiors are educated to silently cooperate with their own demotion out of the cultured social order. Thus males may retain their superficial autonomy at the price of losing Eros.[20]

Viewed like this, pornography permeates all facets of western culture, including monotheistic religions and the cultures of their practitioners. In these cultures the pornographic fantasy simply waits to be enacted because it is built into the religious order. This fantasy is likely to become an event, a series of events, a norm unproblematically built into the social system. Therein lies the danger of pornography: fantasy is not dangerous if it remains just that; its violent enactment is much more of a societal threat, especially since the dialectics of social co-operation dictate that weaker social groups actively participate in the enactment of their masters' fantasy.

At this point I could refer to other feminist critics, like Jessica Benjamin in her book *The Bonds of Love;*[21] or to works by male psychologists and sociologists and anthropologists which imply that females, by definition, hover outside the symbolic, hence social, order. Such views are a faithful description of western culture: whether they constitute a justification of gender relations in that culture is another matter entirely. Instead, I shall return to the 'prophetic' divine husband/human wife image in order to problematize it further.

---

[20] I would like to add, in passing, that the relatively modern phenomenon of female-authored pornography, when it involves hierarchic relations and S/M relationships, is in my view no better than any other type of pornography.

[21] J. Benjamin, *The Bonds of Love* (New York: Pantheon, 1988).

Love, Eros, is indeed being declared by the metaphoric husband. He claims he loves his wife. Is this Eros or pornography? Lo and behold, in a moment we shall be called to witness a violent scene. If 'he' has his way, 'she' will be publicly shamed. She is called whore, deviant, uncivilized; she is animalistic. She is threatened with divorce; loss of status, possessions and children; torture and deportation— before she is taken back by her magnanimous owner. An attempt is made to silence her into submission. Her implied behaviour is graphically described in Jeremiah and, even more so, in Ezekiel. Is this fantasy of female punishment by a [divine] male force a female fantasy?

'She'. The idea of metaphorizing woman into a rejected country, town, nation, land to be punished—an idea that, more often than not, receives readerly consent or at least 'understanding'—is common throughout the prophetic books, as has been pointed out by many commentators. Nevertheless, this common-place idea or image should give us impetus for reflection.[22] Especially so since the metaphoric 'woman' is to have her body exposed as part of her punishment and re-education. The distance between metaphoric 'prophetic' speech and social potentialities is easily bridged here. The transition from one territory or community/'wife' into two territories or communities/ 'wives'—like Judah and Samaria, Ohalah and Ohalibah (Ezek. 23)— is quickly introduced, e.g. in Jeremiah 3 and 5 and Ezekiel 16 and 23. 'They' are imaged as kin, sisters. From here to a stereotypic generalization—i.e., *all* women potentially are like this, of unbridled sexuality and potentially suspect sexual fantasies/behaviour—there is but a short distance. And this brings us back to the question, is the pornoprophetic literature discussed propaganda?

Is prophetic literature propaganda?

There is hardly any doubt that many passages in the so-called prophetic books are propaganda. The form of address bears this out. The literary style is that of an attempt to persuade, to sway public opinion by the techniques and devices delineated above, separately

---

[22] Brenner, *On Gendering Texts*, pp. 182–83; P. Gordon and H.C. Washington, 'Rape as a Military Metaphor in the Hebrew Bible', in Brenner (ed.), *A Feminist Companion to the Latter Prophets*, pp. 308–25.

or mixed together. Stereotyping, name-calling, selection, exaggeration
and half-truths, repetitions, promotion of its own goals as the truth,
promises alternating with threats, examples, generalizations, the
pinpointing of enemies and appeals to divine as well as lesser respected
authorities—all serve the ideology of Yhwh as a single god of his
people and their history. Be the attempts to influence public and
private opinion successful or otherwise, be our own sensibilities in
empathy with the message conveyed or otherwise, the utilization of
propaganda techniques in such texts makes them into just that:
propaganda, an advertising of wares. The fact that the merchandise
is ostensibly spiritual and religious does not invalidate the definition
of the means, or vehicles, of transmission. Furthermore, even if we
agree with the underlying ideological premises, this does not render
the means automatically justifiable. Therefore, the propagandistic
features of the husband/wife metaphor should be examined for
themselves, and for the additional light they might shed on the
significance of this metaphor—not only for its religious ideology but
also for its by-product, gender relations.

Pornography and propaganda, modern and biblical: similarities of techniques

Pornography advertises its wares in much the same ways used for
advertising propaganda. In order to show the similar techniques
deployed, I shall review the ten propagandistic devices listed above
and apply them again to pornographic media. Since it is easier to
accept claims concerning modern pornography than claims concerning
biblical pornography, I shall begin with the former then move back
to the latter.

Stereotyping is part and parcel of pornographic representations,
be they 'soft' (non-violent) or 'hard' (violent), although the stereotyping
becomes more rigid the more violent the representation. Women
and femininity are mostly objectified into types: carnal, submissive,
promiscuous, whores to be conquered, inexperienced-but-waiting-to-
be-taught are some of the recurrent types. The metaphorical/imaged
women hardly have positively valued minds or ethics. They hardly
exhibit independent, self-initiated character development. They are
breasts and genitalia: their behaviour is determined by their essential
sex urges. This stereotyping reaches a climax, so to speak, in the

S/M fantasy of rigid gender roles: passive masochistic [the object who is being asked to agree to, understand and perhaps love the action to be carried out on her body] female; and active sadistic [strong, controlling] male.

Name-calling or name-taking is common. Women are 'whores'. They are de-humanized into minors or playthings or animals, with the accompanying change of address (the Playboy Bunny is an appropriate example). Pornographically represented women figures may even be stripped of a name completely, which signifies a total departure from the social order (as for prison inmates, if not to invoke even more painful historical analogies). Thus, for instance, in the *Story of O*, O is the only character in the book to have no name whatsoever. Whether O stands for 'zero', 'orifice', 'other', 'woman in general' or some other explanation, or all these lumped together, is less significant than the act of name-stripping itself.

In pornography, a dual process of selection occurs. Basically, a single vision of female sexuality is presented: a woman who is turned on by violence. This selected vision excludes other visions of female sexuality almost altogether. Further selection is evidenced by the claim that pornography liberates desire and prevents repression, to the exclusion of pornography's possible harmful effects.

In line with the tendency to stereotype, the fantasy of woman in pornography is not gender-neutral in its applicability. It has little to do with actual women's fantasy, in as much as it is presented as an exclusive vision. A good example is the myth of women's voluntary [group] tendency to enjoy masochism, exploded only recently by woman writers.

The story lines are few and repetitious. Every woman is a whore, given a chance. Women love to have violence practised on their bodies, even if they protest to the contrary. They enjoy being disciplined. They love to perform oral sex. They love and obey strong, assertive males, etc.

Pornography is promoted as erotics, the 'natural' expression of desire that is liberating, even necessary. Its supporters present it as value-neutral or positive, free, uninhibited. Claims for its dissemination under the principles of freedom of speech, civil liberties, adult consent and so on are made often and repeatedly.

In pornography, women are threatened by violence and rewarded by pleasure if they comply with the role arranged for them. Potential consumers (all of us, regardless of gender) are threatened by being

166   CHAPTER SEVEN

labeled 'spoilsport', 'reactionary' or 'radical feminist' if they object to
pornography; and promised the reward of being considered 'politically correct' or 'liberal' if they consent to co-operating with their
role as demanded. Pornography, like propaganda, tends to shame its
target audience into submission while claiming rational attitudes.

Men are the heroes of heterosexual pornography: they are the
active ones. Women are the objects, the anti-heroes. As throughout
my description, I am aware that exceptions to this formula exist as
such—they are exceptional. The majority of pornographic representations follow the principal rules.

The anti-hero is the scapegoat or enemy. Woman, especially
assertive and active woman, is the enemy to be conquered (tamed,
educated) in the pornographic representation. The sighting of this
conquered enemy is a source of bonding for the males within and
outside the pornographic representation/fantasy.

Appeals to authority are made in order to make pornography
respectable and legitimate. The example of Playboy magazine again—
its interviews with prominent public, literary and artistic figures—
springs immediately to the mind. The industry's appeal to science,
literatures and so on is a case in point.

Working back from the generalization of pornographic representation to its underlying ideocontents, the question asked earlier can
be repeated. Is pornography simply about sexual desire? Pornography's
use of specific propaganda techniques excludes such a naive assumption.
It is seen to propagate, even sell, male supremacy while selling itself.
The propagation/sale is indirect, although not necessarily innocent
or self-conscious. According to heterosexual pornographic ideology,
the social group 'women' mostly exists as the agent for or object of
male sexual gratification. Like in other areas of psycho-social relations,
women are thereby dehumanized and de-socialized. Although pornography claims to entertain and to represent non-gendered desire, in
fact it advertises an ideology of female bondage and upholds the
gender split typical of our society.[23]

How are the same criteria applicable to the husband/wife metaphor
in the 'prophetic' passages (Hosea 1–3, Jeremiah 2–5, Ezekiel 16
and 23, some Second Isaiah passages and Revelation 17–18, to name
the most prominent examples)? The frequent depiction of turning

[23] Cf. Benjamin, *The Bonds of Love.*

away from the one true monotheistic god is metaphorized into female 'whoring'.[24] This is stereotyping as well as name-calling. Another instance of name-calling is to be found in Ezekiel, where the names of Samaria and Jerusalem are changed into Oholah and Oholibah (ch. 23), presumably to indicate some property of their relationship with the divine. In Jer. 2.20–24 the land/community/addressee gets to be called whore, animal and more. The shaming mechanism is much in evidence. Only one possible way of female sexual behaviour is selected for presentation, then generalized by enthusiastic repetition (cf. Ezek. 16 and 23) into an unshaken axiom. Exaggeration by repetition and exclusion amounts to a half-truth: the accused party, 'woman', is allowed no independent voice. The idea of violent sexual punishment is promoted as a justified solution, the only one viable.[25] Threats of violence and promises of reward if submission is embraced are essential and often repeated. The woman-people-city-land is pinpointed as the enemy: of themselves, of Yhwh's love. The bonding between the speaker and his target audience, essential to propaganda, is presumably to be achieved by the key reference to the social enemy, woman. Finally, the appeal to authority is absolute. The legitimizing authority is Yhwh himself: in most of the relevant passages he is present[ed] in the speaking mode, he is the 'I' persona.

There is no doubt that, unlike modern pornography, the HB pornoprophetic passages are *not* intended as depictions of female and male desire per se. I would even venture the thought that the depictions are, perhaps, not *consciously* misogynist. That, however, is small consolation. The ideology of male supremacy is indispensable to the husband/wife metaphor: without this ideology the metaphor will not have been understood, much less acted upon. The fact remains that only one type of woman is presented, be she daughter (Ezek. 16) or wife and mother (Hos. 1–2). 'She' is objectified and dehumanized by various means, including loss and expulsion. She is the enemy of positive, godly, male values. The authority appealed to is, ultimately, male authority as symbolized by and symbolizing divine authority. Throughout these pieces of religious propaganda, identification with the male god is sought at the expense of the humiliated, naked 'woman'. In other words, a glimmer of liberation

---

[24] As also in numerous passages of the Deuteronomistic history, notably in Deuteronomy and Judges.
[25] As also in the case of Jezebel, 2 Kgs. 9.

is offered by a model of female submission. Let us now look, then, at the biblical text's invitation to look.

Voyeurism and pornography

In propaganda the addressees are required to assimilate a vision and make it their very own. They, we, are asked to comply with a message. Pornographic representations, be they verbal or visual, involve our senses directly. What about our complicity, our voyeurism of the figures pornography claims to represent, in general and in the relevant biblical texts?

In our dominant western culture, Judeo-Christian and patriarchal and heterosexual, women have been and still are treated as collective or individual object[s] for gazing at. This is borne out by many cultural facets of female socialization. Our clothes, behaviour, art, body image, self-image and so on are preparations for the gaze: not only and simply the male gaze, though; women are also socialized, more so than men, into gazing at themselves and other women as objects of the gaze. Women, at least heterosexual women, are taught to gender themselves as both subjects and objects of the gendered gaze. By common consent, nowhere is this phenomenon more glaring than in American cinema, as succinctly analyzed by the film critic Laura Mulvey.[26]

In this cultural world we recognize the possibility of eroticism wherever women are exhibited, or exhibit themselves, as naked or partly dressed (even outside pornographic representations). Female nudity functions as a social code: an invitation to sexual fantasy and, potentially, to sexual activity. This is not to say that the male body always appears clothed in erotic or pornographic representations, be they visual or verbal. However, the nude male body is treated with much more discretion, that is, coverage. The coverage extends particularly to male genitalia, as if by way of protection. Late at night one can watch films that conjure up such a world of 'erotics' on commercial cable television networks, which means that the films are socially acceptable as erotica or at least 'soft porn'. And erotics

---

[26] L. Mulvey, 'Visual Pleasure and Narrative Cinema', *Screen* 16/3 (1975), pp. 6–18.

is 'healthy', is it not, while pornography is more debatable and hardly tolerated by many social groups.

Clothing distinguishes culture from nature, as Susan Griffin asserts time and time again.[27] Images of females [un]willingly undressed in/ by film have a certain effect. In such representations women are stripped of their cultural identity; they become, literally and figuratively, more 'natural'. The same applies to male images, only that their stripping in art and other visual representations is much less frequent and follows different rules.[28]

Is such a universe of habitual female exposure by the gaze portrayed in the HB and in related literature? Indeed, clothing in the Bible does symbolize culture. Lack of clothing may thus symbolize a state of non-culture.[29]

Where can we view, so to speak, female nudity in the Bible? Where, for instance, can we view female breasts? In the SoS, of course; there is a concentration of breasts there. However, in order to view, touch, feel and handle female breasts *with violence* we must turn to the so-called prophets: to Hosea (ch. 2) and Ezekiel (chs. 16, 21.8, and 23). There female nakedness is highly visible and doubly vulnerable: for being explicit as well as repeatedly threatened. Accusations of female whoring abound in those passages and others (notably also in Jeremiah and other chapters of Hosea); and modern scholarship complies with the accusations by writing copiously about Israelite 'sacred' prostitution.[30] There is a veritable mass of female breasts and total or near-total nudity introduced with violence and verbal abuse. The literary trope of the promiscuous naked woman appeals not only to our implied experience of the female species, but also to the image we presumably have of female corporeality: how can it work otherwise? In turn, the image educates our bi-gender perception of its source. I follow Mieke Bal here to conclude that desire and viewing and the attempt to gain knowledge blend in such images into a kind of epistemology, a ידיעה—of female bodies, of their nature, of their

---

[27] S. Griffin, *Pornography and Silence*.

[28] It is worth noting that such rules obtain, for instance, in the 'soft porn' film shown on European public (that is, general, non-specialized) cable television. Repeatedly and prominently, female nudity is total, including female genitalia. Male genitalia is consistently implied but, by feats of camera acrobatics, not actually visible. The most one can hope to watch is a male behind, or an extremely abrupt and hazy glimpse of a male's under-the-belt front.

[29] See Chapter 3, 'A Body of Difference'.

[30] But cf. M. Gruber, 'The Hebrew *qĕdēšāh*', pp. 17–47; and pp. 147–51 above.

im/proper treatment through silencing and abuse. In the Bible, the man is almost always the subject of the verb ידע, 'know' in the sense of 'have sex'; the woman is more often the verb's object.[31] I suggest that this too reflects a world view: the possessor of knowledge, the one allowed to see and act on the sighting, is the male. Moreover, when a woman 'looks' or attempts to 'look' in the realm of sex, she can meet misfortune: it is implied that Dinah's encounter with Shechem is her fault, for she 'goes out to see' (Gen. 34.1–2).[32] Not to mention what is prescribed when a woman dares to touch a strange man's genitals in public, presumably where her action can be seen by others: her hand shall be cut off for this serious breach of modesty without mercy (Deut. 25.11–12; cf. Pressler).[33] For a textual woman, looking is immoral and touching male genitalia in public even more so. But a male, be he symbolic or otherwise, is invited to look at female private parts continuously and to act, if he so chooses, on the naked body. Women are invited to look at the female body too: Ezek. 23.10 and 46–49 contain explicit addresses for women to look and to learn; not surprisingly, the elusive demarcation lines between metaphor and 'reality' break down and the two worlds, the divine/human and the social, blur into one gendered schism.[33a]

What we, all of us, ultimately see in the woman-community-territory of the divine husband/human wife metaphor is not just a metaphorical woman but a *naked* woman: silent, accused of prostitution, framed for sustaining male violence. And the metaphor is backed up by two uncontested male claims: a claim of love and desire, and a claim for absolute truth.

This image shows too much and too little. Too much female flesh. Too little of the 'female' herself and of the multi-layered motivation of her accusers. Viewed together, by us, against the backdrop of promised violence, the nude female figure and her clothed, self-appointed male mentors constitute an asymmetric S/M pornographic icon. I feel acutely uncomfortable with that paradigmatic icon. It contains an inflexible model for gender relations. I sense it is damaging to my gender and take no comfort in other biblical models for gender

---

[31] As Francis Landy remarked in a conversation, a possible exception is Hos. 2.22. For other exceptions see Chapter 2, 'Love, Desire and Sexual Activity'.
[32] For a dissenter, cf. again Bechtel, 'What if Dinah is not Raped'.
[33] C. Pressler, *The View of Women Found in the Deuteronomic Family Law*, pp. 74–7.
[33a] See above, pp. 41–3.

relations. I wish not only to suspect this pornographic icon that allows women neither knowledge nor unlimited sight, and consequences thereof, but also to resist it. I do not want to join in the game of undressing that woman; I do not want to leer at her uncovered body. I am a heterosexual woman; I would rather view Israel, God's chosen son, being paraded naked in the marketplace. Alas, this is not possible: the son's private parts have been established as linked with the divine. Hence, these private parts are covered, are not visually and linguistically accessible for the likes of me.

In conclusion

For me, a pornographic representation qualifies as such, as a fantasy of pornographic sexual desire to be distinguished from erotic fantasy, when it contains abuse and/or violence. The boundary is very clear: it is less the amount of flesh shown that bothers me but the manner with which it is treated in the representation, since the image created depends on the *how* as well as the *what*. When one of the imaged partners is almost always clothed, retains control, heaps abuse, threatens physical punishment; and the other is naked or threatened with nakedness, on view, not allowed to speak and closely monitored—that is pornographic fantasy, despite the declarations of 'love' uttered, as shown by van Dijk-Hemmes in her article on Hosea.[34] From this perspective, the husband/wife metaphor is a pornographic fantasy of male desire.

The metaphoric and speaking and listening males assume the right to undress the female and to drive knowledge into her gazed-at being, while they remain safely protected by layers of clothing and self-righteousness. This attitude is both reflected in biblical language and the gender and cultural ideologies motivating it, and is perpetuated by that language. If we identify with the biblical speakers' religious position, we also buy their gender position: the two, in their own culture as reflected by its own literature, are intertwined and insepa-rable. Religious propaganda is not divorced from social norms.

Religious propaganda builds on social norms and also perpetuates them. There is more to understanding biblical pornography than at

---

[34] F. van Dijk-Hemmes, 'The Imagination of Power and the Power of Imagination'.

first meets the eye. Not only a gender picture is at stake here, but also our knowledge—preferably not idealized knowledge—of the socio-cultural fabric of ancient Israelite/Judahite societies in general. Our modern sensibilities are all we have to guide us here. Because we recognize that women are excluded, because we see that women's lack of a penis that bears the sign of the divine covenant means that they have no easy co-existence with the divine phallus, we can understand how and why biblical women and woman figurations cannot tell us about their situational location and their views of such texts. Neither can we resort to material evidence or to comparative literatures in this case.

I can see no reason for complying with biblical pornography, even at the price of being considered politically incorrect. Far be it from me to censure erotics. But, together with other feminist critics, like for instance Gordon and Washington in their essay on rape as a military metaphor,[35] I want to expose, thus in effect censure, any representation of violence against negatively-depicted female images—even in the HB—as propaganda and pornography. The insistence, in the Bible and in its interpretations, that a community is censured in the metaphoric image rather than womanhood is not sufficient. That insistence does not obliterate the image and its damaging effects for readers of both genders, even today.

Afterword: is there anything to be gained from reading such texts?

One way of dealing with pornoprophetic texts is to expose and then reject them. This has certainly been the way I have chosen for myself. Quite frankly, I would have loved such pornoprophetic texts to disappear from the book practising Jews and Christians read as one of their inspirational canons. My preoccupation with these texts is a testimony to my deep-rooted conviction that they, as cultural and religious artifacts, still influence my own life as a Jewish, Israeli woman.

Other readers, although willing to employ a hermeneutic of suspicion to the point of exposition and exposure, might not be so willing to reject these texts. Troubled as they may become, they might wish to find an exegetical solution that may be theologically acceptable while neutralizing the texts' harmful effects for gender relations.

---

[35] Gordon and Washington, 'Rape as a Military Metaphor'.

Traditional [male] unproblematizing efforts are well known, and can be found in mainstream commentaries. Other efforts have taken new directions, some of which shall be outlined below.[36]

- Identification with the male-position-in/of-the-text does not necessarily imply acceptance of this position; insights into the male psyche from an M perspective can be critical if and when it is sympathetic. Such insights may be formulated as complements to modern feminist approaches. For instance, this has been the approach chosen by Goldingay regarding Hos. 2.[37]
- Violence, such as the violence contained in the husband/wife metaphoric image, is self-destructive and self-deconstructive. This lesson is as important for assessing biblical theology as it is for assessing biblical sociology—in this case, gender relations. This has been formulated by Landy, again from an M perspective conscious of feminist criticism on Hosea 2.[38]
- Compensatory strategies can and have been applied. Some Bible critics choose to regard such negative, one-sided M texts as lacking and to fill in the gap, thus, paradoxically, turning them into a source of liberation theology for the oppressed and their signifier (woman). Pornoprophetic texts reflect, among other things, human desire. Supplementing those texts with additions on female desire, by way of modern midrash or discussion of other biblical analogies, or insisting on a fuller symbolic, bi-gender epistemology (ידיעה) of human sexuality and love of the divine, can serve to sublimate the pornoprophetic message. So can a viewing of Yhwh as possessing female as well as male attributes.
- Such texts are time-, place- and culture bound. I have chosen to assess the texts' afterlife, so to speak, their timeless influence. However, it is possible to link the texts' message back to their imagined original, 'historical' setting. In this way, their message for modern gender relations can be separated from their

---

[36] I delivered part of this Chapter at a Faculty seminar of the Faculty of Theology at the University of Amsterdam in April, 1995. The 'what to do, where to go from here' approach was discussed at the meeting with great interest. I thank the Faculty members present for their illuminating remarks.

[37] J. Goldingay, 'Hosea 1–3, Genesis 1–4 and Masculist Interpretation', in Brenner (ed.), *A Feminist Companion to the Latter Prophets*, pp. 191–8.

[38] F. Landy, 'Fantasy and the Displacement of Pleasure: Hosea 2.4–17', in Brenner (ed.), *A Feminist Companion to the Latter Prophets*, pp. 146–60.

message about god since, primarily, they are about a society
not just women, much less so about modern women.
- The husband/wife metaphor can be viewed as an economic
  metaphor about land, people and god, rather than about gender
  relations. This path was taken, e.g., by Alice Keefe in a recent
  article.[39]
- Judgment can be deferred until more work is done on sexuality
  and desire in the HB, so as to understand whether the pornoprophetic texts should indeed be exegeted rather than eisegeted
  as pornography.
- Another strategy is to insist, once again, that the husband/
  wife metaphor is primarily directed at a community of *men*,
  since men are the privileged group within the community
  constructed in/by the text, and since women are only indirectly
  implicated: after all, the passages are about the politics of
  religion, not *directly* about the politics of gender relations.[40]

As indicated above, I do not share in the hope or assessment that
biblical texts like the pornoprophetic passages are redeemable for
readers like me. On the balance, I fail to see how the texts' unsavoury
properties can be neutralized and separated from their religious
message. But then, I too am a conditioned and subjective reader—
exactly like those readers who operate on other premises and who
do wish to continue using such disturbing texts as instruction within
their religions and cultural traditions.

---

[39] A. Keefe, 'The Female Body, the Body Politic and the Land: A Sociopolitical
Reading of Hosea 1–2', in Brenner (ed.), *A Feminist Companion to the Latter Prophets*,
pp. 70–100.
[40] For the last two suggestions cf. Carroll, 'Desire under the Terebinths'.

CHAPTER EIGHT

THE GENDERED BODY, 'SEXUALITY' AND KNOWLEDGE: THEOLOGIES AND SOCIAL IDEOLOGIES

As Eilberg-Schwartz[1] and Boyarin[2] point out, there is hardly a demarcation line in the HB between 'body' and what, for lack of a more appropriate English term, can be called 'soul' or 'spirit' or 'mind' or (Heb. רוח, נשמה or נפש; in psychological terms, unobservable and unquantifiable psychic phenomena). Matter (body, flesh) and non-matter, in the HB as in early Judaisms, cannot be differentiated into autonomous beings like they are in external biblical sources and already from early Pauline Christianity onwards. Man is created of the earth and the נשמה ('soul'?) that Yhwh Elohim gives him (Gen. 2.7); life, for animals as well as humans, is having a נפש (non-matter attributes) as well as a corporeal existence (Gen. 1.20, onwards; 2.7). Graeco-Roman influences ultimately were assimilated into Jewish mainstream views. This is already evidenced by the statement and question in Qoheleth 3.20–21—be the question a rhetorical, polemical, an ironic or a straightforward question: 'Everything goes to the same place: everything is of earth and everything goes back to earth. Who knows concerning the human spirit (רוח) whether it goes upwards [to heaven] and the [domestic] animal spirit, whether it goes down to earth'. However, and for most of the HB, the corporeal is bound up with the non-corporeal.

This basic view of a harmonious unity, of a differentiated yet unified being, is certainly problematic theologically. In what ways is humankind differentiated from yet similar to the god that created it (Gen. 1)? Furthermore, what is the meaning of this differentiation-in-unity for human sexual difference and gendered existence, as well as for human gendered relations with its male-gendered god? How can binary differences be reconciled in any religious or social system that constructs such differences as divinely ordained and meant to last (Gen. 1) yet, at one and the same time, as *reconciled* differences

---

[1] H. Eilberg-Schwartz, 'The People of the Body'.
[2] D. Boyarin, *Carnal Israel*, Ch. 1 (pp. 31–60).

(Gen. 2)? For instance, how should god's body be conceptualized, if pure non-matter is absent from everything, thus also from the divine image? does Yhwh require a [female, erotic] mate, as supplied by early as well as later sources?[3] Does unity through difference (bodily and otherwise) imply equality, for instance between the two human sexes/genders? And what about the tensions between opposites like 'good and evil', not to mention spiritual as against carnal love, nature against culture, intellect against the emotion? Platonic influence and Hellenistic thought imply a dualism that is problematic by its privileging the soul/spirit/intellect over the flesh and by defining them as closer to the divine; this is problematic, for in such systems the material is erased, gender and body and sexuality suffer a loss of prestige, reproduction and social continuity as well as social boundaries are damaged or removed. But a non-dual 'harmonious' system which strives to minimize the significance of matter/non-matter and other differences while upholding them 'in unity' is not without its problems too. The discourse of the acknowledged 'other' is not properly heard because it is claimed as 'similar', hence cannot function as a proper mirror of the self. Difference is oppressed, to the cost of oppressed and oppressor. Solutions are introduced, but the basic tensions remain. In 'life', after all, difference—of looks, origins, emotional makeup, age, education, opportunity, status, behaviour, class, gender, sex, circumstances and so on—cannot be ignored. Unified if tense harmony of differences and oppositions is certainly not the way of the world; neither is an insistence on matter/spirit duality, for that matter.

The implications of the separated-yet-fated-to-remain-suspended-in-unity worldview, so dominant in the HB, for gender relations in general and for the references to gendered desire and sexuality obtainable in it in particular, are many and profound. Ontological and genealogical similarity is not enough. On the contrary: similarity threatens boundaries. Therefore, and in order to maintain order, a hierarchy is necessary. To begin with, male and female biological bodily differences and functions are indeed conceptualized as complementary. However, socially and ideologically their 'oneness' and 'unity' are interpreted as the superordination of males over females—as shown by the ending of the hyperbole of the primeval garden. Marriage is

---

[3] Divine consorts like the Shekinah and the Shabbat fulfill an erotic role, thus complementing the godhead. A case in point is the Zohar, in which the divine/ human reflected image theology is anchored in reciprocal male/female and divine erotic and sexual behaviour.

a joining of the separate-yet-unified elements; and yet, order is achieved by establishing a pecking order. Emotion, mind, spirit are recognized. And yet, the yardstick of biological [sexual] difference is simultaneously used for defining gender difference *and* for establishing a unity that has nothing to do with social equality. For the opposite components to hold together, nothing but a rigid framework will do.

Thus, paradoxes are inescapable. For example, since only males have a penis and consequently a phallus, only males can demonstrate their affinity with the divine as marked in their 'flesh'; only males are the true, direct participants in the Covenant. It is possible to evade this assertion by various means, such as a reference to Gen. 1.27 ('male and female he created them', in his own image and likeness); or by insisting that the language of the Law, although typically addressed to males, is inclusive for females also; or by the understanding of Yhwh as bodiless and sexless, hence the 'likeness' of both sexes and both genders. And yet, the 'prophetic' root metaphor of the divine husband/errant wife makes it amply clear that, theologically and sociologically, males and females—as evidenced by their different bodies—are not equal in Yhwh, the way they are not equal in any other level of social existence. The males of the community, not the women, are addressed with the requirement to 'love' their god. And the love and fear of god are the beginning of knowledge (Prov. 1.7).

The apparent unity, the epistemological base for religio-social organization in the HB, across times and places and of course with variations and exceptions but nevertheless with monotonous structural regularity, can only be kept because female sexuality is eradicated. This is a sweeping generalization that, once again, should be substantiated.

I agree with Daniel Boyarin who, following Foucault and others, argues that the HB—and, for that matter, much of later Jewish culture and other cultures in early and later antiquity—belongs to the age before *sexuality* as modern readers conceive of it. Sexuality in the *ancient* world is subsumed under other, more important social requirements like survival, procreation, internal and external boundaries. Modern categories of sexual behaviours such as 'homosexuality', 'adultery', 'prostitution' or 'rape' do not correspond to ancient categories. Love and desire are differently constructed. The visual as well as the carnal body is differently constructed. In all these senses, for us the HB reflects pre-sexuality times.

And yet, in another sense, depictions of males and maleness in the HB do contain more than a kernel of male sexuality/masculinity, although that kernel might be different from ours. In fact, whereas a female is just that (Heb. נקבה), a biological orifice, a male can be or become a man. Males are constructed largely as penetrators, insertive, initiators, active sexual agents; women are constructed largely as penetrated, receptors, passive sexual objects (an active seductress is condemned unless in the service of procreation). Whereas female sexuality is either ignored altogether or presented as negative and uncontrolled, male sexuality is presented as potentially normative or neutral. Males are expected to become responsible sexual agents; women are expected to become irresponsible sexual agents who require supervision by seclusion. Men 'know' women: women might get to the stage when they 'know a man' in some texts (Num. 31.17, 18, 35; Judg. 11.39) but most of them do not. Love and desire are better experienced by men than by women, with the exclusion of the Song of Songs. Sexual pleasure is the prerogative of males: a man can take a wife if he likes her (like Samson), or divorce her if he does not enjoy her any more. Self-restraint, a chief component of masculinity in rabbinic culture according to Satlow,[4] is expected of males but hardly of females in biblical literature too. In short, HB males are depicted as having at least a modicum of independent, autonomous potential for socio-sexual behaviours motivated by desire. HB females are reduced for the most part to biological, procreativity oriented sexual behaviour—if they want their behaviour to be approved of, and unless they inhabit the magical poetic garden of love (in the SoS). Women, then, are much more pre-sexual than men in the HB.

This is not to say that female sexual desire is not recognized as potential or motivational. It is. But, over and apart for the SoS, female desire is presented as natural and instinctual rather than the product of cultural knowledge. Male desire is often, especially in the 'prophetic' metaphor, presented as complying with social sanctions. Sexual knowledge is translated into social control.

Can a HB woman *enjoy* sexual intercourse? I expect so. Is there any explicit reference to it outside the SoS? Only when she is after illicit sex and in the improper place of the initiator (Gen. 39, Prov. 7). A woman who loves well, like Michal, would come to a sorry end—

---

[4] M. Satlow, "'Try to Be A Man'".

again, outside the SoS. Does a HB woman have sexual freedom, in the sense of choosing a partner freely and/or having a number of [male] partners simultaneously, of having a variety of erotic experiences without being censured for it? Never, not even in the SoS. Granted, sexual promiscuity is not recommended for males either;[5] but neither is it punishable in their case if it does not entail damaging another man's (a father or husband) female goods. Is there sexual autonomy for the female hero/es of the SoS? No, as the references to the 'brothers' and 'keepers of the gates' testify.

Some readers have read and will undoubtedly read some biblical passages as more helpful for constructing modern female sexuality than I have. Such readers will find consolation in the creation or garden stories of Genesis, or in the positive aspects of womanhood informing much of the SoS. I fail to see the point. In spite of the beauty of this collection of love lyrics, perhaps because of the beauty, its message of [limited] female sexuality (of a certain age) is not sufficient to counterbalance the dominant views: there is no female sexuality in the HB for women of any class apart from whores, although there is female sexual desire and diminished capacity to love. By comparison, the admittedly limited sexual autonomy or agency accorded to free adult males looks like a huge privilege. If sexuality is a requisite for constructing gender, then the one truly normative gender in the HB is the M gender.

Once more, a good clue to attitudes concerning human sexual desire and its gendering can be gleaned from the garden narrative (Gen. 2–3)—not because it is the *only* or even the most important formulation of gender relations in the HB, but because it seems to be symptomatic of them. It is perhaps no accident that the story is located almost at the beginning of the Bible's very first book. To posit a narratively veiled explanation of gendered relations and desire, as connected to knowledge, 'at the start' among explanations of other crucial experiences of humanity (relationship to the divine, obtaining food and work, life and death) is perhaps a matter of deliberate choice on the part of editors at least, if not of the original author[s]. And

---

[5] Gruber's reading of Hos. 4.12. Gruber, after Ginsberg, interpret the 'stick' and 'rod' mentioned as directing Israelite males' behaviour as their phalluses and penises (Gruber, 'The Hebrew *Qĕdēšāh*', p. 20, with additional references to negative views of male fornication in prophetic literature, and additional bibliography.

so is the choice to present humans as controllers and procreators (Gen. 1) *before* the nature of their coupled relationship narratively, symbolically and socially defined. How is it possible, then, that Eve initiated the eating from the fruit of the 'tree of knowledge, good and bad' and gave her man some, while the outcome points to *her* desire for and subjugation to him and his sexual penetration (knowledge) of her? The narrated outcome reflects a certain social order, ambivalence towards women, fear of the unbridled female, endorsement of male dominance. These are some of the attempts to solve the apparent enigma: knowledge is 'good'; how, then, does disobedience to god's command not to eat from the tree correspond to the asymmetrical gendered outcome? A possible answer is that this text (and others) is informed by a subtext that affirms female *superiority* of discernment and, therefore, of sexual power. It is precisely because of female power that the female, a source of all life, has to be controlled. Not because 'she' is inferior goods but because she is better. Males stand no chance of making their social mark if females are in the lead: they would remain passive followers, like the husband who meekly accepts the fruit from his woman (Gen. 3.5). A deep-rooted male adoration of the female principle can be counterbalanced only by its transference into something else. The way to deal with a subject of desire is to make it into a contained object of desire, to deconstruct it by various strategies. This is what biblical literature does: it contains females in a way that it does not contain males. In that sense, there is no misogyny in the garden narrative, perhaps not in most or the whole of the HB. Psychologically, to distinguish from the social manifestations of psychological states, women are so well loved and so little understood in biblical literature that the only way left to deal with their otherness is to displace the fear and frustration into their opposites: an ideology whereby, as a group, males possess social, intellectual, religious, psychological, intellectual, ethical supremacy as a matter of natural destiny.

Against this background, to dwell upon the supposedly 'liberating' properties of the SoS or the early Genesis texts would be, in my view and in Marsha Hewitt's words after Marcuse and Hokheimer, rather risky. To be exposed to 'the dangers within emancipatory theories' may end in these theories devolving 'into their opposite when their focus is displaced from the concrete realities and operations of domination'.[6] David Clines' suggestion to forego biblical authority is

---

[6] M.A. Hewitt, 'Cyborgs, drag queens, and goddesses', p. 152.

much more to the point. Despite the sexism and despite everything, the Bible continues to influence the world. This does not mean that we ought to either ignore or to apologize for values that would not suit our current needs.[7]

Throughout this book, I have tried to avoid logical leaps that identify textual analyses and the ideologies they might contain with the extratextual phenomena that literature mediates or 'reflects'. It is certainly and logically conceivable that, in 'real' life, desire was gendered differently than in the ways it is presented in various types and shades in various genres of biblical texts. It is helpful to note, in this regard, the recent warnings of many scholars that the world of the rabbis does not necessarily represent well the worlds of antique Judaisms. Similarly, we are still far from a comprehensive knowledge of the world recorded by the authors of the HB—sociologically, historically, religiously and in any other way. Texts, artifacts and methodologies of interpretation are what we have to go by, while personal temperaments and circumstances shape our scholarly judgments. Irrespective of how desire and 'sexuality' were gendered in the world of the 'ancient Israels' that bequeathed the HB to us, the views contained in the HB texts remain influential. One way of defusing or offsetting this influence when it does not suit us is to discover and to uncover the texts. In that sense like in others, the task of feminist Bible scholarship is far from done.

---

[7] D.J.A. Clines, 'What Does Eve Do to Help', in Clines, *What Does Eve Do to Help and Other Readerly Questions to the Old Testament* JSOTSup 94; Sheffield: Sheffield Academic Press, 1990), p. 48.

BIBLIOGRAPHY

Abusch, T., 'The Demonic Image of the Witch in Standard Babylonian Literature: The Reworking of Popular Conceptions by Learned Exorcists', in J. Neusner *et al.* (eds.), *Religion, Science, and Magic: In Concert and in Conflict* (New York: Oxford University Press), pp. 27–58.

Alter, R., *The Art of Biblical Narrative* (New York: Basic Books, 1981).

Amit, Y., *The Book of Judges: The Art of Editing* (Heb.; Jerusalem: Bialik, 1992).

Annas, J., 'Women and the Quality of Life: Two Norms or One?', in M. Nussbaum and A. Sen (eds.), *The Quality of Life* (Oxford: Clarendon Press, 1993), pp. 279–96.

Arens, W., *The Original Sin: Incest and Its Meaning* (New York and Oxford: Oxford University Press, 1986).

Arensburg, B., 'The Skeletal Remains', *'Atiqot* 12 (1977; English series), pp. 81–83.

Bach, A., 'Mirror, Mirror in the Text: Reflections on Reading and Rereading', in A. Brenner (ed.), *A Feminist Companion to Esther, Judith and Susanna* (Sheffield: Sheffield Academic Press, 1995), pp. 81–6.

Bal, M., *Death and Dissymmetry in the Book of Judges* (Bloomington: Indiana University Press, 1988).

——, 'Head Hunting: "Judith" on the Cutting Edge', *JSOT* 63 (1994), pp. 3–34. Reprinted in Brenner (ed.), *A Feminist Companion to Esther, Judith and Susanna*, pp. 253–85.

——, *Lethal Love* (Indianapolis: University of Indiana Press, 1987).

Bar-Efrat, S., *The Art of Narrative in the Hebrew Bible* (trans. from Hebrew; Sheffield: *JSOT* Press, 1992).

Barstow, A.L., *Witchcraze: A New History of the European Witch Hunt* (San Francisco: Harper/Pandora, 1994).

——, 'Women as Healers, Women as Witches', *Old Westbury Review* 2 (1986), pp. 121–33.

Bechtel, L.M., 'Genesis 2.4b–3.24: A Myth of Human Maturation', *JSOT* 67 (1995), pp. 3–26.

——, 'Shame as a Sanction of Social Control in Biblical Israel: Juridical, Political and Social Shaming', *JSOT* 49 (1991), pp. 47–76.

——, 'What if Dinah Is Not Raped', *JSOT* 62 (1994), pp. 19–36.

Becking, B., P.W. van der Horst and K. van der Toorn, *Dictionary of Deities and Demons* (Leiden: Brill, 1995).

Be'er, I., 'Blood Discharge: On Female Im/purity in the Priestly Code and Biblical Narrative', in A. Brenner (ed.), *A Feminist Companion to Exodus—Deuteronomy* (Sheffield: Sheffield Academic Press, 1994), pp. 155–68.

Bendor, S., *The Bet 'Ab in Israel from the Settlement to the End of the Monarchy: The Social Structure of Ancient Israel* (Heb.; Tel Aviv: Afik and Sifriat Po'alim, 1986).

Benedek, T.B., 'The Changing Relationship Between Midwives and Physicians During the Renaissance', *Bulletin of the History of Medicine* 51 (1977), pp. 550–64.

Benjamin, J., *The Bonds of Love* (New York: Pantheon, 1988).

Biale, D., *Eros and the Jews* (New York: 1992; also in Heb. translation).

Bigger, S., 'The Family Laws of Leviticus 18 in Their Settings', *JBL* 98 (1979), pp. 187–203.

Biggs, R.B., 'Medical Surgery', in J. Sasson (ed.), *Civilizations of the Ancient Near East* (New York: Charles Scribner's Sons, 1995), vol. 3, pp. 1911–24.

Bird, P., 'The Harlot as Heroine: Narrative Art and Social Presupposition in Three Old Testament Texts', *Semeia* 46 (1989), pp. 119–39.

——, '"To Play the Harlot": An Inquiry into an Old Testament Metaphor', in P.L. Day (ed.), *Gender and Difference in Ancient Israel* (Minneapolis: Fortress, 1989), pp. 75–94.

Black, J. and Green, A., *Gods, Demons and Symbols of Ancient Mesopotamia: An Illustrated Dictionary* (Austin, TX: University of Texas, 1992).

Bloch-Smith, E., *Judahite Burial Practices and Beliefs about the Dead* (JSOTSup, 123; Sheffield: Sheffield Academic Press, 1992).

Blumenfeld-Kosinski, R., *Not of Woman Born: Representation of Caesarian Birth in Medieval and Renaissance Culture* (Ithaca, NY: Cornell University Press, 1989).

Bovenschen, S., 'The Contemporary Witch, the Historical Witch and the Witch Myth:', in B, P. Levack (ed.), *Articles on Witchcraft, Magic and Demonology* (New York: Garland Publishing, 1992), vol. 10, pp. 83–119.

Boyarin, D., *Carnal Israel: Reading Sex in Talmudic Culture* (Berkeley: University of California Press, 1993).

——, *A Radical Jew: Paul and the Politics of Identity* (Berkeley: University of California Press, 1994).

——, 'Are There Any Jews in "The History of Sexuality"?', *Journal of the History of Sexuality* 5.3 (1995), pp. 333–55.

Braidotti, R., 'What's Wrong with Gender', in F. van Dijk-Hemmes and A. Brenner (eds.), *Reflections on Theology and Gender* (Kampen: Kok, 1994), pp. 41–79.

Brener, T. (ed.), *Feminism and Psychoanalysis* (London: Routledge, 1989).

Brenner, A., 'Aromatics and Perfumes in the SoS', *JSOT* 25 (1983), pp. 71–85.

——, *Colour Terms in the Old Testament* (Sheffield: *JSOT* Press, 1982).

——, '"Come Back, Come Back the Shulammite"', in Y.T. Radday and A. Brenner (eds.), *On Humour and the Comic in the Hebrew Bible* (Sheffield: *JSOT*/Almond Press, 1990), pp. 251–76.

——, 'Female Social Behaviour within the "Birth of the Hero" Paradigm', in A. Brenner (ed.), *A Feminist Companion to Genesis* (Sheffield: Sheffield Academic Press, 1993), pp. 204–21.

——, 'On the Semantic Field of Humour, Laughter and the Comic in the Hebrew Bible', in Y.T. Radday and A. Brenner (eds.), *On Humour and the Comic in the Hebrew Bible* (Sheffield: *JSOT* and Almond Press, 1990), pp. 39–58.

——, 'On Incest', in A. Brenner (ed.), *A Feminist Companion to Exodus to Deuteronomy* (Sheffield: Sheffield Academic Press, 1994), pp. 113–38.

——, 'On "Jeremiah" and the Poetics of (Prophetic?) Pornography', in *On Gendering Texts: Female and Male Voices in the Hebrew Bible* (Leiden: Brill, 1993), pp. 177–93.

——, 'Who's Afraid of Feminist Criticism? Who's Afraid of Biblical Humour? The Case of the Obtuse Foreign Ruler in the Hebrew Bible', *JSOT* 63 (1994), pp. 38–55.

Brenner, A. and van Dijk-Hemmes, F., *On Gendering Texts: Female and Male Voices in the Hebrew Bible* (Leiden: Brill, 1993).

Brown, J.A., *Techniques of Persuasion* (New York: Penguin, 1963).

Burgouts, J.F., 'Witchcraft, Magic and Divination in Ancient Egypt', in J. Sasson (ed.), *Civilizations of the Ancient Near East* (New York: Charles Scribner's Sons, 1995), vol. 3, pp. 1775–86.

Burstein, S.R., 'Demonology and Medicine in the 16th and 17th Centuries', *Folklore* (1955), pp. 16–33.

Butler, J., *Gender Trouble and the Subversion of Identity* (New York: Routledge, 1990).

Carroll, R.P., 'Desire under the Terebinths: On Pornographic Representations in the Prophets—A Response', in Brenner (ed.), *A Feminist Companion to the Latter Prophets*, (Sheffield: Sheffield Academic Press, 1995), pp. 275–307.

——, 'Whorusalamin: A Tale of Three Cities as Three Sisters', in B. Becking and M. Dijkstra (eds.), *On Reading Prophetic Texts: Gender-Specific and Related Studies in Memory of Fokkelien van Dijk-Hemmes* (Leiden: Brill, 1996), pp. 67–82.

Cassuto, M.D., *A Commentary on the Book of Genesis* (Heb.; Jerusalem: Magnes, 1987).
Childs, B.S., *The Book of Exodus: A critical Theological Commentary* (OTL; Philadelphia: Westminster Press, 1974).
Chodorow, N., *Feminism and Psychoanalytic Theory* (Cambridge, MA: Polity Press, 1989).
Clines, D.J.A. (ed.), *Dictionary of Classical Hebrew* (Sheffield: Sheffield Academic Press, 1993, 1996), vols. 1 and 2, letters *aleph* to *waw*.
——, 'What Does Eve Do to Help', in Clines, *What Does Eve Do to Help and Other Readerly Questions to the Old Testament* (JSOTSup, 94; Sheffield: Sheffield Academic Press, 1990), pp. 25–48.
Cohen, S.J.D. (ed.), *The Jewish Family in Antiquity* (Atlanta: Scholars Press, 1993).

Dan, J. (ed.), *Sefer Ha-Yashar* (Heb.; Jerusalem: Bialik Institute, 1986).
Davies, P.R., *In Search of 'Ancient Israel'* (Sheffield: *JSOT* Press, 1992).
——, *The Damascus Covenant: An Interpretation of the 'Damascus Document'* (JSOTSup, 25; Sheffield: *JSOT* Press, 1983).
Demand, N., *Birth, Death and Motherhood in Classical Greece* (Baltimore and London: Johns Hopkins University Press, 1994).
Devereux, G., *A Study of Abortion in Primitive Societies* (New York: International Universities Press, 1955).
van Dijk-Hemmes, F., 'The Imagination of Power and the Power of Imagination: An Intertextual Analysis of Two Biblical Love Songs—The Song of Songs and Hosea 2', *JSOT* 44 (1989), pp. 75–88; repr. in A. Brenner (ed.), *A Feminist Companion to the Song of Songs* (Sheffield: *JSOT* Press, 1993), pp. 156–70.
——, 'The Metaphorization of Woman in Prophetic Speech: An Analysis of Ezekiel 23', in A. Brenner and F. van Dijk-Hemmes, *On Gendering Texts: Female and Male Voices in the Hebrew Bible* (Leiden: Brill, 1993), pp. 167–76.
——, 'Sarai's Exile', in A. Brenner (ed.), *A Feminist Companion to Genesis* (Sheffield: Sheffield Academic Press, 1993), pp. 222–34.
——, *Sporen van vrouwenteksten in de Hebreeuwse bijbel* (Utrecht: Faculteit der Godsgeleerdheid, 1992).
——, 'Tamar and the Limits of Patriarchy: Between Rape and Seduction', in M. Bal (ed.), *Anti-Covenant: Counter-Reading Women's Lives in the Hebrew Bible* (Bible and Literature, 22; Sheffield: Almond Press, 1989), pp. 135–56.
Dixon, S., *The Roman Mother* (London and New York: Routledge, 1988).
Donegan, J.B., *Women and Men Midwives: Medicine, Morality and Misogyny in Early America* (Westport, CT: Greenwood Press, 1978).
Douglas, M., *Purity and Danger* (London: Routledge & Kegan Paul, 1966).
——, *Implicit Meanings* (London and Boston: Routledge & Kegan Paul, 1975).
Durber, S., 'The Female Reader of the Parables of the Lost', in G.J. Brooke (ed.), *Women in the Biblical Tradition* (Studies in Women and Religion, 31; Lewiston/Queenston/Lampeter: Edwin Mellen Press, 1992), pp. 187–207.
Dworkin, A., 'For Men, Freedom of Speech; for Women, Silence Please', in Lederer (ed.), *Take back the Night: Women on Pornography* (New York: Morrow, 1980), pp. 256–58.
——, *Pornography: Men Possessing Women* (New York: Putnam, 1981).
——, 'Why so-called Radical Men Love and Need Pornography', in Lederer (ed.), *Take back the Night*, pp. 148–54.

Eilberg-Schwartz, H., 'The Problem of the Body for the People of the Body', in H. Eilberg-Schwartz (ed.), *People of the Body: Jews and Judaism from an Embodied Perspective* (New York: University of New York at Stony Brook, 1992), pp. 17–46.
——, *The Savage in Judaism* (Bloomington: University of Indiana Press, 1990).
Eliade, M., *The Sacred and the Profane: The Nature of Religion* (New York: Harper, 1961).

Farber, W., 'Witchcraft, Magic and Divination in Ancient Mesopotamia', in Sasson (ed.), *Civilizations of the Ancient Near East*, vol. 3, pp. 1895–1910.

Feldman, D.M., *Birth Control in Jewish Law* (New York: New York University Press, 1968).

Fewell, D.N. and D.M. Gunn, *Gender, Power & Promise: The Subject of the Bible's First Story* (Nashville: Abingdon Press, 1993).

Finkel, D.J., '2. Human Skeletal Remains', in J.D. Seger and H.D. Hance (eds.), *Gezer V* (Jerusalem: , 1988), pp. 129–45.

Fischer, I., '"... und sie war unfruchtbar": Zur Stellung kinderloser Frauen in der Literatur Alt-Israels', in G. Pauritsch *et al.* (eds.), *Kinder Machen: Strategien der Kontrolle weiblicher Fruchtbarkeit* (Wien: Wiener Frauenverlag, 1988), pp. 116–26.

Fitzmyer, J.A. (ed.), *The Genesis Apocryphon* (Rome: Biblical Institute Press, 1971).

Fontaine, C.R., 'Disabilities and Illness in the Bible: A Feminist Perspective', in A. Brenner (ed.), *A Feminist Companion to the Hebrew Bible in the New Testament* (Sheffield: Sheffield Academic Press, 1996), pp. 286–300.

——, 'Hosea' and 'A Response to Hosea', in A. Brenner (ed.), *A Feminist Companion to the Latter Prophets* (Sheffield: Sheffield Academic Press, 1995), pp. 40–69.

——, 'The Social Role of Women in the World of Wisdom' in A. Brenner (ed.), *A Feminist Companion to Wisdom Literature* (Sheffield: Sheffield Academic Press, 1995), pp. 41–5.

Forbes, T.R., *The Midwife and the Witch* (New Haven and London: Yale University Press, 1966).

Fox, M.V., *The Song of Songs and Ancient Egyptian Love Songs* (Madison: University of Wisconsin, 1985).

Frantz-Szabo, G., 'Hittite Witchcraft, Magic, and Divination', in J. Sasson (ed.), *Civilizations of the Ancient Near East* (New York: Charles Scribner's Sons, 1995), vol. 3, pp. 2007–20.

Freud, S., *Moses and Monotheism* (trans. K. Jones; New York: Random House, 1955).

Frymer-Kensky, T., 'Law and Philosophy: The Case of Sex in the Bible', *Semeia* 49 (1989), pp. 92–3.

——, 'The Strange Case of the Suspected Sotah (Numbers v 11–31)', *VT* 34 (1984), pp. 11–26.

Gilligan, C., *In a Different Voice* (Cambridge, MA: Harvard University Press, 1982).

Girard, R., *Things Hidden since the Foundation of the World* (Stanford: Stanford University Press, 1987).

——, *To Double Business Bound* (Baltimore: Johns Hopkins University Press, 1978).

——, *Violence and the Sacred* (Baltimore: Johns Hopkins University Press, 1977).

Glancy, J., 'The Accused: Susanna and her Readers', *JSOT* 58 (1993), pp. 103–16. Reprinted in Brenner (ed.), *A Feminist Companion to Esther, Judith and Susanna*, pp. 288–302.

Goldingay, J., 'Hosea 1–3, Genesis 1–4 and Masculist Interpretation', in Brenner (ed.), *A Feminist Companion to the Latter Prophets* (Sheffield: Sheffield Academic Press, 1995), pp. 191–68.

Gordon, P. and Washington, H.C., 'Rape as a Military Metaphor in the Hebrew Bible', in Brenner (ed.), *A Feminist Companion to the Latter Prophets* (Sheffield: Sheffield Academic Press, 1995), pp. 308–325.

Green, M., 'Women's Medical Practice and Health Care in Medieval Europe', *Signs* 14.2 (1989), pp. 434–73.

Griffin, S., *Pornography and Silence: Culture's Revenge Against Nature* (New York: Harper & Row, 1980).

Gruber, M., 'The Hebrew qĕdēšāh and Her Canaanite and Akkadian Cognates', in M. Gruber, *The Motherhood of God and Other Studies* (Atlanta: Scholars Press, 1992), pp. 17–47.

——, 'The Motherhood of God in Second Isaiah', in *The Motherhood of God and Other Studies*, pp. 3–15.

——, 'The *qādēš* in the Book of Kings and in Other Sources', *Tarbitz* 52 (1983), pp. 167–76 (Heb.).

Gubar, S. and Hoff, J. (eds.), *For Adult Eyes Only: The Dilemma of Violent Pornography* (Bloomington: Indiana University Press, 1989).

Gunkel, H., *Genesis* (Göttingen: Vanderhoeck & Ruprecht, 1918).

Haas, N., 'Anthropological Observations on the Skeletal Remains from Giv'at ha-Mivtar', *Israel Exploration Journal* 20 (1970), pp. 38–59.

——, 'Human Skeletal Remains in Two Burial Caves', *Israel Exploration Journal* 13 (1963), pp. 93–96.

Hachlili, R. and Smith, P., 'The Genealogy of the Goliath Family', *BASOR* 235 (1979), pp. 67–70.

Haraway, D., 'Situated Knowledges: The Science Question in Feminism and the Privilege of Partial Perspective', *Feminist Studies* 14.3 (1988), pp. 575–99.

——, *Simians, Cyborgs and Women: The Reinvention of Nature* (New York: Routledge, 1991).

Hewitt, M.A., 'Cyborgs, Drag Queens, and Goddesses: Emancipatory-Regressive Paths in Feminist Theory', *Method and Theory in the Study of Religion* 5.2 (1993), pp. 135–54.

Horney, K., *Feminine Psychology* (ed. by K. Helman; New York: Norton, 1967).

van der Horst, P.W., *Ancient Jewish Epitaphs* (Kampen: Pharos, 1991). 'Sarah's Seminal Emission: Hebrews 11.11 in the Light of Ancient embryology', in van der Horst, *Hellenism-Judaism-Christianity: Essays on their Interaction* (Kampen: Kok-Pharos, 1994), pp. 203–23.

Hrdlicka, A., 'Skeletal Remains', in P.L.O. Guy and R.M. Engberg (eds.), *The Megiddo Tombs* (Oriental Institute Publications, 33; Chicago: University of Chicago, 1938), pp. 192–95.

Imbens, A. and Jonker, I., *Christianity and Incest* (Turnbridge Wells: Burns & Oats, 1992).

Irving, J., *The Hotel New Hampshire* (New York: Pocket Books, 1981, 1982).

Itzin, C. (ed.), *Pornography: Women, Violence, and Civil Liberties* (Oxford: Oxford University Press, 1993).

Keefe, A., 'The Female Body, the Body Politic and the Land: A sociopolitical Reading of Hosea 1–2', in Brenner (ed.), *A Feminist Companion to the Latter Prophets* (Sheffield: Sheffield Academic Press, 1995), pp. 70–100.

Keil, C.F. and Delitzsch, F., *Commentary on the Old Testament: The Pentateuch* (Grand Rapids: Eerdmans, rep. 1980).

Klein, L.R., 'Honor and Shame in Esther', in A. Brenner (ed.), *A Feminist Companion to Esther, Judith and Susanna* (Sheffield: Sheffield Academic Press, 1995), pp. 149–75.

Klein, M., *The Selected Melanie Klein* (ed. by J. Mitchell; New York: Free Press, 1987).

Kraemer, R.S., 'Jewish Mothers and Daughters in the Greco-Roman World', In Cohen (ed.), *The Jewish Family in Antiquity*, pp. 89–xx.

Kunin, S.D., *The Logic of Incest: A Structuralist Analysis of Hebrew Mythology* (JSOTSup, 185; Sheffield: Sheffield Academic Press, 1995).

LaBelle, B., 'The Propaganda of Misogyny', in Lederer (ed.), *Take Back the Night* (New York: Morrow, 1980), pp. 174–78, 324.

Landy, F., 'Fantasy and the Displacement of Pleasure: Hosea 2.4–17', in Brenner (ed.), *A Feminist Companion to the Latter Prophets* (Sheffield: Sheffield Academic Press, 1995), pp. 146–160.

——, *Paradoxes of Paradise* (Bible and Literature, 7; Sheffield: Almond Press, 1983).
Leach, E., *Structural Interpretation of Biblical Myth* (Cambridge: Cambridge University Press, 1983).
Lederer, L. (ed.), *Take Back the Night: Women on Pornography* (New York: Morrow, 1980).
Lévi-Strauss, C., *The Elementary Structure of Kinship* (Boston: Beacon Press, 1965 = 1969).
——, *The View from Afar* (trans. from French; New York Basic Books, 1985).
Levine, A.-J., '"Hemmed in on Every Side": Jews and Women in the Book of Susanna', in F. Segovia and M.A. Tolbert (eds.), *Reading from This Place* (Philadelphia: Fortress, forthcoming). Reprinted in Brenner (ed.), *A Feminist Companion to Esther, Judith and Susanna*, pp. 303–23.
Lerner, G., *The Creation of Patriarchy* (Oxford: Oxford University Press, 1986).
Loraux, N., 'What Is a Goddess', in P. Schmitt Pantel (ed.), *A History of Women in the West: I. From Ancient Times to Christian Saints* (Cambridge, MA/London: Harvard University Press, pp. 11–44, 481–89.

Malamuth, N.M. and Donnerstein, E., *Pornography and Sexual Aggression* (Orlando: Academic Press, 1984).
Manniche, L., *Sexual Life in Ancient Egypt* (London and New York: KPI, 1987).
Meiselman, K.C., *Incest: A Psychological Study of Causes and Effects with Treatment Recommendations* (San Francisco: Jossey-Bass Publishers, 1978).
Meyers, C., *Discovering Eve: Ancient Israelite Women in Context* (New York: Oxford Press, 1989).
——, 'Gender Imagery in the Song of Songs', *HAR* 10 (1986), pp. 209–23. Repr. in A. Brenner (ed.), *A Feminist Companion to the Song of Songs* (Sheffield: Sheffield Academic Press, 1993), pp. 197–212.
——, 'Gender Roles and Genesis 3.16 Revisited', in A. Brenner (ed.), *A Feminist Companion to Genesis* (Sheffield: Sheffield Academic Press, 1993), pp. 118–41.
——, 'Returning Home: Ruth 1.8 and the Gendering of the Book of Ruth', in Brenner (ed.), *A Feminist Companion to the Book of Ruth* (Sheffield: Sheffield Academic Press, 1993), pp. 85–114.
——, 'To her Mother's House', in A. Brenner [ed.], *A Feminist Companion to Ruth* (Sheffield: *JSOT* Press, 1993), pp. 85–114.
Milgrom, J., 'tōʿba', *Enc. Biblica* (Heb.; Jerusalem: Bialik, 1965–88), vol. 8, pp. 466–68.
Milne, P.J., 'The Patriarchal Stamp of Scripture', in A. Brenner (ed.), *A Feminist Companion to Genesis* (Sheffield: Sheffield Academic Press, 1993), pp. 146–72.
Mulvey, L., 'Visual Pleasure and Narrative Cinema', *Screen* 16/3 (1975), pp. 6–18.
Murphy, R.E., *The Song of Songs* (Hermeneia; Minneapolis: SCM Press, 1990).
Musallam, B.F., *Sex and Society in Islam: Birth Control before the Nineteenth Century* (London: Cambridge University Press, 1983).

Niditch, S., 'The "Sodomite" Theme in Judges 19–20: Family, Community and Social Disintegration', *CBQ* 44 (1982), pp. 365–78.
——, 'The Wronged Woman Righted: An Analysis of Genesis 38', *HThR* 72 (1979), pp. 143–49.

Olyan, S., '"And with a Male You Shall Not Lie the Lying Down of a Woman": On the Meaning and Significance of Leviticus 18:22 and 20:13', *Journal of the History of Sexuality* 5.2 (1994), pp. 179–206.
——, 'Honor, Shame, and Covenant Relations in Ancient Israel and Its Environment', *JBL* 115.2 (1996), pp. 201–18.
O'Neill, O., 'Justice, Gender, and International Boundaries', in M. Nussbaum and A. Sen (eds.), *The Quality of Life* (Oxford: Clarendon Press, 1993), pp. 303–23.

Paglia, C., *Sexual Personae: Art and Decadence from Nefertiti to Emily Dickinson* (New York: Vintage Books, 1991).

Pardes, I., *Countertraditions in the Bible*: A Feminist Approach (Cambridge, MASS.: Harvard University Press).

Peskowitz, M., 'Family/ies in Antiquity: Evidence from Tannaitic Literature and Roman Galilean Architecture', in S.J.D. Cohen, *The Jewish Family in Antiquity* (Atlanta: Scholars Press, 1993), pp. 9–36.

Pinto, L.B., 'The Folk Practice of Gynecology and Obstetrics in the Middle Ages', *Bulletin of the History of Medicine 47* (1973).

Polzin, R., 'The Ancestress of Israel in Danger', *Semeia 3* (1975), pp. 81–98.

Pope, M.V., *The Song of Songs* (*AB*; Garden City, NY: Doubleday, 1977).

Porter, J.R., *Leviticus* (Cambridge: Cambridge University Press, 1976).

Pressler, C., 'Sexual Violence and Deuteronomic Law', in A. Brenner (ed.), *A Feminist Companion to Exodus to Deuteronomy* (Sheffield: Sheffield Academic Press, 1994), pp. 102–12.

——, *The View of Women Found in the Deuteronomic Family Laws* (BZAW, 216; Berlin/ New York: de Gruyter, 1993).

Pritchard, J.B. (ed.), *Ancient Near Eastern Texts Relating to the Old Testament* (Princeton, NJ: Princeton University Press).

von Rad, G., *Genesis* (OTL; rev. edn; Philadelphia: Westminster Press, 1972).

Rashkow, I.L., *The Phallacy of Genesis: A Feminist-Psychoanalytic Approach* (Literary Currents in Biblical Interpretation; Louisville, KY: Westminster/John Knox, 1993).

Reed, E., *Woman's Evolution: From Matriarchal Clan to Patriarchal Family* (New York: Pathfinder Press, 1975).

Reinhartz, A., 'Parents and Children: A Philonic Perspective', in Cohen (ed.), *The Jewish Family in Antiquity*, pp. 61–88.

Riddle, J.M., *Contraception and Abortion from the Ancient World to the Renaissance* (Cambridge, MASS/London: Harvard University Press, 1992).

Risdon, D.L., 'A Study of the Cranial and Other Human Remains from Palestine Excavated at Tell Duweir (Lachish) by the Wellcome-Marston Archaeological Research Expedition', *Biometrika 31* (1939), pp. 99–161.

Rofé, A., *Introduction to the Book of Deuteronomy* (Heb.; Jerusalem: Academon, 1988).

Rollin, S., 'Women and Witchcraft in Ancient Assyria', in A. Cameron and A. Kuhrt (eds.), *Images of Women in Antiquity* (London: Croom Helm, 1983), pp. 34–45.

Rose, E., *A Razor for a Goat: A Discussion of Certain Problems in the History of Witchcraft and Diabolism* (Toronto: University of Toronto Press, 1962).

Sarna, N., *Understanding Genesis* (New York: Schocken, 1970).

Sasson, J. (ed.), *Civilizations of the Ancient Near East* (New York: Charles Scribner's Sons, 1995), vol. 3.

Satlow, M., '"They Abused Him Like a Woman": Homoeroticism, Gender Blurring, and the Rabbis in Late Antiquity', *Journal of the History of Sexuality 5.1* (1994), pp. 1–25.

——, '"Try To Be A Man": The Rabbinic Construction of Masculinity', *HThR* 89.1 (1996), pp. 19–40.

——, '"Wasted Seed": The History of a Rabbinic Idea', *HUCA 65* (1994), pp. 137–75.

Scanlon, T., 'Value, Desire, and Quality of Life', in M. Nussbaum and A. Sen (eds.), *The Quality of Life*, pp. 185–200.

Schüngel-Straumann, H., 'God as Mother in Hosea 11', in Brenner (ed.), *A Feminist Companion to the Latter Prophets*, pp. 194–218.

Seger, J.D. and H.D. Hance (eds.), *Gezer V* (Jerusalem: Annual of the Nelson Glueck Institute, 1988).

Setel, D.T., 'Prophets and Pornography: Female Sexual Imagery in Hosea', in L.T. Russell (ed.), *Feminist Interpretations of the Bible* (Philadelphia: Westminster Press, 1985), pp. 86–95.

Sherwood, Y., 'Boxing Gomer: Controlling the deviant Woman in Hosea 1–3', in Brenner (ed.), *A Feminist Companion to the Latter Prophets*, pp. 101–125.

Showalter, E. (ed.), *Speaking of Gender* (London: Routledge, 1989).

Simpson, C.A., *The Book of Genesis* (IB, 1; Nashville and New York: Abingdon, 1952).

Smith, P. and Zias, J., 'Skeletal Remains from the Late Hellenistic French Hill Tomb', *IEJ* 30 (1980), pp. 109–15.

Snaith, N.H., *Leviticus and Numbers* (New Century Bible; London: Nelson, 1967).

Speiser, E.A., *Genesis: Introduction, Translation, and Notes* (AB; Garden City, NY: Doubleday, 1964).

Stol, M., *Zwangerschap en geboorte bij de Babyloniers en in de bijbel* (Leiden: Ex Oriente Lux, 1983).

Stone, K., 'Gender and Homosexuality in Judges 19: Subject-Honor, Object-Shame?', *JSOT* 67 (1995), pp. 87–107.

de Tarragon, J.-M., 'Witchcraft, Magic and Divination in Canaan and Ancient Mesopotamia', in J. Sasson (ed.), *Civilizations of the Ancient Near East* (New York: Charles Scribner's Sons, 1995), vol. 3, pp. 2071–82.

Teubal, S.J., *Hagar the Egyptian: The Lost Traditions of the Matriarchs* (San Francisco: Harper & Row, 1990).

———, *Sarah the Priestess: The First Matriarch of Genesis* (Athens, OH: Swallow Press, 1984).

———, 'Sarah and Hagar: Matriarchs and Visionaries', in A. Brenner (ed.), *A Feminist Companion to Genesis* (Sheffield: Sheffield Academic Press, 1993), pp. 235–50.

Thurston, T.M., 'Leviticus 18:22 and the Prohibition of Homosexual Acts', in M.L. Stemmeler and J.M. Clark (eds.), *Homophobia and the Judaeo-Christian Tradition* (Dallas, 1990).

van der Toorn, K., 'Female Prostitution in Payment of Vows in Ancient Israel', *JBL* 108 (1989), pp. 193–205.

———, *From Her Cradle to Her Grave: The Role of Religion in the Life of the Israelite and the Babylonian Woman* (Biblical Seminar, 23; Sheffield: JSOT Press, 1994).

Trible, P., *God and the Rhetoric of Sexuality* (Philadelphia: Fortress Press, 1978).

Tyldesley, J., *Daughters of Isis: Women of Ancient Egypt* (London: Penguin Books, 1994).

Walters, S.D., 'The Sorceress and Her Apprentice: A Case Study of an Accusation', *JCS* 23 (1970), pp. 27–38.

Weeks, K., 'Medicine, Surgery and Public Health in Ancient Egypt', in J. Sasson (ed.), *Civilizations of the Ancient Near East*, vol. 3, pp. 1787–98.

Weinfeld, M., *Deuteronomy and the Deuteronomic School* (Oxford: Clarendon, 1972).

——— (ed.), *Leviticus* (Heb.; World of the Bible Encyclopedia; Ramat Gan: Revivim, 1987).

Westermann, C., 'Das Schöne im Altem Testament', in H. Donner, R. Hanhart and R. Smend (eds.), *Beiträge zur alttestamentlichen Theologie: Festschrift für Walther Zimmerli zum 70. Geburtstag* (Göttingen: Vandenhoeck & Ruprecht, 1977), pp. 479–97; repr. in C. Westermann (R. Albertz, ed.), *Erträge der Forschung am Alten Testament: Gesammelte Studien III* (München: Chr. Kaiser Verlag, 1984), pp. 119–37.

Yassine, K. (ed.), *Tel el Mazar: I. Cemetery A* (Amman: 1985): A. Disi, W. Henke and J. Wahle, ch. vi ('Human Skeletal Remains').

Zakovitch, Y., 'Dual Name Play', MA dissertation, The Hebrew University (1971, Heb.).

———, 'Humor and Theology, or the Successful Failure of the Israelite Intelligence (Josh. 2): A Literary-Folklorist Approach', in S. Niditch (ed.), *Text and Tradition: The Hebrew Bible and Folklore* (Atlanta: Scholars Press, 1990), pp. 75–98.

———, *The Song of Songs: Introduction and Commentary* (Heb.; *Miqra le-Yisrael*; Tel Aviv: Am Oved and Magnes Press).

Zakovitch, Y. and Shinan, A., *Sarai and Abram in Egypt* (Heb.; Research Project of the Institute of Jewish Studies Monograph Series, 1; Jerusalem: The Hebrew University, 1983).